Superstates

Superstates

Empires of the Twenty-First Century

Alasdair Roberts

polity

First published in 2023 by Polity Press

Polity Press
65 Bridge Street
Cambridge CB2 1UR, UK

Polity Press
111 River Street
Hoboken, NJ 07030, USA

ISBN-13: 978-1-5095-4447-9 (hardback)
ISBN-13: 978-1-5095-4448-6 (paperback)

A catalogue record for this book is available from the British Library.

Library of Congress Control Number: 2022937025

Typeset in 10.75 on 13 Adobe Janson
by Fakenham Prepress Solutions, Fakenham, Norfolk NR21 8NL
Printed and bound in the UK by TJ Books Limited

The publisher has used its best endeavors to ensure that the URLs for external websites referred to in this book are correct and active at the time of going to press. However, the publisher has no responsibility for the websites and can make no guarantee that a site will remain live or that the content is or will remain appropriate.

Every effort has been made to trace all copyright holders, but if any have been overlooked the publisher will be pleased to include any necessary credits in any subsequent reprint or edition.

For further information on Polity, visit our website:
politybooks.com

Contents

About the Author

Alasdair Roberts is a professor of public policy at the University of Massachusetts Amherst and writes extensively on problems of governance, law, and public policy. He is the author of several acclaimed books, including *Strategies for Governing: Reinventing Public Administration for a Dangerous Century* and *Can Government Do Anything Right?* He received the ASPA Riggs Award for Lifetime Achievement in Comparative Public Administration in 2022, and Canada's Grace-Pépin Access to Information Award in 2014 for his research on open government. He is a Fellow of the United States National Academy of Public Administration.

Sometimes I like to compare the European Union as a creation to the organization of empires. Empires! Because we have the dimension of empires.

José Manuel Barroso, President of the European Commission, 2007

India is such a huge country. It is not a scooter whose direction you can change easily. A forty-compartment train takes time.

Narendra Modi, Prime Minister of India, 2015

One should be mindful of possible danger in times of peace, downfall in times of survival, and chaos in times of stability.

Xi Jinping, President of the People's Republic of China, quoting the *Book of Changes*, 2014

The forces that divide us are deep and they are real.

Joseph Biden, President of the United States, 2021

1

The Experiment

In this century, the world will conduct an extraordinary experiment in politics and government. By 2050, almost forty percent of the planet's population will live in just four places: India, China, the European Union, and the United States. These are superstates: polities that are distinguished from normal states by expanse of territory, number and diversity of people, and social and economic complexity. Never in human history have so many people been crowded into such a small number of polities. The least populous superstate – the United States – will contain almost as many people as the vast British empire did at its peak in 1914.

How should these immense and complex polities be governed – and can they really be governed at all? There are no easy answers to these questions. The superstates themselves do not have much experience to draw upon. The European Union is scarcely thirty years old, and the republics of India and China are less than eighty years old. In the sweep of history that is not much time. Moreover, that short history is not reassuring. Modern India and China suffered from internal upheavals for decades after their creation, governing much smaller populations than they have today. The United States is the oldest of the four super-states, and for most of the last century it has enjoyed political and social stability. But the United States, as the least populous and wealthiest superstate, might also be the easiest to govern. And recently even it appears to be coming apart at the seams.

Looking to other modern states for lessons on governance does not help much either. Political scientists often hold up Denmark as a model of good practice, but it is not immediately obvious how anything we might say about Denmark would apply to China, which has 240 times as many people and 230 times as much land.[1] The Indian capital of Delhi by itself has three times as many people as Denmark. And Denmark is not an unusually small country. As we shall see later in this chapter, the typical modern state has roughly the same population and territory. There is an immense disparity in circumstances between the four superstates and most countries.

We might also look to history for advice on how to govern big and complex polities. In the two millennia that preceded the early twentieth century, empires rather than states were a common form of political organization. Like superstates, empires encompassed vast territories and diverse populations. But anyone looking to empires for lessons on governance will be disturbed by what they find. Empires were fragile enterprises. Imperial rulers were always struggling to prevent collapse. Rulers were fortunate if their empires lasted more than three or four generations.

Of course, superstates are not exactly like empires. The rulers of modern-day China and India have access to technologies that make surveillance and control of people easier than in the age of empires. But rulers of superstates carry heavier burdens too. Imperial rulers did not worry about improving the welfare of ordinary people by providing public services like education and healthcare. The people they governed were not crowded into cities where it was easy to organize against central rule. Subjects of empire could not read or write, they did not have the internet and cell phones, they could not travel and assemble easily, and they were not brought up on the modern-day doctrine of human rights. Leaders of superstates must manage populations that are more restless and demanding.

Superstates are a hybrid form of polity. They carry the old burdens of empire, such as holding diverse communities together and managing other hazards to which empires were unusually susceptible because of their scale and complexity. Superstates also carry the burdens of modern statehood, including the duty to govern more intensively, provide more services, and respect human rights. Superstates are different from other states because they carry these twin burdens.

The aim of this book is to provide a framework for understanding how leaders of superstates might carry this heavy load in theory, and then look at the history of each superstate to see how they have carried it in practice. While doing this, I will try to overcome two divides in scholarship. The first is a divide between countries. Within academia there are China scholars, Americanists, India scholars, and Europeanists. Each group tends to use a distinct vocabulary to examine what are sometimes imagined to be exceptional problems of governance. I will try to bridge this divide by showing how leaders in each superstate grapple with similar problems and sometimes experiment with similar solutions.

The second divide is between past and present. Even though the age of empires has passed, the scholarly literature on the governance of empires has burgeoned in recent years. But this scholarly work is often regarded as a form of purely historical inquiry. The possibility that there might be lessons for the governance of modern states is not recognized. I will suggest that features of empire survive within superstates, and that we can draw on our growing knowledge about empires to understand the tensions that operate within extensive and complex polities today.

Imperial rulers experimented constantly with different ways of holding their empires together. Central control over everyday life would be tightened or loosened, power within the imperial court would be concentrated or diffused, and the imperial creed would be revised and applied with more or less dogmatism. The same sort of restless experimentation goes on within superstates. No superstate is governed as it was one or two generations ago. Moreover, no two superstates are governed in the same way today. China is structured as a centralized authoritarian state. By contrast, the European Union is a highly decentralized polity with a little democracy at the center and a lot of democracy below. India and the United States fall somewhere in the middle, but still with important differences in the structure of government and practice of democracy.

These differences in governing strategy are shaped but not determined by the history of each superstate. Every day, leaders in each superstate make complicated choices, under conditions of immense uncertainty, about the best way of managing hazards that are compounded by scale, diversity, and complexity. Most of the time, leaders appreciate that the wrong choice about regime design could have fatal consequences. Like empires, superstates are perceived as inherently fragile structures. They never achieve the level of stability that is considered the hallmark of successful modern states. Awareness of this persistent fragility is essential to survival because it makes leaders vigilant about new dangers.

Imperial rulers were often tempted to close ranks and tighten control so that they could respond decisively to new threats. This tactic sometimes had the unintended consequence of undermining empire, by overwhelming the capacity of central authorities to make and execute intelligent decisions.[2] The same temptation operates within superstates, accompanied by the same danger of perverse results. But this centralizing tendency poses an additional danger within super-states, which did not trouble most imperial rulers. Democracy and individual freedom might be sacrificed in the attempt to improve the odds for survival. In the eighteenth century, Montesquieu argued that liberty was only possible in states of "mediocre size."[3] Some wonder whether China is proving Montesquieu right today.

We are entering the age of superstates. This book will explore the governance challenges that will dominate this age. We want to under-stand how leaders hold superstates together in the face of extraordinary strains and shocks. We want to speculate about what life within super-states will be like for ordinary people, and how modern ideas about democracy and human rights can be squared with the pressures of governing vast and complex polities.

I will begin by explaining the difference between the states and empires, and how the age of empires gave way to the age of states and next to the age of superstates. Then I will describe the plan for the rest of the book.

Defining States and Empires

Today, states are the most familiar form of rule. Almost all the world's land is claimed by states, and almost all of us are citizens of at least one state. A state is typically defined as an assemblage of institutions – consisting of a leadership group, a civil bureaucracy, an army and police force, and so on – which has effective control over a defined territory.[4] The international community – the "society of states" – generally acknowledges the right of each state to govern its territory as it likes. Recently, though, expectations about the kind of control that states will exercise within their territory have risen. Leaders lose the respect of other states if they fail to maintain internal order and control of their national borders, if they abuse their citizens, and if they cannot adequately monitor economic and social life inside their country.[5]

There is no minimum size requirement for states. Tuvalu is recog-nized as a state even though its three south Pacific islands account for only ten square miles of land and eleven thousand people. However, there is some expectation that people living within a state will share a culture, language, and understanding of history. That is, people are expected to constitute a nation, or at least to have the potential to become a nation. Strictly, this is not a prerequisite for statehood: multinational states do exist. But multinational states are regarded as exceptional and fragile.[6] The world looks sympathetically on ethnic communities within multinational states that demand autonomy because they have been maltreated by the central authorities of those states.

There are no empires in the world today, so we talk about them in the past tense. Like states, empires were constituted by an assemblage of institutions that maintained control over a territory and population.[7] But empires were distinguished from states in five ways. First, size mattered. The territory contained within an empire was vast, by the standards of the time when the empire existed. Indeed, empires tested the limits of how much territory could be governed by a central authority, given the available methods of travel and communication. Over-extension – claiming more territory than it was possible to hold – was a common explanation for the collapse of empires.[8]

Empires also differed from states with respect to the intensity of control exercised over territory. The standard for empires was lower. Often, imperial leaders exercised control over parts of their domain indirectly. When new territories were acquired, local elites were allowed to stay in power so long as they recognized the empire's ultimate authority.[9] One result was that methods of local administration often differed substantially across an empire. Ordinary people might see little difference in everyday life after they had been absorbed into an empire, because local elites and traditional political structures remained in place. Unlike the leaders of modern states, imperial rulers rarely felt a strong obligation to improve the lives of ordinary people throughout the empire. They were not encumbered by the obligation to respect and advance human rights.

Control became even more tenuous at the edges of every empire. This produced a third difference between empires and states. Modern states aspire to have well-marked, well-defended, and stable borders. The edges of empires were often more ambiguous, permeable, and changeable. They were frontier zones that shifted as imperial fortunes waxed and waned.[10]

Empires were also distinguished from many modern states by their sense of self-importance.[11] Elites and denizens of empires often shared the belief that they were charged with propagating a particular vision of social order.[12] In the nineteenth century this was called the civilizing mission of empire. Sometimes this mission was founded on religion, but not always: for example, the British empire was said to be founded on the secular ideals of law, representative government, and free trade.[13] Imperial authorities tried to civilize people already living within the borders of their empire, and they justified imperial expansion as a way of bringing civilization to the broader world.

The civilizing impulse should not be exaggerated. It varied between empires, and over time within empires, depending on circumstances. Furthermore, imperial rulers had limited ability to impose their way of life on subjects. Commands from the seat of empire were often ignored or resisted.

The civilizing mission was especially difficult because of the fifth distinctive feature of empires: the size and diversity of their populations.[14] People living within an empire did not constitute a nation. They were divided in many ways – by culture, religion, language, historical animosities, or race. Imperial rulers might try to temper some of these differences, or to inculcate some sense of a higher common purpose among disparate peoples. But there was no expectation that all differences would dissolve and that a single nation would eventually emerge. Persistent diversity in ways of living was an inescapable aspect of empire.[15]

The Long Age of Empires

"Empires," the American writer Irwin St. John Tucker observed in 1920, "are as old as history itself."[16] More recently, historian John Darwin has described empire as the normal form of political organization throughout most of history.[17] One of the earliest, the Akkadian empire, was formed when Sargon, ruler of Akkad, conquered other city-states in the Tigris-Euphrates valley in present-day Iraq over four thousand years ago. It collapsed within two centuries, maybe because of climate change.[18] Later empires were bigger and sometimes more durable.[19] The Roman empire survived for five centuries and at its peak was seven times larger than the Akkadian. The Mongol empire, which arose in the thirteenth century, was five times larger than the Roman empire but held together for scarcely sixty years. The British empire at its peak was even bigger, spanning oceans and governing one-fifth of the world's population.

Little more than a century ago, empires were still the dominant form of political organization on the planet. Around 1910, Britain and other European imperial powers asserted control over more than eighty percent of the planet's land surface.[20] (See Figure 1.) The Qing and Ottoman empires accounted for much of the remainder. The Qing empire collapsed in 1911, followed by the Austro-Hungarian empire in 1918, and the Ottoman empire in 1922. But other empires survived and even thrived. Tucker, writing in 1920, was certain that empires would continue to play the "leading role" in human history. The British empire reached its zenith in the 1920s. Three states – Germany, Japan, and Italy – tried to construct new empires in the 1930s and early 1940s.[21] World War II put a stop to these projects and led to the collapse of the other European empires as well. But not immediately: Britain was still shedding colonies in the 1980s. Some argue that the long age of empires only ended in 1991 with the demise of the Soviet Union, which had taken over the lands of the Romanov dynasty in 1917.

The World of States

Today we live in a "world of states" rather than empires.[22] The transformation from one dominant mode of political organization to another was gradual. The modern concept of the state began to form in Europe in the sixteenth century. As kings battled one another they tightened their hold on territory and improved their ability to raise armies and collect taxes. The principle that kings were sovereign within their borders was recognized.[23] By the end of the eighteenth century, central authorities in emerging states were busy mapping land, counting people, encouraging industry, and cultivating a common identity among subjects. In the nineteenth century, this process of statebuilding accelerated. The state we know as the United Kingdom was established in 1801, Italy was finally unified in 1870, and so was Germany the following year.

The nineteenth century was a period of transition between the age of empires and the age of states, and terminology was often jumbled.[24] Some European empires of that era were conceived as hub-and-spoke arrangements, with a European state at the hub and colonies at the end of each spoke. This hub-and-spoke model made sense for transoceanic empires, because colonies were thousands of miles away from the imperial seat. But this model did not fit land empires like Russia and Austria-Hungary. These were described simultaneously as empires and states. Similarly, Germany defined itself as an empire after unification in 1871 but was conceived as a single state at the same time. After acquiring overseas colonies in the 1880s, the German empire was also

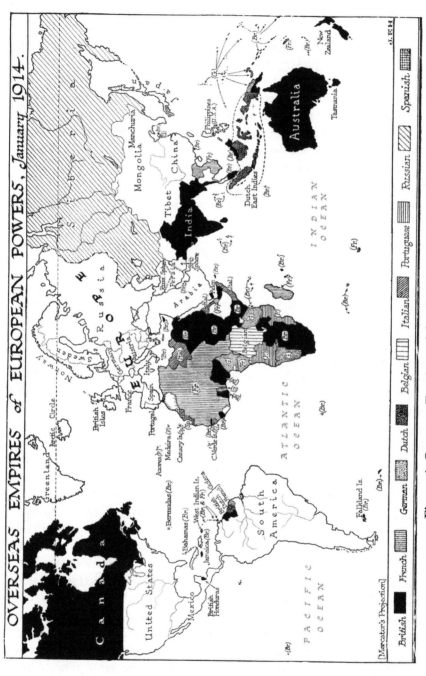

Figure 1 Overseas Empires of the European Powers, 1914.
Source: H.G. Wells, *Outline of History* (New York, Macmillan, 1921).

regarded as a hub-and-spoke enterprise with the German state at its center.

Terminology became simpler after the extinction of empires in the twentieth century. States were recognized as the "basic building block of the world political map."[25] The overseas possessions of hub-and-spoke empires were transformed into states, while provincial boundaries within land empires turned into borders between newly formed countries. More than sixty states were formed as the British empire shrank throughout the twentieth century. Fifteen more were created when the Soviet Union collapsed in 1991. In 1945, when the United Nations was established, there were seventy independent states on the planet; today, there are almost two hundred. Flags of all states now fly in front of the United Nations headquarters in New York City. Most of these flags are less than sixty years old.

Since the turn of the nineteenth century, there has been debate about whether states needed to have some minimum size. This was an argument about what was necessary for a state to thrive, not about legal requirements for statehood. Over the course of two centuries, the dominant view about minimum size has shifted dramatically.

In nineteenth-century Europe, bigness was considered a virtue. European countries were divided into two groups at that time. There were six "great states" – Britain, France, Austria-Hungary, Germany, Italy, and Russia – and several "lesser states" like Belgium, Denmark, Holland, Portugal, and Sweden. The distinction was based on territory and population. Denmark had only two million people in 1880, and Switzerland four million; by comparison, France had forty million and Germany, forty-five million. Many believed that lesser states would eventually be swallowed up by the great states. A French politician claimed this was an inevitable phase of social evolution.[26]

An obvious weakness of small states was their inability to resist the mass armies of great states that swept across Europe throughout the nineteenth century. France mobilized an army of two million men when it declared war on Germany in 1870, and Germany replied with an army of 1.5 million men.[27] By contrast, Denmark marshalled only 70,000 men when it went to war with Germany in 1864 and was crushed as a result.[28] Even in times of peace, small states had little influence. They were doomed to be "nobodies" in international affairs, British journalist Walter Bagehot declared in 1866.[29]

Small countries also suffered from economic vulnerability, especially as great states put up tariffs to protect their own industries. This policy of industrial protection had been recommended by the economist

Friedrich List in the early 1800s. The goal, List explained, was "perfection . . . [of] the various branches of production" within national borders. List warned that his policy could only succeed in states with "a large population and an extensive territory." Small states, lacking a large internal market and access to neighboring markets, could never become rich.[30]

Nor could small states achieve cultural excellence. Bagehot believed that they lacked the numbers necessary to sustain a "vigorous intellectual life."[31] Too many of the best minds would be tied up in government – and even there, a shortage of talent would produce inferior results. "Small politics debase the mind," Bagehot said.[32] Bagehot's compatriot Lord Acton agreed, dismissing small states as "impediments to the progress of society."[33] A small country, said Friedrich List, "can only possess a crippled literature, [and] crippled institutions for promoting art and science."[34]

By the end of the nineteenth, the lesser states appeared to be doomed. "The day of small nations is gone forever," a British diplomat pronounced in 1894.[35] A German economist predicted that the world would be preoccupied with the construction of large states for years to come.[36]

Indeed, some intellectuals speculated about how big countries could be. In 1883, the British historian J.R. Seeley predicted the emergence of "a larger type of state than any hitherto known." Seeley was thinking about the United States and Russia – countries that had ten times as much territory as the great state of France, and twice as many people. New technologies like the railroad and telegraph made it possible to build these new super-sized states. Seeley warned that they would upend international politics. "The old level of magnitude" would no longer be adequate for security, prosperity, and cultural achievement. The great states of the nineteenth century would become "unsafe, insignificant, [and] second rate" in the twentieth century.[37]

The futurist H.G. Wells had a similar vision and thought that the United States was a model of where the world was heading. "This new modern state," Wells said, was "an altogether new thing in history": there had never been "one single people on this scale before." And Wells did not expect the United States to be alone for long. He predicted that Russia, China, India, and a unified Europe would gain similar status by the twenty-first century. "We want a new term for this new thing," Wells said. But he did not say what the new term should be.[38]

States Get Smaller

Seeley and Wells were right in the long run. In the short run, however, gloomy predictions about the prospects of lesser states were mistaken. The "world of states" that emerged in the second half of the twentieth century was very much a world of small states. The median population of the world's states in 2020 was just 8.5 million people – roughly that of Switzerland, which counted among the lesser states in the nineteenth century. Half of the world's states have less territory than Portugal, another of the nineteenth century's lesser states. Some researchers even specialize in the study of micro-states, which have a population of less than a million people.[39] There were only two micro-states in 1960 – Luxemburg and Iceland – but now there are almost forty.[40]

Why were predictions about the demise of lesser states off the mark? Because circumstances changed, so that the disadvantages of smallness were reduced. At the same time, some burdens of bigness became more obvious.

Granted, small states still worried about national defense in the late twentieth century. As in the nineteenth century, they lacked the money and manpower to maintain a strong military force. Even if Estonia conscripted every adult into military service, it would still be outnumbered by the present-day armed services of neighboring Russia; and even if it spent every penny of its national income on defense, it could not match Russia's current military budget. Other small states are outgunned just as badly.

But the odds that powerful neighbors would take advantage of this vulnerability were lower in the decades following World War II than they were before World War I. There were critical changes in attitudes, institutions, and military technologies. Before 1914, national leaders saw war as an acceptable way of advancing national interests. War was more easily justified under international law and soldiering was celebrated in popular culture.[41] Technological limitations meant that wars unfolded slowly. Rulers did not worry that military engagements would turn into total wars threatening the very survival of state and society.

By 1950, the world had changed. New technologies increased the pace of conflict and the risk of escalation. Rulers and citizens understood the horror of total war. As a result, attitudes about the legitimacy of war as an instrument of policy changed radically. International law now defined aggressive war as the "supreme international crime."[42] The principle of non-aggression became a building block of the post-World War II international order.[43] The overall result was a dramatic decline in wars between states after World War II. Small states thrived in this new and more peaceful environment. Of course, Russia's attack on Ukraine in February 2022 might make us wonder whether this environment is collapsing. It is too soon to know. The Russian invasion might prove to be an exceptional case that demonstrates the illegitimacy of aggressive war in the modern age.

The economic challenges of smallness also diminished in the late twentieth century. Consider the case of Singapore, a city-state with a population of only five million people. It cannot produce many of the goods and services that are required by its people. Singaporeans are more dependent on foreign trade than almost any other country in the world. In the nineteenth century, this seemed like a recipe for economic failure. But Singapore prospered after World War II, transforming itself into one of the richest countries in the world, measured by per capita GDP.[44]

This transformation was made possible by changes in the international economic system. Protectionist policies were discredited after the economic crisis of the 1930s. After World War II, leaders of the major economies created international institutions that curbed the ability of governments to impose tariffs and other protectionist measures.[45] This free-trade regime became more robust over the following decades. The average tariff imposed by major trading countries declined from thirty percent before the 1940s to less than four percent by the early 2000s.[46] In this new world, small countries were able to prosper.

Similarly, it was no longer obvious that small states must be cultural backwaters. Because of technological improvements, smallness no longer meant isolation. Intellectuals and artists from small states connected easily with peers in other countries. Citizens could import books, music, and movies, while the cost of producing these things domestically also declined. Because of the boom in international migration, many small countries had large diasporic populations in other countries that were connected to their homelands by the internet and inexpensive air travel.

While the disadvantages of smallness declined over the twentieth century, problems of bigness became more obvious. In particular, the work of unifying big countries – of fusing people into one nation – proved more difficult than expected.

Here, we must remember to be precise about language. Sometimes we talk as though states and nations are the same thing. They are not. A state is a political structure that exercises control over a defined territory, while a nation is a population that recognizes itself as a single community, sharing a language, culture, and understanding of history.[47] A state whose population is unified in this way is called a nation-state. All the great states of the nineteenth century aspired to become nation-states. Their model was France. In the eighteenth century, most people living in territory claimed by the French state did not speak French and knew little about life beyond their own villages.[48] Rulers of the French state worked deliberately to forge a nation by establishing a universal system of primary education, standardizing the language, and many other measures.

At the time, it was widely believed that states could not endure unless their people constituted a nation. German philosopher J.G. Herder dismissed states containing mixed nationalities as "patched-up contraptions" that would inevitably fall to pieces.[49] British philosopher John Stuart Mill maintained that states with diverse peoples could survive only when ruled with an iron fist. "Free institutions," he insisted, "are next to impossible in a country made of different nationalities."[50] But European leaders in the nineteenth century were confident about their ability to avoid such dangers. France, they thought, had shown how to forge a diverse population into one nation.

This confidence was shattered by the late twentieth century. Although states often achieved some degree of commonality among their people, minority cultures were often stubbornly resilient. Scotland still defined itself as a separate nation three centuries after its formal union with England in 1707. In Spain, years of repression could not erase the distinct identity of people in Catalonia and the Basque Country. The authoritarian rulers of Yugoslavia could not forge a common identity among Serbs, Croats, Bosnians, and Slovenes. Old identities persisted in regions of the Soviet Union despite decades constructing a "new Soviet man."

Before World War II, states sometimes used violence as a tool for nation-building. They tried to exterminate minorities or to dissolve their culture by forced resettlement. However, states found it harder to use such tactics after World War II, as ideas about human rights were popularized and entrenched in international law.[51] The Universal Declaration of Human Rights, adopted in 1948, promises protection against state violence and respect for the cultural rights of all people.

Another tool for the integration of great states, economic policy, also proved to be less effective than expected in the late twentieth century. National leaders thought that large countries would hold together if they had a single, integrated economy. This meant careful economic planning. Faith in the capacity of governments to undertake economic planning was strong in the first half of the twentieth century but dissolved in the second half.[52] As capitalism developed, market dynamics were harder to monitor and regulate. After the 1980s, many governments stopped trying to guide their economies so closely. The implications for cohesion within large countries were substantial. Free-market policies produced more inequality between social classes and regions, which fueled political polarization and instability.[53]

The collapse in faith about economic planning was one aspect of a larger problem with big states. Leaders struggled because of the scale of decision-making. The center of government was deluged with problems that were complex and interconnected. This was not an entirely new problem: in 1913, journalist Norman Angell had observed how the Russian empire suffered from "the stupidity of giants."[54] In the mid-twentieth century, leaders in many large states believed that they could overcome this handicap by building computer-powered bureaucracies to tame the tsunami of information. But these bureaucracies often proved to be slow and clumsy. Stress, exhaustion, and distraction at the apex of government often led to bad decisions.[55] Overload within the centralized Soviet state contributed to its eventual collapse.[56]

By the late 1990s, the typical state was not only small; it also appeared to be increasingly inconsequential. Cross-border trade and finance was growing so rapidly that national economies seemed to be melding into one global economy. The internet was knitting together social movements in many countries, producing a new kind of integrated global politics. It seemed that emerging problems like climate change could not be solved by national governments acting independently. States appeared impotent under these new conditions, and some experts predicted that they would simply "wither away."[57] In 1995, Kenichi Ohmae described states as "bit actors . . . [in] today's borderless world."[58] French diplomat Jean-Marie Guéhenno said states had been "bypassed" and no longer functioned as "the natural space . . . of political control."[59]

Even the most powerful state, the United States, seemed to be diminished by globalization. After the collapse of the Soviet Union, the United States was sometimes described as the sole remaining superpower, and even as a hyperpower. But many disagreed. "Globalization affects the United States as it does other countries," the sociologist Anthony Giddens warned in 1993. Giddens believed that the United States was weaker than it had been during the Cold War, and that its power would continue fading away.[60] International law had always recognized the formal equality of states, but globalization appeared to be making them more equal in practice, inasmuch as they were becoming equally irrelevant.

The Age of Superstates

In the new millennium, however, history took another turn. It became clear that reports about the death of the state were premature.[61] After a wave of terror attacks in the early 2000s, governments tightened border controls, extended surveillance activities, and policed their territories more severely. The global financial crisis of 2007 to 2009 led to another bout of governmental activism, involving closer supervision of banks and international capital flows. Pressure from populist movements after 2010 led to further retreats from open-border policies. There was even more governmental action because of the COVID-19 pandemic in 2020. "The state is here, the state is present," Italy's prime minister reassured citizens during the pandemic, as he promised "extraordinary measures" to protect lives.[62]

Power inequalities between states were also accentuated in the new millennium. Following the terror attacks of 2001, the United States asserted its prerogatives more forcefully. It invaded Iraq despite international protests and opposition of allies such as France and Germany. The American political scientist Michael Mandelbaum declared in 2005 that the United States would serve as "the world's government" on matters of security and economic policy. Mandelbaum argued that the United States in the twenty-first century should act like "great empires of the past" by imposing order on world affairs.[63] President Donald Trump retreated from international commitments after his inauguration in 2017, but not because he disagreed about America's pre-eminence within the world of states. The United States, he insisted, was still "the greatest and most powerful Nation on earth."[64]

The United States is not alone in making claims to greatness. So does China. In the first half of the twentieth century, China was a troubled country, debilitated by civil war and foreign invasions. It continued to suffer from economic backwardness and political instability after the proclamation of the People's Republic in 1949. In 1975 China had a smaller economy than Canada, but forty times as many people.[65] Today China has been radically transformed. By some measures it has already surpassed the United States as the world's biggest economy.[66] China's leaders are becoming bolder in celebrating their system of authoritarian rule and claiming a leading role in international affairs.

India, too, is claiming its "rightful place" as a great power.[67] Like modern China, the Indian Republic was born in a moment of violence and struggled to hold itself together for years. A million people may have died in Hindu–Muslim conflict when British-controlled territory was divided between the new states of India and Pakistan in 1947.[68] Fears about "centrifugal forces" – religious, regional, and caste divisions – persisted for decades. Prime Minister Indira Gandhi maintained a state of emergency for two years in the mid-1970s on the pretext that this was necessary to preserve the Indian state. In the last thirty years, however, anxieties about survival have ebbed. India is expected to have the world's third largest economy, after China and the United States, by 2035.[69] It will displace China as the most populous country on earth.

A fourth great polity is emerging as well. The European Union was created in 1993 and now includes twenty-seven countries. The EU contains more land than India and forty percent more people than the United States. It presently has the second largest economy in the world and in 2050 will still count among the top four. The project of economic and political integration in Europe has proceeded in fits and starts, and at moments has seemed likely to collapse. But recent crises have encouraged European leaders to pursue their common interests more deliberately. In 2017, German chancellor Angela Merkel said it was time for Europeans to "take our destiny into our own hands."[70] Some have described the EU as a new type of empire, with a mission to promote democracy, human rights, and well-ordered trade.

The international order that is emerging in the twenty-first century consists of a world of states that is distinguished by dramatic differences in the scale of states. We are repeating the nineteenth-century division of great and lesser states, except the division is more extreme today. In nineteenth-century Europe, there were roughly equal numbers of great and lesser states, and the great states were about ten times larger (by population) than the lesser states. Today, there are about 165 lesser states, and four great states, if we count all the members of the European Union as one. The lesser states have an average population of about 23 million, while the great states have an average population that is forty times larger. China and India each have thirty times more people than did the great state of Germany in 1880.

In some ways, the world is evolving as H.G. Wells predicted a century ago. Granted, Wells did not anticipate the proliferation of smaller states. But he certainly predicted the emergence of a small number of very large polities, including the United States, China,

India, and a unified Europe. Wells was not sure what to call these political forms. I suggest that we call them superstates. They are a new kind of polity, a hybrid of empires and states. Like empires, superstates are distinguished by their size, diversity, and complexity. But superstates cannot govern as loosely as empires often did. Like other modern states, superstates are expected to exercise a high degree of control throughout their territory, and they are expected to treat all their people well. Never in history have we constructed polities that carry such heavy burdens.

Superstates are not the same as superpowers. The superpower concept is concerned mainly with international influence and not the complexities of governance at home. A superpower is a country that has the ambition and capacity to exert power in every part of the globe, and the ability to annihilate enemies by nuclear attack.[71] It is possible to imagine a rich, militarized country that counts as a superpower even though it is not big or diverse enough to count as a superstate. Britain, for example, clung to superpower status for a few years after World War II even though its empire was collapsing and its own territory and population was relatively modest and homogeneous.[72] Conversely, there can be superstates that do not count as superpowers. Presently, neither India nor the European Union have the capacity to use force anywhere they choose, and China's ability to project power is also limited.

H.G. Wells anticipated that Russia would also rank among the gargantuan states of the twenty-first century. But this prediction was not borne out. Russia is still vast, although not so vast as the Russian empire of 1914 or the Soviet Union of 1989. But its population has collapsed. In 2021, Russia had only 145 million people – less than half that of the United States – and its population is expected to decline even more over the next thirty years. Its economic clout has also declined. China, the EU, and the United States each have economies that are eight to twelve times larger than the Russian economy. Without a doubt, Russia still has the capacity to threaten its neighbors, as the 2022 invasion of Ukraine showed. Perhaps it still ranks as a waning superpower. But it is not a superstate. It is what remains after the collapse of the Soviet superstate and a warning to the leaders of other superstates about the fragility of these massive enterprises.

There are a handful of countries that match the four superstates in one way or another, but not in all ways. Some countries, like Canada, Australia, Argentina, and Kazakhstan, have a lot of land but very small populations. Japan has a large economy but cannot match the superstates in terms of territory, population, or diversity. Brazil is a more plausible contender for superstate status. It has vast territory, a growing economy, and a diverse population of about two hundred million. This is impressive, but in all these ways Brazil still falls short of the smallest superstate, the United States. A handful of other countries – Indonesia, Pakistan, Nigeria, Bangladesh – are comparable to Brazil in population but smaller in terms of territory and economy. The vast majority of all other states are much further behind the superstates in terms of territory, population, and complexity.

Should we count the European Union as a superstate? Some European leaders flatly reject the idea. "The European Union is not a super-state," the President of the European Commission, José Manuel Barroso, insisted in 2007.[73] Some scholars go further, denying that the European Union constitutes any kind of state at all, or that it will ever become a state. Barroso thought that it made more sense to think of the European Union as a new kind of empire. Many commentators agree.

I explore this debate about the nature of the EU in Chapter 7. For the moment, we should recognize that it hinges on a disagreement about the essential characteristics of states. People who dismiss the idea of the European Union as a state tend to think of states as highly centralized systems, in which top leaders wield broad authority over societies that are well integrated and homogeneous. Europeans who fear the emergence of an EU superstate have the same notion in mind. Certainly, some states are highly centralized, well-integrated, and homogeneous – but not all. These characteristics are not essential to statehood. If we applied these criteria to the United States, for example, it would not have counted as a state for much of its history and might not even count as a state today. The question is really whether the European regime as a whole, which comprises EU institutions, national and subnational governments, exercises the kind of comprehensive control over European territory that is typical of states. There is no doubt that it does.

However, insisting that the European Union be classified either as a state or as an empire is a mistake. It is a hybrid form. Every superstate carries the burdens of statehood, that is, the duties of intensive governance and respect for human rights that are carried by all modern states. But superstates also carry the burdens of empire, principally the burden of holding together a large and diverse population spread across a vast territory. Superstates are distinguished from ordinary states by problems of governance that are intensified by scale, diversity, and complexity.

Will the Experiment Succeed?

Will superstates survive, or will they fall apart as empires and many multinational states have done? And even if they survive, will they thrive: will they be places where people live well and enjoy fundamental rights? The purpose of this book is to explore these questions.

We start by learning from history. In Chapter 2, I consider what the extensive literature on empires tells us about governing vast and complex polities. The experience of empires is sobering. It has long been recognized that empires were transient phenomena. The fate of all empires, it was agreed, was extinction. Some died quickly, while others survived for centuries; but, ultimately, they all expired.

There is no simple explanation for the rise and fall of empires. Imperial rulers faced a range of elemental hazards, such as war, rebellion, drought, and disease, economic stagnation, and technological backwardness. The scale of empires made them unusually susceptible to a fatal cascade of such hazards. Rulers tried to build regimes that would be effective in managing elemental hazards but this work was difficult and fraught with dilemmas. Methods of governing that were intended to mitigate one elemental hazard often had the effect of aggravating another hazard or of creating entirely new challenges for imperial rulers. Imperial rule was a never-ending exercise in improvisation. It involved the constant renovation of institutions to meet new threats and avoid a fatal cascade of problems. Eventually the skill and luck of imperial rulers ran out, and events conspired to bring the empire down.

Superstates are not exactly like empires, of course. In Chapter 3, I consider whether historical developments of the last two centuries are likely to save superstates from the fate of empires. The answer is not straightforward. There are some ways in which new technologies make it easier for rulers to govern large populations and vast territories. However, modern states are expected to govern their territories more closely, provide more services for citizens, and respect human rights. People are also more restless and resistant to command: they are urbanized, educated, mobile, and interconnected. National economies are more complex and volatile than they were two centuries ago.

On balance, it is not obvious that superstates will be more resilient than empires. They might even be less resilient. Like empires, super-states face a daunting array of elemental hazards. At the same time, dilemmas about methods of governing at scale remain intractable. Leaders of superstates, like imperial rulers, are engaged in a relentless exercise of improvisation for the sake of survival.

Indeed, the strategies that are now being used to govern the four superstates differ radically. Regarding key aspects of regime design – control, leadership, and creed – no two superstates are alike. China emphasizes centralized and intensive control, while the EU empha- sizes radical decentralization. India and the United States fall in the middle, with India more centralized than the United States. In every superstate, leaders are selected and organized in different ways, giving different levels of respect to democratic principles. Similarly, leaders in each superstate have composed distinctive creeds, drawing on a range of cultural resources: old civilizational ideals, modern doctrines about politics and government, and sometimes even appeals to faith and race. Moreover, methods of rule within each superstate have evolved substantially over time. Not one of the superstates is governed as it was forty years ago.

Chapters 4 through 7 explore how leaders in each of the four super- states have addressed the challenges of governing at scale. I consider how leaders in each superstate have renovated their regimes as hazards and dilemmas have risen and fallen in importance. I do not follow a fixed formula while telling these four stories, because history does not unfold so neatly. But several themes will be evident:

- *Commonalities among superstates.* We should put aside the notion that each superstate is exceptional. Leaders in all superstates face the common problem of governing at extraordinary scale, although they approach that problem in different ways.
- *Historical continuities.* The line between the age of empires and the age of states is not so clear after all. Most superstates were once imagined as empires or parts of empire. Some modern-day leaders of superstates recognize that they are still managing age-old problems of empire. And sometimes those leaders adopt methods of rule, and face dilemmas in regime design, that would have been familiar to imperial rulers.
- *Inescapable fragility.* We often think that a well-developed state must be a solid, stable enterprise. Superstates are different. Size, diversity, and complexity mean that these regimes are inherently fragile. Leaders are usually aware of this fragility, even if they do not publicly acknowledge it. Fears about "centrifugal forces" recur in every chapter. Moments in which leaders forget about fragility are usually moments of danger.
- *Need for adaptability.* Indian governance has been described as "an extemporized performance."[74] We can say the same about

governance in every superstate. Leaders are engaged in a never-ending process of adjustment. There is no permanent solution to the question of how to govern because hazards and dilemmas change constantly.

- *Dangers of centralization.* There are pressures in every superstate to centralize, but the capacity of the center to wield power competently is often overestimated.
- *Democracy at the center.* All superstates wrestle with the question of how leadership at the center should be structured, and how, or even whether, democratic principles can be applied without jeopardizing the capacity of leaders to hold the superstate together.

The resilience of empires was often tested by sudden shocks, and the same is true of superstates. The COVID-19 pandemic provides an opportunity to observe how these four superstates, governed very differently, have responded to a common crisis. Millions died in India, the United States, and the European Union, but only thousands in China. Some people feared that the pandemic would trigger the collapse of the European Union, while in the United States and India it widened pre-existing social and political divisions. In Chapter 8, I compare the responses of the four superstates. The questions will be familiar: were centralized systems more successful than decentralized systems, and which form of leadership structure seemed to respond most effectively? As usual there is no neat answer, but the evidence suggests that centralization is the wrong way to assure resilience in face of a hazard like COVID-19.

In Chapter 9, I consider some of the critical choices that leaders must make as they devise strategies for governing at scale. We want a strategy that respects fundamental rights, including the right of ordinary people to select their rulers. However, experience shows that democratic principles must be applied carefully in large and complex systems. Simple ideas about majority rule and the virtues of a strong, directly elected executive are potentially dangerous when applied within superstates. Ways must be found to allow the representation and conciliation of diverse communities. We must also be careful about excessive centralization. This may lead to overload, polarization, and a fatal rigidity in the face of new hazards.

Successfully running a superstate requires a certain way of thinking about the work of governing. Leaders of superstates, like their predecessors in empires, must appreciate the fragility of their enterprise: the danger that strains and shocks will bring the whole edifice down. As in empires, governance is largely concerned with designing and redesigning institutions to put off the day of reckoning. The mindset must be pragmatic, recognizing the need for constant adjustment and sometimes for unorthodox policies. Often it must also be reserved, because candor and belligerence can undermine sensitive negotiations to maintain internal peace.

The mindset might also be uninspiring. A nineteenth-century imperial politician, Eduard Taaffe, described his approach to governing as "muddling through."[75] But Taaffe was not a democratically elected leader, and he did not live in the digital age. Today, leaders are expected to tell a compelling story about their grand ambitions. The challenge is to square this expectation with the gray realities of superstate governance.

2

Empires Always Die

Throughout history, empires have been perceived as fragile enterprises that were doomed to collapse sooner or later. This seemed self-evident to the philosopher Zou Yan as he surveyed Chinese history in the third century BCE. For centuries, China had been riven by war, with power shifting frequently between dynasties. Like many later scholars, Zou searched for an explanation of why dynasties rose and fell. He concluded that every dynasty had a distinctive virtue corresponding to one of the five elements: earth, wood, metal, fire, and water. This virtue was strongest when a dynasty was new, and it enabled the dynasty to dominate others. Eventually the virtue weakened so much that the dynasty collapsed, to be replaced by another dynasty representing the next element in the sequence. Zou thought it possible to predict when a dynasty would end. Understandably, further pursuit of this research was discouraged by later emperors.[1]

A century later, the Greek historian Polybius reached a similar conclusion about the ephemerality of empires. Polybius watched as his patron, the Roman general Scipio Aemilianus, ordered the destruction of Carthage in 146 BCE. Scipio burst into tears as Carthage burned, realizing that Rome itself would meet the same fate eventually. Empires like men must die, Scipio said. Polybius developed his own theory about the cycle of growth and decay that governed empires, which he thought was determined by the corruptibility of political institutions. Polybius agreed that Rome would collapse some day. This was the natural order of things.[2]

Ibn Khaldun also had a theory about the rise and fall of empires. He completed his great book the *Muqaddimah* in Tunis, only a few miles from Carthage. By that time, the Roman Empire had been extinct for almost a millennium. Ibn Khaldun devised his theory based on the history of Islamic regimes over the previous seven hundred years. These empires, he observed, had "a natural life span like people." They became senile and died when rulers lost their "desert toughness." By Ibn Khaldun's calculations, dynasties survived about 120 years, and less time if they included diverse peoples.[3]

Ibn Khaldun had a like-minded contemporary, Luo Guanzhong, a writer in northeast China. In the 1500 years since Zou Yan, China had oscillated between periods of calm and upheaval. Luo himself witnessed the collapse of the Yuan dynasty in 1368. Seeking solace in history, Luo wrote a novel, the *Romance of the Three Kingdoms*, about the demise of the Han dynasty around 200 CE and the reunification of China one hundred years later. Luo blamed court intrigues for the Han collapse but did not see it as a surprise. "Empires arise from chaos and empires collapse back into chaos," Luo explained. "This we have known since time began."[4]

Intellectuals in Istanbul, writing three hundred years later, knew nothing about Luo but shared his view that empires were "subject to the laws of growth and decay."[5] Some feared that their own Ottoman empire was entering its final phase. An Ottoman ambassador who visited the opulent courts of European empires in the 1790s wondered whether they, too, were suffering from the "loss of virility" that Ibn Khaldun had said was a symptom of decline.[6]

Europeans themselves felt this apprehension. Four months after the outbreak of the American Revolution, the chaplain to King George III warned that empires were like waves in the ocean, "successively rising and disappearing again." The Right Reverend George Horne reassured the king that God looked more kindly on empires whose rulers honored the true religion.[7] A few years later, the French philosopher Constantin de Volney also explored the "secret causes" of the rise and fall of empires. One important cause of decline, Volney suggested, was the tendency of rulers to use harsh methods as they struggled to control vast territories.[8]

This age-old certainty about the fragility of empires was tested as Britain reached the apex of its power in the late nineteenth century. On one side were classicists who hewed to the traditional view about rise and fall. On the other side were statesmen who insisted that the British empire had discovered how to escape the usual fate of empires.[9]

The historian Arnold Toynbee recalled watching Queen Victoria's jubilee celebrations in 1897: "Here we are on top of the world. There is a thing called history, but history is something unpleasant that happens to other people."[10] As late as 1929, Lord Birkenhead predicted that British rule over India would last another century at least.[11] But India was independent eighteen years later, and the whole empire was gone soon after. Historians now tell the story of the British empire as another example of rise and fall.[12]

In the 1970s, an Estonian political scientist, Rein Taagepera, picked up the project of calculating the lifespan of empires. Taagepera identified seventy-eight empires and carefully measured changes in their size over time. He found that the average size of empires increased over the centuries because of improvements in technology. But the average lifespan of empires did not change. Remarkably, the average lifespan was 130 years, not far from Ibn Khaldun's estimate of 120 years. There was variation though. Most empires were short-lived, and only one-fifth survived more than three centuries.[13]

The age of empires ended conclusively with the collapse of the Soviet Union in 1991. But scholarly interest in empires boomed after that. Modern-day theories of empire are more sophisticated than the five-element model of Zou Yan, but in one respect theorists have moved an inch. Empires are still perceived as fragile and transitory enterprises. "No empire is permanent," observes political scientist Michael Doyle.[14] "The fundamental reality of empires," agrees Timothy Parsons, "is that they are unsustainable."[15] Every empire, says fellow historian Charles Maier, is an "epoch of entropy."[16] Throughout history, the question has never been whether an empire will die. This was taken as a certainty. The question was only: how soon, and for what reason?

Elemental Hazards

The problems that bedeviled empires fell into two categories. First, there were elemental hazards that arose out of the times and circumstances. These hazards could not be avoided but they could be dealt with through statecraft – that is, by building institutions to anticipate and manage them. However, bad choices about the design of imperial institutions could inadvertently intensify some hazards and even create new ones. A miscalculation about regime design might itself bring an end to empire. Worse still, the distinction between good and bad choices about regime design was rarely clear. Rulers were thus confronted with a set of elemental hazards, and a set of potentially fatal dilemmas about methods of imperial governance.

The greatest elemental hazard was attack from outside the empire. This hazard was severe because of the scale of empire. For example, Chinese emperors wrestled constantly with incursions along thousands of miles of frontier. China's Song dynasty collapsed in 1279 after a Mongol invasion from the west, which resulted in the incorporation of Chinese territory into the empire of Khubilai Khan; similarly, the Ming dynasty fell four centuries later after a Manchu invasion from the northeast.[17] Imperial rulers often faced several enemies on fronts that were far removed from one another. Rulers in the Habsburg empire were obsessed with defending four frontiers.[18] In the mid-seventeenth century, Mughal emperors battled Safavids and Uzbeks in northwest India, the Ahom kingdom in the northeast, and Muslim sultanates in the south.[19] At the same time, the Portuguese fought to protect their maritime empire against the French in South America, the Dutch in southeast Asia, and the English in western India.[20]

In fact, warfare was eventually fatal for the whole age of empires. In the nineteenth century, the Ottoman Empire was called the "sick man of Europe" because of its internal troubles, but it was war with other empires in 1914–1918 that finally finished it off, along with the Habsburg, German, and Russian empires. World War II was another inter-imperial conflict that destroyed the nascent Nazi, Italian, and Japanese empires and exhausted the other European empires.[21]

The second elemental hazard, also aggravated by scale, was rebellion within subject territories. Indeed, rebellion was a chronic condition in most empires. The British suffered an uprising in the American colonies in 1775–1783, Ireland in 1798, Jamaica in 1831, Canada in 1837–1838, north India in 1857, South Africa in 1880–1881 and 1900–1902, and Ireland again in 1916.[22] Generally, rebellions could be managed if they were infrequent and dispersed. But some empires suffered from more severe internal divisions. The Safavid empire that ruled present-day Iran between 1501 and 1736 was a delicate construction plagued with uprisings and civil wars.[23] Chinese history has also been punctuated by periods of violent disintegration – most recently between the end of the Qing empire in 1911 and the establishment of the People's Republic in 1949.

Other hazards undermined empires less directly. Climate change was one of these. Periods of drought were dangerous for early empires that depended mainly on agriculture. Crop failures led to famine, mass migrations, and peasant uprisings. In these periods, central authorities struggled to collect taxes to maintain an army, and became easy prey for neighboring powers as a result. This may have been the fate of the Akkadian empire that collapsed in the Tigris-Euphrates valley around 2100 BCE. Volcanic eruptions in present-day Turkey choked the atmosphere with dust, causing a centuries-long drought that turned farmland in the valley into desert, and weakening the Akkadian empire so much that it was easily overrun.[24]

Many other instances of imperial strain caused by climate change have been documented. The crisis that seized Roman empire in the third century CE – a period known as "the anarchy" – may have been aggravated by climatic instability that caused cooler weather and droughts. In the fourth century CE, worsening weather on the Eurasian Steppe drove nomadic groups westward, putting pressure on Roman borders that ultimately proved fatal to the empire.[25] Long periods of cold and dry weather in the tenth century contributed to the fracturing of the Abbasid empire and also collapse of China's Tang dynasty.[26] Drought in northern India triggered rebellion in the Delhi Sultanate in the fourteenth century, while another drought two hundred years later weakened the Suri empire and allowed the Mughal emperor Humayun to regain power.[27]

Large "composite states," historian Geoffrey Parker says, were particularly vulnerable to shocks like climate change. They had "lower boiling points."[28] Parker has linked a period of global climatic disruption in the seventeenth century with upheavals in several empires. In China, the Ming dynasty collapsed because of famine and rebellion.[29] At the close of the nineteenth century, India was struck by devastating droughts caused by shifting weather patterns across the Indian and Pacific oceans. The failure of the British empire to provide relief spurred the movement that won independence for India fifty years later.[30]

Disease was another elemental hazard that was more pronounced in empires. Historian Kyle Harper observes that empires created their own "disease ecologies": as they moved troops and encouraged trade over long distances, imperial rulers accelerated the spread of disease as well.[31] The Roman and Byzantine empires were struck by three terrifying epidemics between the second and sixth centuries. The last, according to the historian Procopius, "destroyed the greater part of the peasantry." The decline in agricultural production during each epidemic led to famines, while stricken imperial armies struggled to resist invasions.[32]

The collapse of the Khmer empire in southeast Asia in the fourteenth century has been attributed to repeated epidemics of cholera, malaria, smallpox, and other maladies. This empire was "a virtual hot zone for the transmission of diseases."[33] The Spanish conquest of the Aztec and Incan empires in the sixteenth century would not have been accomplished so easily if those empires had not been debilitated by the smallpox virus that accompanied Europeans.[34] By contrast, the advance of European empires in the tropics was slowed by the vulnerability of Europeans to unfamiliar diseases. A Portuguese explorer said that sub-Saharan Africa was protected by "a flaming sword of deadly fevers."[35] Four hundred years later, Europeans still debated whether "white colonization" was possible in tropical territories.[36]

Economic shifts were an elemental hazard for empires too. The power of the Ottoman and Venetian empires in the late Middle Ages hinged on their control of trade from Asia through the eastern Mediterranean to Europe. When Portuguese explorers opened a new maritime route around Africa to Asia in the sixteenth century, the eastern Mediterranean turned into "a stagnant backwater through which the life-giving stream of world trade no longer flowed."[37] The Safavid empire was similarly weakened by this shift in global trade patterns.[38]

Economic shifts inside an empire could be destabilizing as well.[39] The loyalties of imperial subjects waivered when they traded more intensively with foreigners than compatriots, and trading provinces within empires often demanded more autonomy as they became richer. Ming emperors in Beijing may have imposed their ban on maritime trade because of doubts about the loyalty of trading communities in the distant Yangtze delta.[40] The Dutch revolt against Spanish rule in the 1600s succeeded because Dutch provinces had grown rich through trade with northern Europe while Spain itself stagnated, partly because its American colonies were trading more with each other than with the Spanish homeland.[41]

A final hazard for empires was technological backwardness: not just regarding physical or hard technologies – tools, machines, weapons – but also social technologies, or methods of organizing people. The safety of an empire could be jeopardized if rivals had better weapons or better ways of organizing soldiers. A clear example is provided by the rise of industrialized European empires in the nineteenth century.[42] Empires could also be endangered by a decline in wealth relative to rivals. This created pressure on laggard empires to adopt new methods of organization for more efficient use of land, people, and capital. But broad reform programs were particularly hard to execute in sprawling empires.

Technological disparities also intensified internal tensions. Imperial rulers always competed for power with provinces and social classes inside their empires. Territories or groups that adopted innovations more quickly would increase their power relative to the center, as the Dutch provinces did within the Spanish empire in the seventeenth century.[43] One solution for imperial rulers was to upgrade their capacity for centralized control, by modernizing bureaucracies and adopting new communication and surveillance technologies. Chinese empires were pioneers in this work two millennia ago.

The scale of empire meant that imperial rulers were constantly wrestling with elemental hazards of one kind or another. Worse still, hazards were more likely to cascade in large and complex polities: that is, one hazard would trigger or aggravate other hazards.[44] For example, famine made an empire more susceptible to plague. Plague weakened armies, making the empire a more tempting target for invasion. Invasions presented rebels with an opportunity to advance their own cause. War and rebellion disrupted trade and reduced imperial revenues. Hazards might compound in innumerable ways. This is one reason why it is difficult to provide a universal theory for the rise and fall of empires. As historian J.B. Bury suggested, every imperial collapse has unfolded "as a series of contingent events."[45]

Dilemmas of Governance

Imperial rulers worked relentlessly to manage elemental hazards and avoid a fatal cascade of problems. They did this by constructing a regime that had three critical components: an *administrative system* designed to control everyday life within the territory; a *leadership structure* that generated decisions about how power should be exercised; and an *imperial creed* that described the empire's aims and justified imperial rule.[46] Designing these three components was not an easy exercise. In each respect, leaders were confronted with choices that had potentially fatal consequences. Although intended to counter elemental hazards, a poorly designed regime might actually intensify them, and generate new problems too.

The First Dilemma: Control

In the abstract, the ways of managing elemental hazards were straightforward. To repulse invasions and suppress rebellions, imperial rulers could maintain a strong army and navy under central command. Ideally, these armed forces would be large enough, and so widely dispersed, that invaders and rebels would be deterred from launching attacks on the empire. Rulers could also build defensive works: walls and fortresses on the frontier, and outposts in fractious provinces. They could construct roads, canals, and railroads to move troops quickly from one place to another, and armories to build and improve weaponry.

Rulers could also stockpile food and supplies to support the empire in moments of distress. They could build irrigation systems to protect against drought, and regulate prices so that subjects were not gouged in times of shortage. They could proscribe behavior that spread disease. They could force landowners and workers to produce essential goods or adopt more efficient ways of working. To improve cohesion and self-sufficiency, rulers could encourage internal trade – by guaranteeing security for travelers, regulating weights and measures, and establishing a common currency. And they could promote internal cohesion by restricting foreign trade as well.

But all these projects required the close regulation of everyday life in the empire. Taxes had to be levied for pay for these projects, subjects had to be conscripted to serve in the army or construct works, and people had to be monitored and punished when they engaged in proscribed forms of production and trade. An administrative system had to be built for the purpose of regulating behavior in desired ways. Often this involved the establishment of an imperial bureaucracy to make and enforce rules throughout the empire.

The first dilemma confronting imperial rulers related to the intensity of control that should be exerted by means of the administrative system as they sought to manage elemental hazards.[47] Pursuing all projects that might reduce hazards meant exercising intensive control of many aspects of everyday life. But intensive control could easily produce undesirable results, for example by triggering unrest. The other approach was loose control, but this might allow some elemental hazards to fester. Sometimes rulers alternated between intensive and loose control as they balanced the risks associated with each approach.

A policy of centralized and intensive control was pursued by the Qin dynasty more than two millennia ago. This dynasty established its claim over the Chinese heartland in 221 BCE, bringing an end to two centuries of war between contending powers. Its rulers aimed to create a "total state" in which social and economic life was regimented to support a powerful standing army. An extensive bureaucracy prohibited non-essential commerce, regulated the size of households and movement of people, conscripted vast numbers for imperial service, and punished violations of the law severely. The philosophy underlying Qin rule became known as Legalism. One of its proponents said that an emperor should control his subjects "as the metalworker controls metal and the potter clay."[48] Another philosopher observed at that time that Qin rulers "allow their subjects to sustain their lives in very limited ways . . . They impose draconian laws on them, terrorize them with authority, embitter them with hardship, seduce them with rewards and intimidate them with punishment."[49]

The Assyrian empire may have been governed with the same rigid discipline. It has been described as the world's first militarized society.[50] Later empires also experimented with periods of more centralized and intensive control. After the chaos of the third century BCE, Diocletian attempted to restabilize the Roman empire by tightening control, and Philip II sought to restabilize the Spanish empire in the same way in the early seventeenth century.[51] The modernization programs under-taken by several empires – Habsburg, Ottoman, Qing, Russian – in the eighteenth and nineteenth centuries were also intended to centralize and intensify imperial control.

These attempts at intensive control had practical limits. The vastness of empires made it difficult for authorities to detect violations of central commands, and the financial incentives for subjects to evade taxes or trade restrictions were often powerful.[52] Indeed, imperial rulers may have imposed draconian penalties for lawbreaking to compensate for the low probability that lawbreakers would be caught.

Intensive control also aggravated the hazard of rebellion. Qin rulers constructed a powerful war machine, but the regime was shattered by insurrections after only fifteen years.[53] Assyrian rule also ended in "an upsurge of the oppressed."[54] Later attempts to tighten control provoked reaction as well. Philip II's centralization effort fueled uprisings in Spanish-controlled Portugal, the Netherlands, and Catalonia. The modernization project of Habsburg emperor Joseph II in the late eighteenth century triggered the worst crisis the empire had faced since the Prussian invasion of the 1740s.[55]

Controls on economic activity and trade were often intended to improve unity and security in the short run, but they also increased the risk of technological backwardness in the long run. Provincial elites and entrepreneurs were denied freedom to adopt new ways of working. Entrepreneurship itself was often stigmatized. Status and wealth were attained through service in the imperial bureaucracy, which despised variation and preferred to maintain traditional ways of life.[56]

Intensive control of economy and society required more bureaucracy, but bureaucracy itself created new problems of control for imperial rulers. Bureaucrats were supposed to assure that subjects in distant lands complied with imperial commands, but bureaucrats themselves often failed to respect instructions. In extensive empires, it might take months or years for messages to be conveyed between the imperial seat and the frontier, and bureaucrats often had good reason for ignoring commands that were no longer workable when they arrived. As a Dutch official in the East Indies explained, when presented with orders from home: "We do here, what seems best and most advisable to us."[57] Officials who were posted for a long time in distant places might also "go native" and develop excessive sympathy for the people they were supposed to rule. Or they might become corrupt, bending rules and lying to superiors about conditions.

Bureaucratic rule on an imperial scale was difficult and unreliable. Imperial rulers were constantly inventing ways to keep the machine running smoothly. Selecting officials who were competent and loyal was a critical task. Sometimes, authority was divided in remote provinces, so that one official could check the misconduct of another. Schemes were invented for collecting reports from the territories, conducting inspections, conferring rewards and levying punishments, and rotating officials to avoid their absorption into local society. In other words, a second bureaucracy was constructed to maintain the integrity of the first, and that second bureaucracy could be flawed too.[58] The burgeoning cost and inefficiency of bureaucracy itself became a hazard to empire.[59]

Extensive bureaucracy created another hazard as well: the danger that bureaucrats would capture imperial power rather than simply weighing it down. Emperors during the Han dynasty appointed eunuchs to critical administrative posts, expecting that they would be loyal to the emperor alone. But the eunuch class gained such influence that they were eventually in the business of toppling emperors.[60] Abbasid rulers of the ninth century created a bodyguard of captured slaves, the Mamluks, on the premise that these slaves would have loyalty to no element of Abbasid society except the ruler himself. But Abbasid rulers became "mere puppets" of the Mamluks.[61] In the fourteenth century, Ottoman rulers also created a corps of slaves, the Janissaries, with similar hopes about their fidelity. The Janissaries became an independent force in Ottoman politics, prone to mutiny and sometimes deposing rulers.[62]

The dilemma of intensive control was recognized by the philosopher Lao Tzu. The imperial domain, he said, could be lost if it was grasped too tightly. The best policy was to resist extremes.[63] After the collapse of the Qin dynasty, Chinese rulers experimented with looser control as they sought to restore order. The experiment took two forms: devolution of authority to fiefdoms headed by the emperor's kinsmen, and a loosening of rules on commerce. The formula worked for a few decades, until emperors became uneasy about the rising power of princes and merchants, and control was intensified again.[64] Chinese history has been distinguished by repeated experiments with liberalization as rulers balanced the hazards to empire, although the baseline has always been relatively intensive control.[65]

Many other empires engaged in bolder trials of loose control. The Roman empire at its zenith in the second century CE had a population roughly equal to that of the Han empire, about sixty million people. Both empires had armies of similar size, about 250,000 men.[66] But the Han civil bureaucracy counted 130,000 while the Roman was a few thousand at most.[67] Romans governed their territories lightly, often working through local elites and traditional power structures. One result was that the form of rule varied substantially from one place to another. Another was that ordinary subjects rarely dealt directly with civil representatives of the empire.[68]

Eighteen hundred years later, the British empire was run in a similar way. "In administrative terms," says John Darwin, "the British presided over a ramshackle empire, full of contradictions and quirks, and with a control apparatus that was spasmodic at best."[69] Some parts of the empire were organized as largely self-governing settler colonies while other parts were governed by a system of "cooperation with native rulers."[70] At the height of empire, there were only 1,200 British administrators in British-ruled Africa and another 1,300 in India.[71] British colonial administration was narrow in its reforming ambitions, largely because it was so dependent on local elites.[72] The whole empire was also prone to rebellions, as we have noted. This "loosely constructed building" required adroit management in moments of danger, of which there were many.[73]

The Second Dilemma: Leadership

At the apex of every empire was a relatively small group of people who were responsible for defining imperial interests and deciding how power should be exercised to advance those interests. The most important of these people was the emperor himself. Typically, he would be served by an imperial court, consisting of kinsfolk, representatives of powerful elements in the societies contained within the empire, and senior bureaucrats and military commanders. Interactions within this group were always structured to some degree. There were routines for decision-making in which people played assigned roles.

Given the fragility of empire, the design of the leadership structure was immensely important. A structure that generated bad decisions – or failed to generate timely decisions – could easily bring the empire down. But there was no clearly superior way of organizing imperial leadership. Every design could produce fatal outcomes under some circumstances. The challenge was designing a leadership structure that minimized the risk of imperial collapse in the long run.

The principle of rule in many empires was autocratic, dynastic, and patriarchal. At the start, a military commander would establish control over vast territories and then claim absolute authority within his new empire. When this emperor died, title would pass to his son or another kinsman. Obviously, emperors themselves had an interest in perpetuating a system of autocratic rule, because it kept power in their hands. But emperors also claimed that autocratic rule benefited the empire as a whole. This was held to be true for two reasons. Because emperors were positioned above all the communities contained within their empire, and sometimes did not belong to any of them, they could arbitrate disputes between communities more easily. Emperors might even protect ethnic or religious minorities against persecution by provincial elites.[74] In addition, emperors could respond to dangers quickly and firmly, precisely because authority to act was entirely in their hands.

The capacity for decisiveness was judged to be especially important in empires because they were vulnerable to severe and cascading hazards. Roman general Marcus Agrippa and Arab philosopher Ibn Khaldun concurred that a vast and diverse population required autocratic rule.[75] "Only undivided authority," Russian empress Catherine II agreed, "can function conveniently over the expanse of a vast empire."[76] Some American writers of the eighteenth century also saw this as a clear lesson of history: extensive territory required autocracy.[77]

However, autocratic rule had its dangers. Emperors could be overwhelmed with work: reading reports from the provinces, receiving embassies, judging petitions, drafting correspondence and edicts, and performing ceremonial functions. Because of this workload, there was a risk that emperors would make bad or inconsistent decisions, become absorbed with immediate crises rather than looking ahead, or fail to make decisions at all.[78] This risk was magnified when empires pursued a policy of intensive control, which increased the load of decision-making at the center of the regime, and also as technological improvements increased the volume of information flowing to the seat of empire.[79]

Philip II, ruler of the Spanish empire for forty years, was celebrated for having "the largest brain in the world." But Philip struggled to manage the deluge of documents generated by his regime, and the pressure often caused him to make critical miscalculations.[80] Sometimes, failures in decision-making could be fatal for an empire.[81] According to historian John Fairbank, the Qing empire "demanded a superman at the head of affairs," and the lack of supermen became an important factor in its collapse.[82]

Indeed, hereditary rule meant that empires often lacked leaders of ordinary competence. J.B. Bury believed that one of the factors that doomed the Roman empire was the accession of the "feeble-minded" emperor Honorius. His reign was punctuated by attempted coups and the humiliating sack of Rome by the Visigoths.[83] The Ottoman empire was also crippled by weak rulers in the sixteenth and seventeenth centuries – including Selim II, a "drunken incompetent"; Mustafa, deposed because of insanity; and Ibrahim, "weak and eccentric, if not insane."[84] The last emperor of Russia, Nicholas II, had "maddening faults" including lack of vision and an inability to learn from mistakes. "I try not to ponder over anything," Nicholas explained. "I find that is the best way to rule Russia."[85]

Empires were also endangered when rulers died. The incentive to challenge a line of succession was substantial because the new ruler's authority would be absolute and indefinite. Some new emperors killed or imprisoned their rivals as a matter of routine, which sharpened the incentive among potential claimants to fight for power.[86] Succession struggles often degraded into civil wars and created moments of confusion that could be exploited by rebellious provinces and rival powers.

Broadly, there were two ways of remedying the defects of autocratic rule. One was power sharing, which in the extreme meant abandoning the autocratic model entirely. But power sharing rarely had satisfactory results. At different points, the Roman empire experimented with governance by a Senate, by triumvirates of powerful politicians and military leaders, and by a system of co-emperors. None of these experiments survived for very long. The last one resulted in civil war and contributed to the eventual splitting of the empire.[87] Similarly, the organization of the Mongol empire into four khanates superintended by a Great Khan eventually resulted in breakup of that empire.[88] The decline of the Dutch maritime empire in the eighteenth century was accelerated by the difficulty of coordinating policy within a highly decentralized republic.[89]

The other technique for remedying the weaknesses of autocracy was the construction of an imperial court, consisting of trusted advisors, leading noblemen, and senior bureaucrats. Work could be divided among specialists and routines could be developed for the handling of the emperor's business. In some empires, courtiers even established themselves as counterweights to the emperor himself. They sought to protect the empire against bad rulers by limiting the ruler's influence over major decisions. Han emperors were encouraged by courtiers to play "a passive rather than an active role" in governance.[90] Historian Yuri Pines sees a general tendency in every Chinese dynasty for emperors to be "deactivated" in this way as the dynasty grew older.[91]

Deactivating emperors might have been a reasonable policy during quiet times when courts could be trusted to perform their work properly. But courts were prone to failure too. Often, they became bloated and inefficient. Procedures intended to speed decision-making became complex and ritualized instead.[92] Courts were often riven by factional struggles and intrigues. Advisory positions that were once filled by merit became heritable, so that the quality of personnel declined. The entire court frequently became isolated and self-satisfied.[93]

To remain effective, a court had to be properly managed. But a deactivated emperor could not do this. Moreover, a deactivated emperor could not rise above court rituals in moments of crisis. Here was another illustration of the dilemma of leadership. On one hand, an emperor without a substantial court was more likely to jeopardize the empire through rash decision-making. On the other hand, an empire might also be jeopardized by a broken court and an enfeebled emperor.

The Third Dilemma: Creed

In the nineteenth century, advocates of European imperialism spoke about the "civilizing mission" of European empires. European states did not exploit their overseas colonies, it was claimed. On the contrary, they improved colonies by teaching new ways of life. European empires were not alone in making such a claim. Almost every empire in history has been guided by a distinctive creed: that is, by a set of ideas about the proper organization of society that rulers had a duty to propagate.[94] But how dogmatic should empires be about their creed – or putting it the other way around, how tolerant should they be of non-conforming ways of life within the empire? This was the third dilemma of imperial rule.

Some imperial creeds were based on religion. Indeed, a major innovation in the governance of empires is said to have happened around the third century BCE, when rulers realized how faith could be effective in unifying their domains.[95] When people share a faith, Ibn Khaldun said in the fourteenth century, "nothing can withstand them, because their outlook is one and their object one of common accord."[96] Ottoman rulers commanded respect in the sixteenth century because they also performed the role of caliph, head of the Islamic community. As caliph, an Ottoman ruler was expected to promote the Muslim faith and honor Sharia, the sacred law.[97] At the western end of the Mediterranean, meanwhile, rulers of the Spanish empire presented themselves as militant defenders of Catholic Christianity. Catholic faith was a "strong unifying force" welding the disparate parts of the empire together.[98]

Imperial creeds were not always based on faith. Roman rulers promoted a way of living that came to be known as *Romanitas* – a broad vision of civilized life that encompassed politics and social behavior, and modes of thought and expression, but which did not involve rigid views about religious practices, at least until the final years of the empire.[99] Similarly, Chinese rulers promoted a form of Confucianism, a formula for maintaining a harmonious society that was "more a this-worldly ethical system than a transcendental religion."[100]

Concepts of civilization that were promoted by European empires in the nineteenth century also placed less emphasis on religion. The French version, more directly influenced by Enlightenment rationalism, aimed at improving humanity through systematic governmental action.[101] The British creed, sometimes known as Anglo-Saxonism, was less ordered. It stressed the rule of law, "good government," and limited self-rule – sooner for colonies dominated by white settlers, and much later for colonies populated by "backward races."[102]

At minimum, a creed was essential as operating software for governing an empire. Elites in the imperial seat and provinces had to share a common understanding about the rituals and purposes of government.[103] Creed was a glue that held elites together in difficult times.[104] It was also employed to rally subjects in times of war. In the Middle Ages, caliphs launched jihads while Western rulers launched Crusades; a millennium later, European leaders launched innumerable "wars for civilization," culminating in the world wars of the twentieth century.

A compelling creed was essential to manage the elemental hazards faced by all empires. It was necessary as a counter to subversive ideologies that periodically spread through the population, sometimes with the encouragement of rival empires. These subversive ideologies also came in religious and secular form. In stressful times, messianic leaders emerged in the provinces to promote new faiths that questioned the legitimacy of imperial rule. Nationalism – the idea that every people with a common culture and history should be permitted to govern themselves – played a similarly subversive role in the nineteenth and twentieth centuries.[105]

In some ways, promoting the imperial creed was just one part of the larger project of intensifying central control throughout the empire. An administrative apparatus was necessary to propagate the creed and suppress rival ideologies. A religious and educational establishment would be set up, and churches, temples, and schools would be constructed. At the same time, heterodox churches and temples would be torn down. Imperial laws often proscribed immoral behavior. Religious minorities were encouraged and sometimes forced to convert to the official faith. Minorities could be punished with taxes, driven into ghettos, expelled from the empire, or exterminated. One of the last empires, Nazi Germany, was also the most deliberate in constructing a bureaucracy to destroy non-conforming ways of life.

However, there are important ways in which the promotion of a creed differed from other problems of imperial control. There was a qualitative difference in the character of control. It is one thing to impose taxes, restrict trade, seize property, or conscript labor; it is another thing to demand that individuals abandon their beliefs, identity, and traditional ways of living. More effort was required by imperial rulers to achieve these fundamental changes, and the magnitude of the project was compounded by the diversity that was found in empires. The probability of evasion or resistance was also higher, because of the seriousness with which subjects regarded matters of faith, identity, and community.

Indeed, attempts to enforce an imperial creed often backfired. At the turn of the fourth century, the Roman emperor Diocletian reversed the traditional practice of tolerating Christians and launched an intensive persecution throughout the empire. The persecution produced great suffering but failed anyway. Diocletian's proscriptions were easily evaded, and in some places triggered a fierce backlash. The persecution was quickly abandoned and probably strengthened the Christian Church.[106] Diocletian's successor converted to Christianity a few years later. The Mughal emperor Aurangzeb, an orthodox Muslim, also reversed a policy of religious accommodation in the late seventeenth century, again with unintended results. Hindu and Sikh rebellions contributed to the empire's decline in following decades.[107]

Creedal dogmatism had another consequence. The bureaucracy that emerged to enforce this policy sometimes acquired autonomy and acted as a continuing check on the emperor's power. If the imperial creed was founded on faith, rulers who deviated from orthodoxy for reasons of state could expect sharp criticism from religious leaders.[108] And programs of religious persecution could acquire their own momentum.[109] Added to this was the growing cost of the religious bureaucracy. This became a significant drag on the Roman Empire after the establishment of Christianity as the state religion, and on the Ottoman Empire as well.[110]

Many rulers, sensitive to the hazards of dogmatism, adopted a policy of limited tolerance within their empires. Subjects with unorthodox beliefs were left alone so long as they recognized imperial authority. The Dutch empire was formally committed to Calvinist Protestantism, but anti-Catholic laws were loosely enforced, and the overseas work of Calvinist missionaries was restricted where it seemed likely to cause unrest.[111] The Ottoman empire devised a system by which Christian and Jewish communities governed themselves through their own institutions, although they were still treated as inferiors to their Muslim neighbors.[112] Russian emperors in the nineteenth century professed a form of orthodox Christianity and persecuted non-believers in the Western empire, but often left Muslims in the Eastern empire alone.[113]

The British, through their practice of indirect rule, tolerated practices that were completely at odds with Anglo-Saxon ideals of good government. When India gained independence in 1947, after two centuries of British rule, almost forty percent of its territory was still governed by hundreds of semi-feudal "princely states," which were propped up by British administrators. India's first prime minister, Jawaharlal Nehru, described these as "sinks of reaction and incompetence and unrestrained autocratic power, sometimes exercised by vicious and degraded individuals."[114]

Rulers often deviated from creed for purely practical reasons, weighing the virtues of doctrinal purity against administrative and political realities.[115] Some scholars have suggested that a policy of accommodation was the surest path for survival of an empire.[116] But this path was treacherous. Rulers who strayed from the imperial creed by accommodating provincial elites and minorities could be accused of faithlessness by clerics or intellectuals, as the Mughal emperor Akbar was in the sixteenth century.[117] Or imperial rulers might be accused of hypocrisy by subjects like Nehru, who saw how ground realities fell short of imperial rhetoric.[118]

The ruling class itself could be demoralized by too much compromise. This might have been one of the ailments of the Habsburg empire in its final decades. The empire's sense of purpose dissipated in the late nineteenth century as its leaders cobbled together remedies for one internal crisis after another. Nationalist pressures were rising, and one leading Habsburg minister complained that the empire had been reduced to "the politics of the bazaar."[119] Habsburg politics and culture was affected by a sense of drift and disintegration even before the First World War dealt the empire its fatal blow.

Plotting Against History

Edward Gibbon, the great historian of Roman empire, said that the puzzle was not why it collapsed, but how it survived so long. The reasons for its demise, Gibbon said, were "simple and obvious." The empire was a vast and unwieldy enterprise, straining under its own weight, and some combination of accidents was bound to cause its collapse eventually.[120] Other empires suffered similar maladies. Another historian has observed that most Chinese dynasties were "mathematically unmanageable."[121] Scale, diversity, and complexity made empires unusually susceptible to a range of hazards that could easily combine in a fatal cascade. Rulers struggled to design regimes that would be effective in anticipating and managing hazards, but uncertainty plagued calculations about the best design. Efforts to build a resilient regime often resulted unintentionally in the production of entirely new dangers.

Successful emperors were those who thought about governance in a certain way. Attentiveness to dangers was an essential skill, and complacency a serious defect. Emperors had to take care not to believe their own propaganda. Empires needed to parade their strength and durability for subjects and rival powers, but this was usually a bluff.[122] The actual practice of government had to be predicated on the understanding that imperial authority was fragile. The "submerged mind of Empire," as novelist J.M. Coetzee called it, was preoccupied with the question of "how not to end, how not to die." Emperors were always plotting against history.[123]

The mix and severity of hazards to empire changed constantly, and the architecture of empires had to adjust accordingly. Often the renovations were dramatic. Frontiers expanded and contracted, with the result that weight of imperial responsibilities increased or declined. Rulers experimented with more or less intensive control over provinces, markets, and communities. At the same time, they experimented with different modes of decision-making at the apex of the empire. Rulers adjusted the substance of the imperial creed and their tolerance of non-conforming ways of life.

The project of renovation was never-ending. The aim of imperial reform was never to achieve a permanent political settlement – because no such settlement was possible – but only to "keep the game going."[124] Rulers had to be good at improvisation and had to avoid attachment to specific ways of governing.[125] There was a danger of seeing institutions as permanent solutions to problems of imperial governance, when they were merely temporary fixes.[126] There was a danger, too, that the whole regime might settle into a form that compromised its ability to adapt to new challenges. The resilience of an empire could be undermined by a dysfunctional imperial court, powerful vested interests, or outdated ideas.

It is tempting to think that problems of empire belong entirely to history. Among other things, superstates have access to technologies and resources that vastly improve their capacity to manage scale, diversity, and complexity. But the balance sheet is not so straight-forward. Superstates do have advantages over empires – but carry new burdens too. And in the end, they too may be vulnerable to the fate of empires.

3

Are Superstates More Durable?

There are no empires left in the world today. The remaining European empires died in the decades after World War II. The Soviet Union, which collapsed in 1991, has been described as the very last of the empires, but I will argue that it is more accurate to see the Soviet Union as a failed superstate. Some experts claim that empires are also obsolete, in the sense that they could not exist under modern-day conditions. "Stable imperial rule" is said to be impossible today because it requires a form of authoritarian rule that is untenable in a world that takes human rights seriously, and in which minorities have easy access to weapons, money, and moral support from abroad.[1]

This argument is not quite right. Undoubtedly, human rights and globalization have made it harder to sustain authoritarian rule over an extensive territory containing diverse peoples. Harder, but not impossible – as the example of China illustrates. China is an authoritarian system that has successfully suppressed movements for autonomy in Xinjiang, Tibet, and Hong Kong. Indeed, some argue that the current regime is simply the latest in a series of empires that have ruled China for more than two millennia.

But it is not helpful to think of China strictly as an empire. Certainly, it encompasses diverse populations within a vast territory. However, it also carries the burdens of any twentieth-century state, large or small. Modern-day China is expected to govern its territory more intensively and has a more complex administrative apparatus for that reason. China is an example of a superstate: a hybrid empire/state form, or alternately, an adaptation of empire to realities of the modern world.

The question is whether this hybrid model is more durable than the model of empire, or whether superstates are just as susceptible to decay and collapse. Chinese leaders claim to have no doubts on this question. Publicly, they boast about the durability of their regime. "Time and momentum," President Xi Jinping said in 2021, "are on our side."[2] Of course, British rulers said the same about the British empire in 1921.

One way to approach the question of superstate durability is to identify important ways in which the world has changed over the last century, and then to consider how these changes affect the hazards and dilemmas that we identified in the last chapter. We will see that there is no compelling reason to think that superstates are more robust than empires. While superstates have some advantages, mainly in methods of control, they also have many serious disadvantages. The collapse of the Soviet Union in 1991 was a warning that superstates are mortal too.

A Changed World

The world has transformed since the last of the great empires reached maturity in the eighteenth and nineteenth centuries. Some of these changes make it easier to govern scale, diversity, and complexity – but many make it harder. We can enumerate some of the most important shifts:

Demography and public health. Global population has increased dramatically since the eighteenth century. In 1800, the population of the Qing empire might have been about 300 million; China's population today is almost five times larger.[3] In 1910, the population of the British empire today was about 400 million; if the empire still existed today, its population would be about 2.5 billion.

People also live more closely to one another. As late as 1920, the vast majority of the world's people was dispersed across the countryside. In Asia, only six percent of the population lived in towns of 20,000 or more.[4] Today, most people live in urban areas, even in Asia.[5] Many urban residents are also slum dwellers. In China today, one-quarter of the urban population lives in slums. In India, the proportion is one-third.[6]

The governed population has changed in other ways too. Because of advances in medicine and public health, people suffer less illness and live longer lives. They are also better educated. Most people who lived in empires could not read or write.[7] As late as 1950, almost half the world's adults were illiterate, and in Asia, two-thirds of all adults.[8] But almost all adult Chinese are literate today, and India is moving quickly toward universal literacy as well.[9]

Science and technology. Advances in scientific knowledge have done more than improve public health. They have also given policy-makers a better understanding of the territory they govern. This includes better understanding of natural processes – relating to geography, hydrology, climate, and ecosystems – and social processes such as the economy. Modern governments collect more data about everyday life and have a better (but still imperfect) understanding of how governmental actions will affect nature, society, and markets.

At the same time, critical technologies have improved dramatically. Fernand Braudel has observed that distance was "the first enemy" of empires.[10] As late as 1914, it took more than forty days to travel from the seat of the British empire to the administrative center of its most distant possession.[11] Travel times have shrunk from weeks to hours, and electronic communication is instantaneous.

Military technologies are also more effective. Nuclear weapons are the most dramatic illustration of this change. But even a single infantryman, equipped with rapid-fire rifle, body armor, mapping device, and night vision goggles, is more deadly than a century ago. The technology of bureaucracy has improved too, although not so radically. Methods of selecting employees, organizing work, and limiting misbehavior are more effective than they once were.

However, technological improvements have not been monopolized by governments. Ordinary people have access to powerful new technologies as well. For example, most subjects of empire rarely traveled. They lived and died near the place they were born. Today, we live in the era of mobility. The average American travels more than 13,000 miles a year.[12] A 2017 study estimated that nine million Indians migrate between states in search of work every year.[13] During the forty-day travel season around China's new year, Chinese citizens undertake the world's biggest annual human migration, completing three billion journeys with a total distance of nearly eight hundred million miles.[14]

People are wired as well. In 1923 the Indian capital, Delhi, had only 1,247 telephones.[15] By 2023, about 700 million smartphones will be in use in India. This exceeds the number of conventional telephones in the entire world in 1995.[16] Forty percent of the Indian population also had an internet subscription by 2019, and twenty percent were actively engaged in social media.

Access to new communication technologies has made it easier to organize social movements within countries and across national borders. It is also easier to organize "dark networks" whose aim is to destabilize states through violence.[17] These subversive movements often have access to powerful weapons, obtained legally or through black markets. A 2019 United Nations report estimated that civilians around the world now own 850 million firearms, vastly more than the number owned by military and police forces combined.[18]

Geopolitics. Much of the history of empires was absorbed by wars to acquire new territories and keep control of vast borderlands. Aggression was more likely because empires had a weak hold on their frontiers and military disparities between rival powers were often large.[19] But transportation and communication improvements in the nineteenth and early twentieth century improved the capacity of rulers to move military forces along their frontiers. The weapons gap also shrank, partly because weaker societies were destroyed, and partly because of the diffusion of new weapon technologies among the remaining powers. The two world wars of the twentieth century – a thirty-year period of struggle among empires – demonstrated how aggressive war had become less useful an instrument of imperial policy. World War II was followed by a long period of unusual calm that has been called the Long Peace.[20]

The two world wars also triggered the development of a thicker corpus of international law and new international organizations like the United Nations, the World Bank, and International Monetary Fund, and many others. The expanding body of international law includes condemnations of imperialism, prohibitions on aggressive war, restrictions on the use of force against a state's own subjects, and obligations on states to control private organizations within their borders that threaten other states. International law has its limitations as a check on bad behavior, but international organizations have become more effective in exposing violations of international norms. The number of nongovernmental international organizations that watch for abuses of governmental power has burgeoned since World War II.

Ideology. Conventional wisdom about politics and government has changed substantially since 1800. In previous chapters, for example, we noted the rise of nationalism – the idea that people who share a language, culture, and history should be allowed to govern themselves. As nationalist movements gained strength in the nineteenth and twentieth centuries, empires began to look like unnatural constructions. However, enthusiasm for the nationalist principle was tempered in the late twentieth century after people saw how it fueled war and persecution of ethnic minorities.

Another idea, constitutionalism, also gained influence in the nineteenth and twentieth centuries.[21] Constitutionalists argue that basic rules about the exercise of political power should be contained in a single written document. Often, constitutionalists have tried to replace autocracies with governments built on a "separation of powers," including a representative assembly to make laws, an executive to execute laws, and an independent judiciary to monitor compliance with constitutional restrictions. Constitutions are usually designed so they can be revised, but not easily.

The doctrine of liberalism has gained influence too.[22] Originally, this doctrine said that individuals should be protected against arbitrary state action and that there should be some part of private life that is free from government interference. After World War II, the doctrine expanded in meaning, so that governments had a duty to provide individuals with basic services such as education and healthcare. Governments are also expected to protect individuals from criminal violence, workplace hazards, poverty in old age, and other threats. The 1948 Universal Declaration of Human Rights is one of several international charters that enumerate the ways in which governments should protect people. The raised status of individuals is reflected in the now-universal practice of calling them citizens rather than subjects.

One of the basic human rights is that of selecting rulers through free elections.[23] This is the democratic ideal, and it too was consolidated after World War II. By the late 1990s, some people were celebrating the global triumph of democracy, anticipating that forms of non-democratic rule, such as monarchism, theocracy, fascism, communism, technocracy, and military dictatorship, would fade away.[24] This celebration turned out to be premature. Confidence in democracy has weakened over the last decade, and many forms of non-democratic governance persist.

Economy. The dominant form of economic activity has transformed over the last two centuries. In 1800, more than eighty percent of the world's population lived in extreme poverty.[25] Methods of production were crude, and trade was sharply limited: families produced much of what they consumed or bartered within their local communities.[26] Over the next two hundred years, household and local production declined in importance. People relied more on the marketplace and long-distance trade. Production technologies became more complicated and required more up-front investment. The work of raising and investing capital became an increasingly important part of daily life.

The expansion of market capitalism made most people richer. Per capita GDP increased fourteen times between 1820 and 2018.[27] But the global economy is also extraordinarily complex. Today, production chains routinely span countries and continents. International trade as a share of global GDP has doubled over the last fifty years.[28] China's central bank recorded more than 400 billion electronic transactions through financial institutions in just the last three months of 2019.[29] In many countries, though, a large portion of market activity still goes unobserved and unregulated by government.[30]

The modern market economy is also volatile. Its tendency is to accelerate the rate of technological change, which means that entire industries and the communities that depend on them may flourish and decline quickly. The economist Joseph Schumpeter called this the process of "creative destruction."[31] Left on its own, the market system also produces severe inequalities in income and wealth.[32] The entire system is susceptible to cycles of boom and bust.[33]

Climate. The last and most critical transformation of the last two centuries is climate change. Over that period, the world burned an increasing amount of fossil fuels, with the result that an increasing amount of carbon dioxide has been released into the atmosphere. The build-up of carbon dioxide in the atmosphere impairs the release of heat from the earth's surface into space, causing an increase in temperature of the atmosphere and the world's oceans.[34]

Without significant effort to reduce the emission of carbon dioxide, the planet's surface temperature is expected to be four degrees Centigrade hotter in 2100 than it was in the late 1800s. The effects of this change would be devastating. Sea levels would rise, flooding coastal cities. Rising temperatures would make some cities nearly unlivable. Persistent drought would jeopardize supplies of food and fresh water, triggering mass human migrations. People around the world would experience more extreme weather events such as heatwaves, cyclones, and wildfires. Many of the planet's species would become extinct.[35]

Avoiding these outcomes requires dramatic changes in everyday life, aimed at reducing carbon dioxide emissions to nearly zero by 2100.[36] Governments have understood the dangers since the late 1980s and often promised to reduce emissions. But they have been reluctant to adopt measures that might slow growth, disturb domestic politics, and reduce their country's standing in the global economic order. The result is that the global emissions continue to rise. Delay in curbing emissions means that even more radical measures will be necessary to avoid the worst effects of climate change.[37]

Persistent Hazards

Bearing in mind this catalog of transformations, can we say with confidence that superstates are more robust than empires were? The answer is clearly no. We observed in the last chapter that empires were fragile for two reasons: because they faced an array of elemental hazards, and because the business of designing a regime to manage those hazards was fraught with dilemmas. Rulers of superstates face a similar predicament. The range of elemental hazards is just as daunting, and dilemmas of regime design are just as profound, as in the age of empires.

Consider the range of hazards that afflicted empires. The first was attack by a neighboring power, or by several powers, moving on far-removed frontiers at the same time. We might think that rulers of superstates worry less about external threats, given the deterrent effect of nuclear weapons, the increased mobility of their forces, the restrictions on aggressive war in international law, and the extent of economic interdependence among superstates. We have seen a remarkable reduction in aggressive war over the last seventy years. But history has seen such quiet interludes before, which have ended suddenly. The restraining effect of international norms and economic interdependence has been overestimated in the past.[38] And superstates themselves clearly see external attack as an ongoing hazard. Each superstate maintains armed services employing at least 1.3 million active-duty personnel.[39]

What about rebellion, the second hazard? The motivation for rebellion, the desire of subject populations to gain autonomy from central authority, has not diminished in significance. On the contrary, a well-educated population can draw on a broad inventory of ideas about national self-determination, anti-colonialism, and human rights to justify demands for autonomy. The world also has higher expectations about the services that should be provided by government, which makes it easier for minorities to demonstrate neglect or discrimination. Several factors, such as urbanization, mobility, and interconnectedness, had made it easier for people to organize against central authority. Impediments to collective action have been dramatically reduced.[40]

Today, every superstate wrestles with resistance to central authority. China faces demands for autonomy in Xinjiang, Tibet, and Hong Kong; the European Union, Brexit and similar national movements; India, Naxalism and pressures from linguistic-minority states; the United States, anti-Washington populism and a surge in right-wing extremism. Resistance to central authority can be managed through political accommodation by the center, but also by investing in domestic surveillance and policing capabilities. Investment of this type has increased substantially in all superstates in the last quarter-century and is a measure of how seriously leaders view the hazard of domestic unrest.

The third hazard faced by empires was climate change. We do not need to spend much time debating whether this hazard is worse today than it was during the age of empires. Clearly the climate threat that will confront superstates in coming decades is profound. A 2021 report by the US National Intelligence Council warned that climate change would deepen societal cleavages and contribute to instability around the world.[41]

Until recently, the fourth hazard – disease – might have seemed less grave than in the age of empires. The twentieth century was marked by growing confidence about the capacity of governments to control communicable diseases. The high-point was the late 1970s, when a worldwide public health campaign achieved the complete eradication of smallpox.[42] "The most likely forecast about the future of infectious disease," a 1972 textbook explained, "is that it will be very dull."[43] However, the following decades witnessed the failure of other eradication efforts, as well as outbreaks of new diseases that spread rapidly because of urbanization and increased human mobility.[44] China fell into political crisis because of its bungled response to the SARS epidemic in 2002–2003.

More devastating than SARS was the COVID pandemic, which killed more than five million people in 2019–2021 and plunged the world into its deepest economic decline since World War II. This pandemic demonstrated how globalization has made the world more vulnerable to communicable diseases. COVID-19 was first identified in China in December 2019 and found on every continent except Antarctica within the next twelve weeks. By contrast, an outbreak of bubonic plague in southwest China in 1855 took forty years to reach Hong Kong, two more years to reach India, and another three years to arrive in the United States and Europe.[45]

The fifth hazard for empires was shifts in patterns of production and commerce. The vitality of empires could be undermined if they were relegated to the margins of the global economy. In addition, internal tensions could be aggravated if inequalities between regions intensified, or if border provinces developed stronger economic ties with traders abroad than they had with other provinces inside the empire. Imperial economies were constantly mutating, if slowly, and these mutations were potentially destabilizing.

The last three decades have demonstrated that this hazard might be even more substantial today than in the age of empires. The globalized market economy creates, destroys, and reallocates wealth with unprecedented speed. Regional and class inequalities have increased in all superstates since the 1980s, fueling conflict between haves and have-nots. Suspicion of "denationalized cosmopolitans," that is, people in trading regions whose loyalty to the homeland has been weakened by globalization, is common to all superstates.[46] Political tensions have intensified during periods of economic turmoil like the global financial crisis of 2007–2009; one of a succession of economic crises that have marked the era of globalization.[47]

The final hazard for empires was technological backwardness. Imperial rulers worried that rivals might gain a military advantage because of superior weaponry or an economic advantage through more sophisticated methods of production and commerce. This anxiety has not abated over time. If anything, we have seen growing fears among leaders about the pace of technological innovation in rival superstates, and more efforts to limit rivals' access to critical technologies. Concerns about economic and national security have driven China and the United States into a "technology cold war" since 2018.[48]

Persistent Dilemmas

Leaders of superstates, like their predecessors in empires, are preoccupied with building a regime that will be effective in managing elemental hazards. As we noted in Chapter 2, any such regime has three critical components: an administrative system for exercising control, a leadership structure, and a justificatory creed. Designing a durable regime is difficult, because measures to control one elemental hazard might have the perverse effect of aggravating another hazard, or of creating entirely new dangers. Governing superstates, like governing empires, means wrestling with unending dilemmas.

The First Dilemma: Control

Superstates exercise tighter control over their territories than empires did. Like all other modern states, they monitor social and economic life more closely, and try to shape daily life in more detail. Similarly, they are more active in monitoring and shaping the elements of nature

– land, water, weather – where possible. One reason that states govern more intensively is simply that they can. Improvements in technology have made it easier to collect data, monitor behavior, and enforce rules.

But states also govern more intensively because they are expected to. As the doctrine of liberalism has developed, governments have been pushed into new realms of service delivery and regulation, such as education, healthcare, protection against discrimination, workplace and consumer safety, and environmental conservation. The international community of states also imposes its expectations on national leaders. Governments are expected to control activity that may affect other countries, such as terrorism, cross-border trafficking, infectious disease, migration, and pollution, and in general to know what is happening within their borders.

More intensive governance means a larger administrative apparatus. One rough measure of the scale of this apparatus is the number of civilian workers employed by governments in each superstate:

United States	22 million
European Union	24 million
India	18 million
China	45 million.[49]

These estimates are probably low, because they exclude millions of workers in state-owned enterprises and businesses that are contracted to do government work. One study estimates that the contractor workforce for the US federal government might include almost ten million people.[50] It is likely that the public sector workforce in China today rivals the total population of the Han empire in the second century CE.

Superstates have not overcome the challenges that accompany intensive control. On the contrary, some of these problems are more severe, because bureaucracies are more sprawling, the tasks they perform are more complex, and the burdens which they impose on ordinary people are more onerous. Symptoms of bureaucratism – wastefulness, corruption, heel-dragging, infighting and incoordination – are found in every superstate. Complaints about central control, heavy taxes, and the sclerotic effect of regulation are commonplace.

In fact, the modern history of all superstates has been absorbed with the dilemma of establishing the right amount of control over everyday life. From the late 1940s to the 1970s, the emphasis in all places – India, China, the United States and Europe – was on intensification of central control and the concomitant expansion of bureaucracy. A backlash against this project arose in the 1970s and gained strength over the next two decades. Bureaucratism and over-regulation were blamed for economic stagnation and the collapse of public trust in central authorities. Political leaders faced a "crisis of governability."[51]

By the end of the twentieth century, political leaders in all superstates had reduced their control over private life, the marketplace, and sub-central governments.[52] This meant reducing the size and influence of government bureaucracies as well.[53] Today, however, there is evidence that the pendulum is swinging the other way, as governments respond to shocks like the resurgence of terrorism in 2001–2005, the global financial crisis of 2007–2009, and the pandemic of 2020–2022. Political leaders in all superstates now worry more about the destabilizing effects of loose-reined government than about the political and bureaucratic costs of intensive control.[54]

The Second Dilemma: Leadership

As we have seen, empires also suffered from dilemmas of leadership. The typical model of leadership in empires was dynastic monarchism. This model had potential advantages, such as decisiveness in the face of crises, but also severe disadvantages, including the risk of overload, succession struggles, and incompetent heirs. Reforms that were intended to counter these disadvantages, such as schemes to divide power or strengthen courts, often backfired.

Our thinking about political leadership has been transformed since the age of empires. Democratic principles dictate that ordinary people should have some way of influencing the selection of leaders through free elections. The doctrine of separation of powers says that authority ought to be split, so that separate branches of government are responsible for making laws, executing laws, and judging whether laws are properly applied. The concept of constitutionalism also says that the basic operating rules for a regime should be codified and not easily changeable.

Rulers of superstates must pay homage to this bundle of ideas, even if they do not apply them rigorously. No superstate is ruled by a hereditary autocrat. On the other hand, no superstate has a ruler who is selected directly by popular election either. Every superstate, even the United States, which relies on an electoral college, tempers the democratic principle in some way. Similarly, all superstates are flexible about separation-of-powers doctrine, sometimes allowing one branch of government to play two or more roles. Superstates also have different views about how much detail needs to be contained in a constitution, how strictly a constitution should be followed, and how hard it should be to make revisions.

In every superstate, the leadership structure has changed substantially over decades. A notable tendency has been the reconcentration of power in the hands of the chief executive. In the United States, the historian Arthur Schlesinger described the emergence of an "imperial presidency" in the early 1970s.[55] Concerns about the imperial presidency were revived in the early 2000s. In India, many prime ministers since 1947 have been criticized for "personalizing" state power.[56] China has swung from autocratic rule under Mao between 1949 and 1976, to forms of collective rule for the next three decades, and back to a reconcentration of power after 2012 with Xi Jinping as the country's "core leader."[57] In moments of stress, the European Union has often relied on ad hoc arrangements for decision-making that short-circuit the procedures prescribed in the Union's founding treaties.

Executives have defended the concentration of authority in very old terms, as a measure necessary to preserve the integrity of their superstate in the face of extraordinary dangers. In 1975, Indira Gandhi said that increased executive powers were essential to counter the "forces of disintegration" within India, while Xi Jinping defends his authority today as the antidote for "deep-rooted problems undermining stability" in China.[58] President George H.W. Bush's reach for increased power after 2001 was justified as the only way of protecting a country that was "tied down like Gulliver by a thousand legal strings."[59]

Critics of executive power have invoked equally familiar arguments. One is the old danger of overload: the inability of executives to make well-considered decisions on all the problems that land on their desks. Granted, the bureaucracy that directly supports modern executives is substantial. In the United States, the White House employs almost two thousand people. On the other hand, the scope of responsibilities has expanded too. Technological change has increased the volume of information arriving at the center of government and accelerated the pace of decision-making.[60] As President Barack Obama observed, chief executives must respond to events that unfold at "warp speed."[61]

The danger that power will be concentrated in the hands of an incompetent ruler is not so great as it was in the era of hereditary monarchs. But the risk of incompetence at the apex of government has not been eliminated entirely. Dynastic tendencies still operate in several superstates: scions of great families are more likely to gain power despite modest abilities. And, as recent American history has reminded us, elections may produce leaders who lack the ability to grapple with complex problems. Similarly, risks associated with leadership successions have been reduced but not eliminated. China still struggles to devise methods of orderly succession, while the assault on the US Capitol in January 2021 showed that the succession process cannot be taken for granted in the United States either.

Centralization of authority can also undermine support for a regime, if the ruling group is perceived as alien and unaccountable. After the 2016 election, many Americans insisted that Donald Trump was "not my president," while others said the same about Joe Biden after 2020.[62] Some Indians deny that Narendra Modi is truly their leader, while some European populists reject a "Brussels elite which has lost touch with reality."[63] Dissent is ruthlessly suppressed in China, but there are still signs of discontent with a system that concentrates authority in the hands of a small and ethnically homogeneous group of leaders in Beijing.

The Third Dilemma: Creed

Every empire needed a justificatory creed, which was a set of ideas that explained why the empire was organized as it was, and what higher purpose it served. Often the imperial creed was founded on the defense of a specific faith or conception of civilization, and in some instances the creed was bolstered by ideas about racial superiority. A well-crafted creed held an empire together. A badly crafted creed, rigidly enforced, could split an empire apart. Imperial rulers often threaded the needle by adopting a policy of qualified tolerance. For example, religious minorities were allowed some freedom so long as they acknowledged imperial authority and accepted second-class status within the empire.

Superstates, like empires, need a justificatory creed. They are too large and diverse to define themselves easily as nation-states, that is, as states that exist as the homeland for one people unified by culture, language, and history. But some other binding agent is necessary. Indian intellectuals search for "the idea of India," a construct that is understood to be essential for "unity, survival, and progress."[64] Similarly, advocates of European integration look for "the idea of Europe," a "vision of political and social order" that will build support for institutions of the European Union across the continent.[65] In the United States, observers worry about the loss of a "sense of common purpose," that "underlying adhesive" that is essential for the country to function properly.[66] Chinese leaders also try to propagate a story about national goals, which is what they call the "China Dream," to unite the country and justify their own leadership.[67]

The range of potential creeds has changed since the age of empires. Creeds based on crude theories of racial superiority are no longer defensible. A creed built on the advancement of a specific faith collides with freedom of religion, one of the fundamental rights recognized in international law and the basic laws of all superstates. The old policy of qualified tolerance, which involved second-class status for minorities, is also hard to defend in the age of human rights.

Because of the legacies of nineteenth-century imperialism, European and American leaders are more cautious about describing their goal as the advancement of Western civilization or Anglo-Saxon ideals, although there are moments when Western leaders continue to do this.[68] But leaders in India and China still appeal to anti-imperialist sentiments as they justify their own rule. China and India have also been defended as civilization-states, that is, states whose mission is to defend values that transcend ethnic, religious, and linguistic differences within those countries.[69] Whether these civilizational values can be identified with adequate precision, and whether a "civilizational mission" can be effective in rallying popular support for the Chinese and Indian regimes, are open questions.

The advance of human rights has also enabled a new justificatory creed: a purely secular ideology premised on the defense of liberties, and the improvement of living conditions, for all people throughout the superstate. Citizens are expected to show loyalty to the regime because it safeguards their rights and provides them with the means to realize their potential. This form of loyalty is sometimes called constitutional or liberal patriotism.[70] Once again, though, it is an open question whether this secular liberal ideology can be effective by itself in sustaining support for central authorities within a superstate.[71] Critics have dismissed it as a cold and unappealing doctrine, contrasted with hot doctrines that play on faith or ethnicity.[72]

Leaders of superstates must have ways of instilling their creed in the minds of the governed population. They can do this by propagandizing in favor of the creed, regulating everyday life so that it conforms to the creed, and repressing non-conforming ideas and behavior. In practice, though, instilling a creed may be more difficult today than in the age of empires. Centuries ago, it might have been enough to persuade a small number of people within metropolitan and provincial elites; today, the broader public must be brought along as well. And the governed population is a tougher audience because it is better educated and has more ways of gaining access to information. Liberal norms make it harder for governments to control the usual channels of indoctrination, such as media, schools, and churches, and to punish heterodox speech and conduct.

The secular liberal creed seems, at first, to lighten the burden on central authorities, because it celebrates a diversity of opinions and does not require intensive control of speech and behavior. In fact, though, the secular liberal creed can impose a very heavy burden. If they want to be taken seriously, central authorities must assure that citizens are treated equally wherever they are. Illiberal social and economic practices must be curtailed throughout the territory. People must have similar access to education, healthcare and other services that are regarded as essential in an advanced liberal society. Imperial rulers never felt pressure to treat their subjects in such an even-handed and generous way. A British colonial official conceded in 1910 that a policy of protecting and improving every human life would be noble – "but its execution inevitably increases the difficulty of government."[73]

The Long Soviet Shadow

The Union of Soviet Socialist Republics died in December 1991, when leaders of its most powerful constituent republics (Russia, Ukraine, and Byelorussia) declared that it had ceased to exist. In fact, it had been coming apart for several years. The Soviet Union was routinely described as the last of the empires, the successor to the Russian empire of the Romanov dynasty, and its collapse was heralded by some as the true end of the age of empires.

In some ways, it did make sense to think of the Soviet Union as an empire. It encompassed vast territories and a large and diverse population, just as the Russian empire had. And many of the problems that contributed to the Soviet collapse were inherited from the Russian empire. Most vexing was the age-old "nationalities problem," which was the demands of ethnic groups for more autonomy. Like the Romanovs, Soviet leaders also struggled with overload at the apex of government, a troublesome bureaucracy, and technological backwardness in relation to rival powers.

But Soviet problems also differed in important ways from Romanov problems. For example, the Soviets tried to engineer the economy with more precision, through a system of centralized planning. The Soviets also had more radical ambitions for social change, including the abolition of religion and diffusion of a new socialist culture. And the Soviets were more dogmatic about the organization of government, insisting that similar forms of rule should be adopted throughout their territory. All of this meant more intensive control, more bureaucracy (and thus more bureaucratism), more pressure on central decision-makers, and more reasons for resistance from the general population.

It may be tempting to describe the Soviet Union as an empire whose leaders made fatal miscalculations about control, leadership, and creed. But the Soviet predicament was complicated because it was not just an empire. It was one of the first superstates. Soviet rulers could not govern as casually as the Romanovs did. They had to make some show of modernizing society and improving the condition of the Soviet population. At the same time, Soviet leaders had to keep pace with a more dynamic global economy. And over the decades, changing circumstances made it increasingly difficult for Soviet leaders to hold the Union together by force alone.

The Soviet Union became the first failed superstate, and other superstates tried to learn from its failure. The Republic of India, for example, had emulated some aspects of the Soviet model in its first forty years. It also engaged in central economic planning, although Indian controls were never as stringent as Soviet ones. As the Soviet Union collapsed, Indian intellectuals and policy-makers struggled to understand what had gone wrong. They wondered whether India might also be destroyed by bureaucratism, stagnation, and "inherent fissiparous forces."[74] India was already experimenting with economic and political reforms in the 1980s, but the Soviet collapse led to an acceleration of reforms in the 1990s.

Chinese leaders studied the Soviet collapse but drew different conclusions. The Chinese regime faced growing pressure for intro-duction of Western-style liberal democracy in the 1980s. In April 1989, thousands of people crowded into Tiananmen Square in central Beijing to demand reforms. After initial hesitation, Chinese leaders brutally suppressed the protest. They were watching the intensifying crisis in the Soviet Union and its satellite states and feared similar trouble in China. "The overwhelming need" in China, paramount leader Deng Xiaoping told President George H.W. Bush shortly before the crackdown, "is to maintain stability."[75]

Chinese leaders were alarmed as the Soviet Union disintegrated over the next two years. The lesson, they decided, was that the authority of the Chinese Communist Party should be fiercely defended while economic reforms were advanced.[76] Thirty years later, Chinese leaders are still dogged by "the nagging feeling that what happened in the Soviet Union portends [China's] own mortality."[77]

The death of the Soviet Union cast a shadow on European integration as well. The treaty establishing the European Union was finalized two weeks before the dissolution of the Soviet Union in December 1991. The Soviet collapse endangered the project of building the European Union in many ways. Some expected that elimination of the Soviet threat would reduce the incentive for Europeans to work together.[78] The reunification of Germany complicated its relations with France, while the breakup of Yugoslavia led to war in the heart of Europe. Integration of former Soviet satellite countries into the European Union meant that its internal differences were larger than ever before.[79]

Years later, the Soviet Union still casts its shadow on Europe. In 2012, Prime Minister Victor Orbán stirred up supporters by warning that Hungary was being colonized by Brussels just as it had been by Moscow.[80] "There is nothing scandalous in comparing the Soviet Union and the European Union," Estonia's finance minister insisted in 2019: "In both cases, only one 'correct' ideology applies, and opponents of this ideology are considered enemies that must be repressed."[81] Even defenders of the European Union make this comparison. George Soros warned in 2019 that the European Union's leadership was "reminiscent of the Politburo when the Soviet Union collapsed," blind to dangers and "sleepwalking into oblivion."[82]

At first, the lesson that most Americans took from the Soviet collapse was that their model of governance had demonstrated its superiority and robustness. This air of triumphalism persisted for several years. But there were always dissenting voices. George Kennan, who as a young diplomat in the 1940s had warned of the Soviet threat, observed in 1993 that the Soviet Union and the United States had something in common. They were both "monster countries," whose size made them vulnerable to crises of popular legitimacy and cohesion. "There is a real question," Kennan said, "as to whether bigness in a body politic is not an evil in itself."[83]

That same year, Senator Daniel Moynihan warned that internal divisions were likely to sharpen within the United States just as they had in the Soviet Union, and that America would soon "know more than it has known of grief."[84] Foreign-policy analyst Robert Kaplan agreed that the crack-up of the Soviet Union would reverberate within the United States. Kaplan described the United States as a vast and fragile polity that might not survive the next century. "It is exactly at such prosperous times as these," Kaplan warned in 1997, "that we need to maintain a sense of the tragic."[85]

By 2021, it was no longer hard for Americans to do this. Triumphalism had disappeared, and a feeling that things were coming apart was all-pervasive. "The forces that divide us are deep and they are real," President Joe Biden said in his inaugural address in January 2021, as he acknowledged "the harsh, ugly reality that racism, nativism, fear, and demonization have long torn us apart."[86]

The Soviet collapse was a warning about the fragility of superstates. The first decades of the twenty-first century have provided even more evidence that the task of governing superstates is no less perilous than that of governing empires. Specific hazards may have shifted in relative importance, but the cumulation of hazards is still fearsome. And the possibility of a fatal cascade of hazards (economic collapse combining with angry populism combining with pandemic, for example) is still real. Meanwhile, the dilemmas of superstate governance persist in full strength.

As we shall see in the next four chapters, leaders in superstates have addressed these hazards and dilemmas in fundamentally different ways. And, within each superstate, opinions about the right way to govern have shifted substantially over decades. Imperial rulers would recognize the kind of work that the leaders of superstates are doing today: juggling hazards, improvising solutions, and struggling to put off the day of reckoning.

4

The United States
An Old Hazard Returns

In May 1933, eight weeks after the inauguration of President Franklin Roosevelt, the Pulitzer Prize for history was awarded to Frederick Jackson Turner for his book *The Significance of Sections in American History*. The Pulitzer jury said that it explained "the evolution of American civilization in a thorough and fresh way."[1] Turner's premise was that the United States should not be thought of as a single nation. It was better to think of the United States as an empire, "comparable to all Europe in area, with settled geographic provinces which equal great European nations."[2]

Turner usually referred to these "geographic provinces" as sections. He counted eight in twentieth-century America: New England, the Middle States, the Southeast, the Southwest, the Middle West, the Great Plains, the Mountain States, and the Pacific Coast. Each section consisted of several states sharing a common economy, culture, and politics. Turner thought the differences between sections were growing, and that they were "more and more the American version of the European nation."

In fact, Turner's conception of the United States was not new. People had talked about sections since the country's founding. Turner simply honed the sectionalist view of America. The whole of American history, he said, should be understood as contest between "rival societies." Politicians were sent to Washington to protect their own section and wrangle with representatives of other sections. Turner compared these politicians to European diplomats, Congress itself to the League of Nations, and laws adopted in Washington to "the diplomatic treaties of European nations."

Turner advanced a theory about how the United States, "a vast and varied union of unlike sections," had been governed since independence. The theory was built on the premise that the main hazard confronting American leaders was conflict between different parts of a vast empire. Every choice that leaders made about the design of the American regime, about the amount of control exercised by central authorities, the organization of leadership in Washington, and the national creed, was made with the aim of containing this hazard and preserving the union.

Turner thought that this way of governing the United States had been effective and would continue. But he was mistaken about its prospects, at least for the next few decades. Roosevelt's inauguration signaled the advent of a new theory about how to govern the United States. Over the next half-century, central government intensified its control over everyday life, power was redistributed among the players in Washington, and the national creed was reimagined. This broad renovation of the American regime seemed possible because the old hazard of sectionalism was fading away. Central government could work more energetically for a country whose parts were increasingly alike.

Unfortunately, reports of the death of sectionalism were greatly exaggerated. By the early 2000s, the old hazard of sectional conflict was back, but in modified form and with a new label: red/blue polarization. The regime that had evolved since the 1930s was not built to accommodate this reality. In Turner's world, sectional differences were managed by limiting the role of central government and giving national leaders the task of "conciliating the conflicting interests of the different sections." In present-day Washington, however, there is a mismatch between regime design and underlying political realities. The federal agenda has expanded, and there are deep divisions between sections about many of the policy questions on that agenda. At the same time, though, there is a reduced capacity in Washington to negotiate peace treaties between the sections.

The result is political instability. Some observers take an extreme view of what might result. "We are closer to civil war than any of us would like to believe," a specialist on political violence said about the United States in 2022.[3] A former chair of the US National Intelligence Council agreed: "It seems plain that a civil war is coming, and the only question is whether it will be fought with lawsuits and secessions or with AK-15s."[4]

The Hazards of Empire

Turner called America an empire, and this also followed tradition. In 1783, at the end of the Revolutionary War, General George Washington hoped that the American states would form an "extensive empire," and speculated about where the "seat of empire" should be.[5] Officers in Washington's army organized an association to defend "the future dignity of the American Empire" once the war was over.[6] Washington also described the United States as a "rising empire" in his 1799 will.[7]

In the Federalist papers, which was a series of essays written by Alexander Hamilton, James Madison, and John Jay to promote ratification of the constitution, the United States was often described as a "great" and "immense" empire. Hamilton called it "the most interesting [empire] in the world." The three authors argued that strong central government was necessary to "preserve the Union of so large an empire," acknowledged that the "fabric of the American empire" must be built on the consent of the people, and promised that Congress would include "representatives of every part of the empire."[8]

The Federalists were writing to win support for ratification and did not believe that talk about empire would alienate readers. Their opponents, though leery of centralized power, still agreed the aim was to establish some form of empire. Thomas Jefferson, third president of the United States, insisted that the country should form an "extensive empire."[9] In the following decades, the practice of describing America as an empire – vast, great, expansive, or continental – pervaded newspapers. *The Boston Courier* pronounced the United States to be "the largest and most varied empire on earth."[10]

The United States was born in the age of empires, and it was natural for Americans to describe their own country this way. As the constitution was drafted, everyone looked at other empires for lessons on how to govern a vast territory. George Washington wanted the United States to have "weight in the scale of empires."[11] Added to this was the reality that the United States was embarked on a program of expansion familiar to any student of empires.

The embryo of the American empire, as Hamilton called it, was a European population that settled on the Atlantic seaboard after the late sixteenth century.[12] This population grew twenty-fold between 1700 and 1800. White migration over the Appalachians was initially obstructed by resistance from indigenous peoples and restrictions on settlement imposed by London. These restrictions became ineffectual after the American rebellion of 1775–1783, and leaders of the new American empire began a program of colonization in the Ohio and upper Mississippi valleys.

These lands, Turner wrote, were like newly conquered provinces.[13] The American army drove indigenous peoples further west to allow white settlement.[14] At first, a simple form of military rule was established in the new Northwest Territory, with a promise that new states would be created once a part of the Territory had enough white settlers.[15] Five new states were formed out of the Territory and joined to the union between 1803 and 1848.

The American empire spread further westward, encompassing all the land now known as the continental United States, between 1783 and 1867. This land was already claimed by other powers – Britain, France, Spain, Mexico, and Russia – and occupied by indigenous peoples. But American migration westward made it hard for other powers to enforce their claims on land, and all these claims were eventually extinguished through negotiation or war. (The Supreme Court affirmed that the national government had the power to acquire territory "by conquest or by treaty.")[16] Once its claim on new territory had been confirmed, the US army drove indigenous peoples into ever-smaller enclaves, while Congress established more territorial governments that were converted into states once they had enough white settlers. The admission of New Mexico and Arizona as states (eventually done in 1912) was delayed until it was clear they would be controlled by white majorities.[17]

The final phase of imperial expansion came with the occupation of the Philippines, Cuba, Puerto Rico, and Guam following the Spanish–American War of 1898. Cuba gained independence in 1902 but the other territories remained under US control. It was understood that English-speaking white majorities could never be established in these territories and there were no plans for statehood. These new possessions were administered through the War Department. Many Americans celebrated the acquisition of an overseas empire to match those of the European powers, seeing this as a logical step along the path that had been followed since 1783. "The Federal Empire," an American jurist explained in 1902, was a "naturally evolved, permanent, and complete form of political organism," comprising both mainland states and overseas possessions.[18]

Throughout its history, this American empire was threatened by two major hazards. The first was a hostility toward centralized power that was manifested in a powerful though unsuccessful campaign against the new constitution, and a string of popular rebellions in the 1790s. The second and even more serious hazard was conflict between sections. Hamilton warned that the alternative to an American union might be three confederacies – the North, Middle States, and South – that would have "frequent and violent contests with each other."[19] The threat of rupture persisted long afterward. There was talk of secession by northern states during the war of 1812.[20] In the 1830s, southern states threatened to ignore laws passed in Washington.[21] In the 1840s a leading jurist anticipated a breakup into four confederacies: north, middle, south, and west.[22] In 1861, southern states finally seceded, triggering a bloody civil war.

The most profound disagreement between sections was over slavery. Many northerners regarded slavery as an abomination, but the profitability of southern plantations depended on slaves, numbering nearly two million by 1860. Many southerners believed that northerners wanted to use the power of central government to abolish the slavery system. There were other disagreements too. Southerners favored free trade because they exported cotton and imported manufactured goods, while infant industries in the North wanted tariff protection against overseas competitors. Northern bankers liked high interest rates and low inflation, while indebted plantation owners in the South liked easy credit and high inflation.[23]

The American regime was carefully designed to manage the two hazards of popular resistance to central power and sectional conflict. One crucial tactic was structuring the administrative system of the new empire so that the national capital did not exercise tight control over everyday life. This meant that there were fewer reasons for popular protest and fewer fights between sections over the details of national policy.

The governance technique that British imperialists called indirect rule was firmly embedded in the American constitution. Powers of the central government were limited, while states retained broad authority to rule within their borders.[24] Moreover, the Supreme Court gave a narrow interpretation to powers allocated to central government.[25] The Bill of Rights, which was added to the constitution in 1791, included an assurance that powers not explicitly given to the center were "reserved to the States . . . [or] the people."

Of course, there were limits to the passivity of central government. President Andrew Jackson, usually a skeptic about centralized power, threatened South Carolina with military action in 1833 if federal taxes could not be collected. Such action, Jackson said, was essential to preserve the union.[26] And in 1861 the central government went to war to prevent destruction of the union. The civil war was followed by a military occupation of southern states. Washington undertook an intensive effort to reconstruct southern societies and protect the rights of freed slaves. However, this burst of central energy collapsed once it was clear that the threat of secession had passed. White rule re-established itself in southern states.[27]

"For the sake of perfect Union," a scholar explained in 1888, the role of the federal government had to be strictly limited: "A federal government attempting to do a great many things . . . is sure to arouse warring interests and clashing influences."[28] James Bryce, a widely respected observer of American politics, explained how small a role the federal government played at the end of the nineteenth century. An American could go through life without ever being reminded of the federal government, Bryce wrote, "except when he votes at presidential and congressional elections, lodges a complaint against the post-office, and opens his trunks for a custom-house officer on the pier at New York when he returns from a tour in Europe."[29] And few Americans ever toured Europe.

From the start, the leadership structure of the American empire was structured to avoid inflammation of sectional conflicts. Every state was guaranteed an equal number of seats in the Senate, so that sections did not have to worry about loss of influence because of shifting population. The allocation of votes in the Electoral College, which selected the president, was also skewed to favor less populous states.

At the same time, the democratic principle was limited so that Washington politicians were not driven by "mob sentiment" in their home states.[30] Senators were selected by state legislatures, not directly by voters. The president was supposed to be chosen by an Electoral College consisting of men of refinement, selected by methods that protected them from the "heats and ferments" of public opinion.[31] After 1820, these presidential electors were typically chosen through popular elections, but voting rights were limited to white males and, before 1840, only those who owned property. Just one-quarter of white adult males voted in the presidential election of 1824.[32] Members of the House of Representatives were chosen by the same limited electorate.

The British journalist Walter Bagehot thought it was a mistake for Americans to fracture the leadership structure of their central government into so many parts – the president, two legislative chambers, and the judiciary – because it undermined the ability of national leaders to manage sectional conflicts.[33] In practice, though, power was arranged to facilitate sectional accommodation. Most of the time, the president was not the most influential player in Washington. James Bryce compared him to "the managing clerk in a large business establishment." The center of gravity in Washington was the Senate, the main forum for sectional negotiations. The Senate was deeply engaged in executive as well as legislative functions, the same "fusion of powers" that Bagehot admired in the British system. Much of the Senate's deal-making was performed behind closed doors.[34]

The formal division of powers in the American constitution was also moderated by social realities. Washington was a small city, deliberately removed from commercial centers. Politicians could not easily travel back and forth from home states. The *Washington Times* observed in 1915 that the capital operated "like a village in its mental processes."[35] The Supreme Court was included in this dense social network. Many nineteenth-century justices were former lawmakers, and the line between politicking and adjudication was not well drawn.[36]

Politics in Washington was also shaped by a distinctive mentality, a way of thinking about the task of governing, which compensated for the potential weaknesses of the separated-powers model. One aspect of this mentality was an obsession with unity, comparable to the present-day concern of Chinese leaders with harmony and stability. In 1830, during his confrontation with South Carolina, Andrew Jackson gave a toast at a Washington banquet: "Our Federal Union, it must be preserved!"[37] This was the leitmotif of the century.[38]

This obsession with unity was combined with celebration of compromise.[39] American history was written as succession of bargains that were struck to keep peace between sections: the Great Compromise of 1787 (about the constitution), the Compromise of 1790 (about national debt and location of the capital), the Compromises of 1820 and 1850 (about slavery in new states), the Compromise of 1833 (on tariffs), and the Compromise of 1877 (ending reconstruction). Compromise was generally regarded as an honorable act, and the most admired politicians were those skilled in crafting such bargains.

"The first duty of an American statesman," John Quincy Adams explained, was "to conciliate and unite" the sections.[40] Frederick Jackson Turner agreed: statesmanship in the United States emphasized "the need for toleration, for cooperation, for mutual sacrifices," in the search for "formula[s] that will bring the different regions together."[41] Henry Clay, regarded as the epitome of this type of statesman, was celebrated as the Great Pacificator. Politicians who stood firmly on principles of any type were disdained as radicals and "one-idea men." Politics driven strictly by principles was understood to be dangerous to the union.

National leaders also sought to define a creed that would bind the new empire together. Thomas Jefferson conceived of an "empire of liberty" united "by the sheer majesty of ideas and ideals."[42] Essential to this national creed was the idea that government as a whole should be limited, and states and localities should have extensive freedom to govern as they liked. Liberty and self-government were conceived as part of the cultural inheritance of white Americans, passed down from their Anglo-Saxon forebears.

By the end of the nineteenth century, the American creed was expressed in language much like that used to justify the British Empire: a commitment to rule of law, small and decentralized government, and self-rule for white populations. In fact, some believed that the two empires were engaged in the same civilizing project. The ambition of the American empire, within the continental United States and in its overseas possessions, was to propagate Anglo-Saxon ideals, just as the British did within their possessions.[43]

The principles of liberty and self-rule did not apply to indigenous peoples and African Americans, who were not considered ready for self-government. These groups were the usual victims of the compromises that held the union together. In the early twentieth century, restrictions on the voting rights of African Americans were still justified on the pretense that they were "unfit for the suffrage."[44] A Bengali scholar living in the United States observed in 1923 that the United States had created their own caste system.[45] By the early 1900s, the population that was perceived to require improvement by means of Anglo-Saxon rule also included Latinos in the southwest United States, southern European immigrants in major American cities, and peoples of the country's overseas dependencies.

Building an American Superstate

The regime that was constructed to govern the American empire was morally abhorrent because it supported slavery and discrimination. But it was internally coherent. The regime was designed to address a single great hazard, conflict between sections, and it did this through light central control, a leadership structure designed to promote sectional bargaining, and adherence to a creed that emphasized white self-rule.

Even after World War I, this regime seemed durable. Many still conceived of the United States as a "budding empire."[46] In 1925, Turner defined the country as "an empire, a federation of sections, a union of potential nations."[47] In fact, though, the imperial regime was breaking down. The United States was transforming into a superstate. Over the next half century, all elements of the regime – administrative system, leadership structure, and creed – were altered fundamentally.

The administrative system was transformed through an expansion of the role of central government. Washington acted in more spheres of policy and controlled everyday life in more detail.[48] Defense illustrates the trend. The military establishment, negligible in 1890, comprised three million uniformed and civilian personnel by 1980, while millions more worked for defense contractors. The federal government also tightened control over state militia, and for thirty years in the twentieth century it used conscription to fill the ranks of the military. Defense spending led to the introduction and expansion of a federal income tax. In 1916, less than one percent of adult Americans filed a federal tax return; by 1950, most did.[49]

Washington's role in guiding the economy increased as well. New agencies were created to regulate major industries, protect consumers, and preserve the environment. The Federal Reserve system, a form of central bank, was established to regulate currency and major financial institutions. After the 1930s, it became acceptable for federal government to "prime the pump" of the economy by borrowing and spending. By the 1950s, the idea that federal government was responsible for "fine-tuning" the economy through monetary and fiscal policy was accepted by Republicans and Democrats alike.[50]

More controversial was the expansion of federal programs to improve the economic security of Americans.[51] Still, the federal government created a new system of old-age pensions and expanded programs to help the unemployed and poor families. In the 1960s, it added programs to provide medical services to the poor and elderly. Federal laws and expenditures on education also increased after World War II. In the 1970s, all these forms of social expenditure displaced defense spending as the main part of the federal budget.[52]

At the same time, central government moved more decisively to protect Americans against maltreatment by state and local governments, as well as private enterprises.[53] In the 1950s, federal authorities enforced Supreme Court decisions that overturned racial segregation in state and local services. The Civil Rights Act of 1964 and the Voting

Rights Act of 1965 expanded federal powers to prevent segregation and scrutinize state and local practices that denied the vote to African Americans. Federal authority to prevent sex discrimination was recognized in 1964 and expanded in 1972.

Now and then, there were reversals in central government activity. The federal role in economic planning expanded during both world wars but contracted immediately afterward. Prohibition, an extraordinary effort at economic and social control, launched in 1920, was abandoned after fourteen years. American control over the Philippines was ceded in 1946. Youth resistance to conscription led to its abolition in 1972. Disillusionment with federal programs and anger over taxes led to a slowing of central government expansion in the 1970s. Despite all this, however, the intensity of central governance increased radically between 1900 and 1980.

The leadership structure of the new American superstate also differed from that of the American empire. Roles were demarcated more sharply. The Senate abandoned its old practice of secret meetings and operated more like a conventional legislative chamber.[54] And the Supreme Court became more independent. It gained more control over the cases it reviewed, kept more distance from the practice of everyday politics, and invalidated federal laws more frequently.[55]

Meanwhile the power of the presidency expanded immensely. The White House, rather than the Senate, became the center of gravity in Washington. This was partly a result of the president's constitutional role as commander-in-chief of an expanded military establishment.[56] But the president had more power in domestic policy too, because Congress drafted legislation in broad strokes and left it to the executive branch to fill in details. The White House exercised more control over budgeting, personnel, and other aspects of administration throughout the executive branch. The number of federal employees directly supporting the president grew from one hundred in 1933 to 1,800 in 1993.[57]

More federal control meant a larger bureaucracy. The federal civilian workforce grew from roughly two hundred thousand employees in 1900 to two million in 1980.[58] At the same time, there was an increase in the proportion of the federal bureaucracy that was appointed through civil service rules rather than political patronage. But the top positions of federal departments and agencies were still filled by political appointees who came and went at the pleasure of the president. By the early 1970s, the apex of the federal bureaucracy comprised more than two thousand political appointees.[59]

The third element of the American regime, its justificatory creed, also changed between 1900 and the 1970s. It was still understood that the purpose of the regime was to advance the welfare and liberty of Americans. But the benefits of citizenship were less likely to be described as an Anglo-Saxon inheritance, and unequal treatment of citizens because of race, sex, and location became less unacceptable.[60] This shift was slower in the South, however: segregationists like George Wallace continued to defend the "Anglo-Saxon heritage" throughout the 1960s.[61]

The American regime changed in the twentieth century because the country faced three new hazards, and because one old hazard – sectionalism – seemed to be fading away. One of the new hazards was the threat of war, especially after 1941. The Axis powers, and then the Soviet Union, threatened fundamental American interests. "This is the kind of enemy," an Ohio newspaper said about the Soviet Union in 1948, that "will destroy us and our way of life by whatever means are available."[62] This existential danger unified the country and justified a military buildup by central government. The ideological war with the Soviets also bolstered the campaign for civil rights within the United States.[63]

The second new hazard was posed by the transformation of the American economy. The foundation of the economy shifted from agriculture to capital-intensive industry in the late nineteenth century, while technological improvements led to massive increases in interstate trade.[64] The new form of economy was prone to booms and busts. It also threatened political stability because of violent conflicts between owners and workers, especially during hard times. Federal action was necessary because states by themselves seemed unable to take the steps required to preserve economic and political stability.

The third hazard to the regime was posed by a demographic transformation and an accompanying revolution in public expectations about the role of government. Over the course of the twentieth century, the American population became healthier and better educated. Its conception of the good life became more elaborate.[65] After 1920, most Americans also lived in cities. New technologies made it easier to learn about national affairs and organize social and political movements. Demands on central government increased, especially after government itself imposed burdens like income tax or conscription. The country also experienced a "rights revolution" after World War II.[66] Americans were more likely to make claims on government for due process or privacy, government services, or participation in government decision-making, using the language of entitlements.

Leaders could not ignore these rising expectations, especially when political reforms made their tenure increasingly dependent on popular support. Democratic ideals shaped the leadership structure of central government more profoundly in the twentieth century. In 1913 the constitution was amended to provide for direct election of senators. The direct primary system was introduced to select candidates for the presidency and Congress, undermining the power of party organizations.[67] Election procedures were overhauled to guarantee the secrecy of individual voting. And voting rights were extended three times: by enfranchising women in 1920, removing barriers to African American voting in the 1960s, and lowering the voting age to eighteen in 1971.

Transformation of the American regime in the twentieth century was not just a response to new hazards, however. Another critical factor was the apparent decline of an old hazard: the danger of conflict between sections. Frederick Jackson Turner, it was argued, had got the future wrong: differences between regions were diminishing and the danger of a national crack-up had passed. The apparent emergence of a common political culture after the 1930s reduced the imperative for sectional brokerage and widened the possibilities for action by Washington.

Ironically, the reaction against Turner's sectionalist vision began soon after the award of his Pulitzer Prize. It was encouraged by Franklin Roosevelt's landslide victory in the 1932 presidential election. Roosevelt won all the Electoral College votes in all sections of the country but one, the Northeast, and even in that section he won the popular vote. This result encouraged the idea that national politics might be reorganizing itself on some basis other than sectional interests. In September 1933 a professor of government at Harvard University, Arthur Holcombe, argued that sectionalism was rooted in the difference between agrarian and industrialized economies, and that sectional interests would converge as industrialization spread across the country.[68]

The decline of sectionalism became a popular theme over the next two decades. Another Harvard political scientist, V.O. Key, agreed that sectionalism would fade as the economies of the south and west became less dependent on agriculture. These sections would become "more like the rest of the United States," and the era of "one-party areas" would come to an end.[69] E.E. Schattschneider, a fellow political scientist, concurred that sectionalism was dying. He argued that politics had been "nationalized" by the economic crisis of the 1930s and World War II.[70]

The idea that American politics was becoming less fractious became well established after World War II. In his 1960 book *The End of Ideology*, Daniel Bell also announced the death of sectionalism and suggested that national leaders were now concerned with largely technical decisions about running a complex economy.[71] President John Kennedy developed the same theme in a 1962 speech. Politicians of the nineteenth century, Kennedy said, spent their careers "grappling with a few dramatic issues on which the Nation was sharply divided." But the country had changed:

> Today these old sweeping issues very largely have disappeared. The central domestic issues of our time are more subtle and less simple. They relate not to basic clashes of philosophy but to ways and means of reaching common goals.[72]

Kennedy's rival in the 1960 presidential election, Richard Nixon, agreed that the era of sectionalist politics was over. "Our disagreement is not about the goals for America," Nixon said during the 1960 presidential debates, "but only about the means to reach those goals."[73] Nixon explained what the end of sectionalism implied: that the president could "take an activist view . . . [and] be deeply involved in the entire sweep of America's public concerns."[74]

But, if sectionalism was dying, it was not going easily. Conscious of the power of Southern Democrats in Congress, Franklin Roosevelt quietly crafted another grand compromise as the New Deal was constructed. Progressive economic legislation came at the price of inaction on civil rights for African Americans. Federal laws to provide pensions and strengthen unions excluded the types of jobs often held by African Americans in southern states. Programs to help the poor were delivered through the states, so that discrimination in benefits persisted. And southerners were given key posts in Washington that allowed them to discriminate within federally administered programs.[75]

Howard Odum, a southern sociologist, was a contrarian who argued in 1947 that the growth of federal activity was intensifying sectional conflicts, because white southerners resented the effort "to make the South over" so that it conformed to Washington's conception of civilized life.[76] There was evidence to support Odum's case. Opposition to the civil rights proposals of President Harry Truman split the Democratic Party and jeopardized his 1948 presidential campaign. Presidents

Eisenhower and Kennedy were compelled to deploy troops to enforce Supreme Court decisions against segregation.[77] The adoption of strong civil rights legislation in 1964–1965 was possible only because of a "highly unusual" alignment of political conditions.[78] The Democratic Party paid the price for that achievement in the 1968 presidential election, when it lost every southern state but one.

The continuing effects of sectionalism could be seen in other areas of public policy as well. As federal programs for the poor were expanded in the 1960s, the New Deal compromise of working through the states was continued, which meant that access to benefits varied substantially between regions.[79] As new federal regulatory programs were established, states were allowed to enforce rules themselves rather than being subject to direct enforcement by federal agencies. The Nixon administration called this approach the New Federalism. An advisor to President Nixon said that it would allow states to "respond to local custom and idiosyncrasy."[80] Critics called it pandering to the old Southern doctrine of states' rights.[81] Again, the result was variation between regions in the application of federal law.[82]

Despite this evidence, however, most people rejected Odum's views about the persistence of sectionalism. More often, instances of sectional resistance were dismissed as the "last gasps of a dying era."[83] The prevailing assumption was there would be a gradual convergence in culture and politics. The New Federalism, for example, was described as a technique for promoting "adjustment . . . and gradual acceptance" of national goals in recalcitrant regions.[84]

The apparent death of sectionalism made possible the reconfiguration of the American regime. E.E. Schattschneider said in 1960 that it was producing "virtually a new government" in Washington.[85] Previously, it would have been dangerous to extend the range of subjects in which federal government was involved, because this would have created more opportunities for conflict between sections. Limiting the federal agenda had been a method of peacekeeping. The erasure of sectional differences meant that the federal agenda could safely grow.

The apparent emergence of a national political consensus in the years after World War II also reduced potential problems with the evolving leadership structure of the American superstate. A century earlier, Bagehot had worried that the separation of powers would undermine the capacity of Washington to act decisively. Indeed, some post-war trends threatened to widen the gaps between the branches of government. However, the possibility of a collision between branches was reduced if the sectionalism was dying and the entire political class shared essentially the same worldview. The growth of presidential power was less worrisome if party differences were small and any president was likely to govern in essentially the same way.

In any case, Washington still operated a village until the 1970s. The Washington establishment still had "a clubbiness, a close-webbed intimacy . . . that oiled the wheels of compromise and made government workable."[86] John Kenneth Galbraith observed that "pivotal figures" in all major institutions knew each other well, agreed on national priorities, and exercised a "disciplinary force" on the whole regime.[87] In this environment, shifts in power between branches, or between political parties, did not matter so much. Few believed that the preservation of their way of life hinged on a presidential election, control of the Senate or House of Representatives, or the next appointment to the Supreme Court.

The Sectionalist Revival

After 1980, however, governing the United States became a more complicated task. The main trend of the preceding eighty years, which was intensification of central control over everyday life, continued despite some minor reversals. But sectionalism did not fade away as expected. On the contrary, national divisions intensified. Parts of the country developed increasingly distinctive ideas about the American creed and the role of central government. The old problem of the American empire, managing sectional conflict, returned with force. But the leadership structure of the American superstate, as it had developed over the twentieth century, was not built to manage sectional clashes. The result was gridlock and rancor at the center of the American regime.

Granted, there was some effort to limit the role of central government in the late 1970s. Public frustration mounted over rising taxes, economic stagnation, and the mixed performance of federal programs. The administration of President Jimmy Carter began the work of reducing the federal role in the economy. Ronald Reagan, inaugurated as president in 1981, pushed this program of economic deregulation a little further. But Reagan's promise to "curb the size and influence of the federal establishment" largely failed.[88] In 1989, federal government employed more people and consumed a larger share of GDP than it did in 1979.[89]

In many ways, Washington's role expanded after Reagan. In the 1990s the federal government extended its role in criminal law and policing, areas usually left to state and local governments.[90] Throughout the 1990s and 2000s, Washington asserted a much larger role in responding to natural disasters across the country.[91] The No Child Left Behind Act of 2001 increased federal influence over education, another function traditionally left to state and local governments.[92] After the terror attacks of 2001, the Bush administration further increased the federal role in policing, adopted new rules for vulnerable infrastructure such as power grids, and expanded the military to launch wars in Afghanistan and Iraq.[93] The financial crisis of 2008–2009 led to a restoration of controls on the financial sector and a massive economic stimulus program.[94] The Affordable Care Act of 2010 was one of several measures that have expanded the federal role in healthcare since the 1980s.[95] The federal government also intervened in debates over abortion rights, same-sex marriage, and transgender discrimination.[96]

Washington is now doing much more that the country can argue about. And the country is more strongly disposed to argue about what Washington is doing. Since the early 1990s, political attitudes of Americans have become more polarized. Individuals are more likely to have consistently conservative or liberal opinions about contentious issues, rather than a mix of conservative and liberal opinions. At the same time, liberals are more likely to identify with the Democratic Party, and conservatives with the Republican Party, so that the ideological gap between parties is widening too.[97]

Polarization can be seen in Washington as well. Over decades, the number of legislators in Congress who can be classified as moderates has declined. Republican lawmakers have become increasingly alike in their opinions, as have Democratic lawmakers; and the ideological distance between the two groups has widened.[98] Not since the late nineteenth century has the gap between parties been so vast. Each camp is well entrenched because the proportion of contested seats in Congress has declined.[99] In presidential contests, the number of states that are solidly Republican or Democratic has also increased. Presidential elections are now decided in a small number of battleground states.[100]

Moreover, ideology is strongly connected to geography. States in the northeast and on the Pacific coast are reliably Democratic, while states in the south and central United States are reliably Republican. Of course, there are Democratic enclaves in Republican regions, notably in urban areas.[101] And there are Republican enclaves in Democratic regions too. This sort of interspersing was also seen in the heyday of nineteenth-century sectionalism.[102] Nonetheless, there is a clear difference between regions on basic questions of government and society. The national map shows similar patterns when we look at variations in a range of state government practices, such as the size and professionalism of state legislatures and bureaucracies, the extent of economic and social regulation by state agencies, and state compliance with federal laws.

Commentators have offered several theories to explain the resurgence of polarization over the last thirty years. One hypothesis is that polarization has been aggravated by growing economic inequality because of deregulation and globalization.[103] Another is that polarization is caused by technological changes that allow conservatives and liberals to live within their own informational bubbles.[104] Other theories are that polarization is deepened by internal migration, so that like-minded people increasingly live together, and that it is inflamed by the political manipulation of electoral boundaries and weak campaign finance laws.[105]

Often, these theories operate on the premise that polarization since the 1990s is an anomaly in American politics. The alternative approach would be to recognize internal division as the historical reality of American politics, as Frederick Jackson Turner suggested a century ago. Political scientists who argued in the 1930s that sectional conflicts were simply a product of fading differences in economic structure were mistaken. Political culture has proved to have staying power. Republican and Democratic partisans, ensconced in regional bases, have distinct views about proper structure of society – that is, about family, gender roles, faith, race relations, and public order – and about the place of government in everyday life.[106] The expanding scope of federal action has resulted in more collisions at the national level between these different worldviews.

After 1990, historian Jill Lepore has suggested, national politics in the United States turned into "a domestic cold war," an "uncompromising, all-or-nothing, life or death" struggle for power.[107] Over decades, supporters of both major parties have developed increasingly hostile feelings toward the opposing party.[108] In a 2020 survey, more than half of Republicans and forty percent of Democrats said that they viewed members of the other party as enemies and that their "entire way of life" would be threatened if the other party gained power.[109] In another study, eighty percent of Trump voters in 2020 said they had a fundamental disagreement with Biden voters about "core American values." The same proportion of Biden voters felt that way about Trump voters.[110]

Forty percent of voters in the 2020 elections said that the goal of politics was "ensuring the survival of the country as we know it" rather than simply "enacting good public policy."[111] This belief about the rising stakes of national politics may explain a growing tolerance for political violence. In a 2020 study, one in three Americans said that violence could be justified to advance their party's political goals.[112] In a 2021 survey, most Republican voters agreed with the statement that "the traditional American way of life is disappearing so fast that we may have to use force to save it."[113]

The problem of sectionalism has revived in the United States. It has been aggravated by the extended role of central government. However, the leadership structure of central government has changed so that its capacity to manage sectional conflicts is diminished. Drafters of the constitution looked for ways of assuring that decision-makers in Washington would be protected from the "heats and ferments" of public opinion so that it would be easier to negotiate peace treaties between sections.[114] But the advance of democracy, and loose controls over key aspects of the democratic process like voting, campaign financing, and media activity, means that modern-day decision-makers in Washington are directly exposed to those heats and ferments. We live in the era of the permanent campaign.[115] Legislators organize constantly to prevent primary challenges even when they come from solidly Republican or Democratic regions.

The rise of the presidency also intensifies sectional rivalry. The office of the president is more important than a century ago and is allocated in a winner-takes-all contest. No surprise, then, that presidential elections have come to be interpreted as immensely consequential events. Most voters in the 2020 election believed that the country would suffer "lasting harm" if their presidential candidate lost.[116] Fears about losing the presidency are aggravated by conventional wisdom about how newly elected presidents are supposed to behave. Presidents are expected to move boldly after their inauguration to achieve sweeping legislative victories within their first hundred days.[117] This might have been reasonable advice when differences between parties were small. In a divided society, it stokes anxiety among followers of the losing candidate.

This hundred-day benchmark was popularized after the election of John Kennedy in 1960s. It was Kennedy who declared an end to the age of sectionalism and the obsolescence of a mentality of governing that was preoccupied with preserving the union.[118] But the old mentality served a purpose. As Walter Bagehot had observed in the 1870s, a leadership structure premised on the separation of powers and robust democratic accountability was prone to mismanagement of sectional conflicts. The old mentality encouraged decision-makers to anticipate this danger. The post-Kennedy mentality, with its emphasis on presidential activism, did not.

Other safeguards against sectional conflict have also weakened. The end of the Cold War meant that the country was not tied together in an existential struggle against an external adversary. Meanwhile, the informal bonds among national decision-makers have dissolved. The Washington establishment is gone. Legislators no longer move their families to the capital or stay there when Congress is not in session. Congress has compressed its work into fewer days so that members can spend more time away from Washington.[119] Trust among lawmakers has declined markedly, undermining their ability to reach agreement on legislation.[120]

In some countries, the career bureaucracy provides some assurance of continuity in government when political leaders are at loggerheads. But the US federal bureaucracy cannot perform this function well because of its heavy dependence on political appointees in leadership roles, and the distrust with which it has always been regarded by many Americans. Hostility toward the federal bureaucracy has intensified over the last decade, particularly among Republicans.

Complaints about the dysfunctionality of political institutions in Washington, about the inability to resolve disagreements, respond to immediate problems, and prepare for long-term challenges, have been mounting for years. Some observers even describe the United States as a failed state.[121] Public trust in central government has been lower over the last decade than in any other period since World War II.[122]

This dysfunction is the result of a collision between new governmental responsibilities and old political realities. Central government has involved itself in a broader range of issues that matter intensely to Americans. No student of empire would be surprised that intensification of central control has been followed by a general decline in trust. In the American case, however, the predicament of central government is aggravated because regions have distinct views about how this broader central agenda should be managed, and because the capacity of central institutions to manage sectional differences has eroded. The leadership structure of the contemporary American superstate is not tuned to manage an old hazard of American empire.

Dilemmas at the Center

There is no simple solution to a governance problem that has developed over decades. One solution that is sometimes suggested is simply browbeating Republicans until they "recognize the reality" that intensive central governance is necessary.[123] But there is no evidence that browbeating over the last three decades has produced the expected results. Polarization has intensified instead.

Another approach would be to force the red–blue conflict to a final resolution. This would be done by adjusting the rules of the political game so that one side clearly dominates the other. For example, selecting the president by popular vote rather than through the Electoral College, a difficult reform to achieve, would improve the odds of long-term Democratic control of that office. Alternately, the Senate filibuster could be eliminated so that a Democratic majority can adopt voting rights legislation that would improve the prospects for Democratic candidates in future elections. But measures like these might easily backfire, intensifying resentments among Republicans and aggravating political instability.

A third approach is simply to wait for social and economic change to end the conflict. The premise is that immigration, urbanization, and fertility rates will eventually reduce the power of the Republican party's white rural base. Alternately, a prolonged economic recovery might introduce a new era of good feelings. Arguments like these, which suppose that long-term social and economic forces can destroy sectionalism, were also advanced in the 1930s. The resilience of political cultures was underestimated in the 1930s, and perhaps today as well. This approach also assumes that the United States can tolerate dysfunction for the years that it would take for social and economic forces to alter the sectional balance of power.

Sectional conflicts could also be managed by the old technique of reducing the intensity of central control.[124] Washington would leave more functions to states and supervise the states less closely. This could be done by refusing to legislate in certain areas or drafting laws so that states have more freedom to decide how they should be enforced.[125] Progressives who want to expand the role of government would pursue their reform projects at lower levels. But this solution to sectional conflict has problems as well. States vary substantially in their willingness and capacity to shoulder responsibilities that are devolved from Washington. Government services that are widely viewed as basic rights, such as education and healthcare, would vary between states even more than they do today. Increasingly, citizenship would mean different things in different places. People in more liberal states would be expected to tolerate restrictions on civil and political rights in other states that they consider to be morally objectionable.

The last approach for improving governance in Washington involves reform to the leadership structure so that it is better at managing sectional conflicts. A variety of changes have been proposed, such as extending the term of office for congressmen, reverting to the indirect selection of senators, eliminating congressional primaries, or even adopting a parliamentary system of government.[126] Of course, we can question the feasibility of such reforms. The process for amending the United States constitution is unusually cumbersome. Moreover, public support would be tepid because these reforms would limit the capacity of citizens to control leaders through elections. Unity would be purchased at the price of democratic principle.

Leaders in superstates are always confronted with painful tradeoffs and deep uncertainties. Most people agree on the need for unity, effective government, democratic accountability, and equal treatment of citizens. The difficulty is that all these things may not be easily achieved at the same time in a supersized polity. Tradeoffs in regime design are necessary. But it is hard to decide what the right tradeoffs are, or to reach agreement about those tradeoffs; and calculations about tradeoffs change over time. The most dangerous circumstance is one in which leaders do not recognize the need for tradeoffs, and central institutions do not allow tradeoffs to be made. This may be the case in Washington today.

5

India
The Centralizing Reflex

In the waning days of their empire, the British elite described India much as Frederick Jackson Turner described the United States. Winston Churchill counted the provinces of India as "separate nations comparable in magnitude and in numbers with the leading powers of Europe."[1] A British general described India as "a congeries of nations" even more varied than those in Europe.[2] A senior British bureaucrat, John Strachey, said that "the differences between the countries of Europe are undoubtedly smaller than those between the countries of India."[3]

For the British, the main hazard in India was that this "congeries of nations" would break apart. Americans, facing a similar hazard, had designed a regime that limited the role of central government and provided mechanisms for negotiating differences among sections. British rulers in India took a different approach. The essential condition for good government in India, they insisted, was that authority should be firm and concentrated. Only a strong central authority could make and enforce the "delicate and difficult" decisions required to "weld the country into a whole."[4] Churchill claimed that the "central imperial executive" was detached from all the creeds and classes of India and therefore able to act as an impartial arbiter between them. If central authority in India was weakened, "chaos would come again like a flood."[5]

The British regime in India was built to reinforce central authority. The British army provided the "ultimate basis" of imperial power in India.[6] It was supported by a centrally controlled police force. The civil administration was similarly centralized and described as the "iron framework" of imperial rule.[7] Most of the territory was divided into districts, each governed by a centrally-appointed district officer who exercised plenary powers over a million or more people – keeping the peace, collecting taxes, and acting as judge for many offenses. Complete separation of administrative and judicial duties was considered a luxury that India could not afford.

Not all India was governed in this way. In some places, British rulers kept hereditary princes in place so long as they followed instructions from British advisors. One-third of the subcontinent was still under princely rule at the start of the twentieth century. British interest in improving life within these "feudatory states" was limited. Their inhabitants were not counted as British subjects. British ambitions for social reform outside the princely states were scarcely more ambitious. Throughout rural India, life continued without much change. British magistrates often applied the customary law of Muslim and Hindu communities.[8]

India was transformed into a superstate when it achieved independence in 1947. Its new rulers shouldered a heavier burden than the British, assuming all the duties associated with statehood in the mid-twentieth century. They absorbed the princely states and promised to govern the whole of India's territory in the same way. The Indian constitution made bold promises about eliminating discrimination and inequality, improving services, and respecting liberties. The constitution reflected the expansive promises of the Universal Declaration of Human Rights, adopted only a year earlier. Indian leaders were also committed to economic planning that would accelerate development and establish real independence from the West.[9]

But India's new rulers did not shake off the past entirely. The imperial preoccupation with cohesion persisted. Indians, freedom fighter Balkrishna Sharma said in 1948, "have been chronic patients of centrifugalities, a tendency to fly away from the Centre. This tendency of the various limbs to break off from the body politic is a chronic illness from which our country has been suffering for centuries." Echoing imperial administrators, Sharma said that the task for India's leaders was to "weld the nation" together.[10] Another freedom fighter, Asoka Mehta, warned in 1949 against "fissiparous tendencies" that could "destroy the integrity and independence of our country."[11] Seven years later, Prime Minister Jawaharlal Nehru cautioned that India must "integrate or perish."[12]

The imperial solution for managing the hazard of disintegration, strong central authority, has persisted as well. Certainly, there have been critical amendments to the British method of rule, including the introduction of free elections. And there have been periods in modern Indian history in which central control over economy and society has loosened considerably. But there is also a tendency in moments of stress for the regime to return to the old formula of concentrated power. This puts intense pressure on central institutions, especially because superstates try to do more than empires ever did. Sometimes leaders are overloaded and decisions are not well executed. Unable to govern effectively, leaders look for easier ways of stirring up popular support, such as appeals to faith-based nationalism.

A distinguished journalist, Selig Harrison, questioned in 1960 "whether any Indian state can survive at all," and suggested that the price of survival might be the sacrifice of democracy.[13] Today, few worry that India will soon fall to pieces. But Harrison's other fear, that survival of the Indian superstate might involve the sacrifice of liberal democracy, persists.

Nehruvian Continuities

We can identify four phases in the evolution of the Indian regime since independence. The first was closely associated with Jawaharlal Nehru, who played a critical role in the independence movement and served as the republic's prime minister from 1947 until his death in 1964. In many ways, the Nehruvian regime continued the approach that had been taken by imperial rulers for the preceding century. It emphasized strong central control and was capped by leadership structure in which democratic forces were carefully managed, all for the purpose of preserving a fragile union.

Certainly, democracy was an important part of the Nehruvian creed. More than one hundred million people voted in the nation's first election, held over four months in 1951–1952. But the results of that election were never in doubt. Nehru's party, the Indian National Congress, won more votes than all others combined, and an overwhelming majority of seats in the national assembly, the Lok Sabha. The party achieved similar results for the next twenty years. Congress dominance provided a guarantee of political stability despite free elections. Powerful constituencies resolved their differences within the Congress apparatus and not by tussling on the hustings.[14]

There were other ways in which democratic ideals were disciplined. The upper chamber of India's Parliament, the Rajya Sabha, is indirectly elected by state assemblies, as the American Senate was before 1913. The influence of the popularly elected lower chamber, the Lok Sabha, is also limited. Under the parliamentary model, the party holding a simple majority in the lower chamber forms the executive, which in turn regulates the business of the chamber. This is the fusion of executive and legislative powers that Walter Bagehot recommended in 1867.[15]

Power in a parliamentary system is concentrated in the hands of the executive, a body that includes the prime minister, other ministers in the cabinet, and senior bureaucrats who support their work. In the early years of Indian independence, power was held tightly even within this small group. Nehru's record as a leader of the independence movement gave him extraordinary influence. He "became India" after 1947.[16] Nehru enjoyed immense popularity and dominated his Cabinet. He also served as external affairs minister, periodically as defense minister, and as de facto head of the Congress party. Critics called Nehru the last Viceroy of India.[17]

In theory, executive power was constrained by the new Indian constitution. But the constitution proved a malleable document. In some cases, it could be amended by central government alone, and otherwise with agreement of just half the states. Under Nehru, the constitution was amended sixteen times. The constitution also allowed the Cabinet to declare an emergency, during which fundamental rights might be limited and the entire country directly ruled from Delhi. The first of India's three emergencies was declared during the brief India–China war of 1962. It ended six years later.[18]

Even in normal times, the central government's capacity to establish order throughout the country was substantial. Before independence, Congress leaders had attacked the empire's centralized bureaucracy and police system as instruments of oppression. In the 1930s, Nehru insisted that these systems must "disappear completely." In power, his attitude changed. "First things must come first," Nehru said in 1947, "and the first thing is the security and stability of India."[19] The civil service and police systems were preserved without much change. The military, also inherited from the British, was deployed to occupy the recalcitrant princely state of Hyderabad, suppress rebellion in Telangana, and defend Kashmir from Pakistani attack.

Nehru's government gradually strengthened its law-and-order capabilities. In 1950, it adopted the Preventive Detention Act, which allowed imprisonment without trial to preserve state security. The legislation was targeted at communists in Bengal and southern India who could not be dealt with "in terms of ordinary law."[20] The next year, the constitution was amended to allow restrictions on speech and assembly in defense of public order.[21] This was followed in 1958 by the Armed Forces (Special Powers) Act, which allowed the suspension of civil liberties and use of deadly force in "disturbed areas" such as India's northeast. The law was based on a pre-independence British ordinance designed for use against Congress itself.[22] In 1963, constitutional freedoms were again restricted to defend the "sovereignty and integrity of India." This measure was targeted at regional leaders who campaigned for "secession from India or disintegration of India."[23]

In 1942, a Congress committee said that India should have a federal system in which states had "the largest measure of autonomy."[24] This was not the system adopted after 1947. Restrictions on state power in the new constitution were so substantial that the system has been described as "quasi-unitary" rather than federal.[25] B.R. Ambedkar, India's first law minister, explained in 1948 that the country was divided into states solely for "convenience of administration."[26] The constitution enables central government to act in almost all areas of importance and gives it control over key sources of revenue.[27] Delhi can reorganize states without their consent. In addition to declaring general emergencies, Delhi may also suspend government in individual states when it believes that constitutional government has broken down. This power was invoked seven times under Nehru.[28]

Nehru's government also exerted tight control over some parts of the national economy. Critical industries, the "commanding heights" of the economy, were government-owned.[29] Private enterprise was steered by a strict licensing regime, and foreign investment and trade were severely restricted. The whole process of economic development was guided by five-year plans based loosely on the Soviet model. These were developed by the Planning Commission, a powerful body of technocrats based in Delhi. Nehru served as chair of the commission. "The idea of a planned society," he had explained in 1946, was accepted "by almost everyone."[30]

But central intervention had its limits. Plans for reform of agriculture were modest. Central government improved irrigation and encouraged new farming techniques but hesitated about addressing the underlying problem of land ownership. Dramatic reforms were anathema to rural landowners, who provided essential support to the Congress.[31] India made no attempt at agricultural collectivization as the Soviet Union and China did. Measures to redistribute land were limited. The result was that severe inequalities in land ownership persisted. Many farms were unprofitably small, and the number of landless laborers remained large.[32]

Nehru was also cautious in his approach to caste discrimination. The new constitution reserved legislative seats and government jobs for Dalits and allowed reservations for other "backward classes" in the bureaucracy and higher education.[33] The technique of reservations was invented during British rule and Nehru's government continued it with ambivalence. Nehru himself said he "dislike[d] any kind of reservation."[34] His government rejected proposals for extension of reservations and other measures to remedy caste-based discrimination, worrying that an emphasis on caste differences would "foster divisive tendencies."[35] The national census limited the collection of data about caste identities after 1951, an unusual example of willful ignorance in a regime that often fetishized statistics.[36]

Nehru's government quashed groups that wanted more radical reforms of the social order in rural India. Between 1946 and 1951, the Indian military and police brutally repressed a peasant movement in Telangana that was inspired by developments in communist China.[37] And in 1959, Nehru invoked emergency powers to dismiss a freely elected communist government in Kerala that had launched radical reforms.[38] Nehru worried about the destabilizing effects of radicalism. "We have too many fissiparous tendencies," he explained in 1958, "for us to take risks."[39]

Hindu–Muslim relations were managed with similar concern for stability. The constitution promised a secular state, but this had a distinctive meaning in the context of Indian independence.[40] Secularism did not mean that the state was blind to religion as it made law: rather, it meant that the state would guarantee the ability of communities to practice their faith in peace. Hindu and Muslim communities continued to live by different laws about family life, while central government suppressed extremism on either side. This was a policy of carefully managed toleration, with the Nehruvian state continuing the old imperial role of umpire.

Breakdown and Emergency

Nehru's ambition had been to build a state that was truly independent, prosperous, and reasonably respectful of fundamental rights. Above all, he wanted to protect the country from destruction by "centrifugal pressures." For this purpose, Nehru and his colleagues built a regime that was highly centralized, modestly democratic, intrusive in some domains, and restrained in others. Almost immediately, though, the Nehruvian order began to crack apart. When it collapsed entirely, the country plunged into crisis. The result was even more centralized rule under Indira Gandhi.

Between the 1950s and early 1980s, India's central government was preoccupied with multiple hazards. The first was attacks from abroad. In 1962, China seized the Aksai Chin, a territory on India's north-western frontier. China attacked India's northeastern frontier as well, but later withdrew its forces. India was surprised by these assaults and failed to repulse them.[41] India also fought a short and inconclusive war with Pakistan in 1965, triggered by Pakistan's attempt to foment an uprising in Kashmir. The two countries fought again in 1971. Indian defense spending grew tenfold between 1960 and 1978.[42]

India's grip on frontiers was challenged by separatist movements as well. In the northeast, armed groups demanded autonomy for Mizos, Nagas, and other ethnic minorities. Delhi responded with a mix of repression and political concessions, including the creation of two new states, Mizoram and Nagaland.[43] In the northwest, meanwhile, Delhi thwarted demands for Kashmiri independence by manipulating elections, imposing emergency rule, and adopting counterinsurgency measures. In the Punjab, the center's violent suppression of a Sikh secessionist movement led eventually to the assassination of Prime Minister Indira Gandhi by Sikh bodyguards in 1984.[44]

Another hazard confronting the regime was resistance to central control from the Indian interior, especially in the south. South India contains many societies that were never tightly integrated into the British empire or the Mughal empire before that. These societies have their own languages, distinctive ideas about religion and social order, and long histories of struggle for autonomy. Southerners resented the domination of central government by politicians and bureaucrats from Hindi-speaking northern states, and the tendency of those states to see themselves as "the center from which all other states derive their ideas and their culture."[45] To many southerners, the centralized Nehruvian regime threatened to become an instrument for imposing an alien conception of civilization.

Regional anxieties came to the fore as central government began to redefine state boundaries in the 1950s. The boundaries inherited at independence were arbitrary and clearly required adjustment. But what should be the basis for reorganization? If states were merely administrative conveniences, as Ambedkar suggested, then boundaries should be determined by practicalities of governance as determined by the center.[46] Regional leaders disagreed, believing that states should be instruments for the protection of distinct communities defined principally by language.

Nehru opposed the idea of reorganizing states on linguistic lines. But political pressure was intense and he relented. The practice of reorganizing states by language, and later by other aspects of identity, has continued over decades.[47] Regional politicians have learned how to use the apparatus of state government to defend sub-national identities. The reconfigured Madras state, renamed Tamil Nadu in 1968, was conceived by activists as a homeland of the Tamil people.[48] Bombay state, redesignated as Maharashtra in 1960, was similarly imagined as a homeland of Marathi-speaking people, and Andhra Pradesh as an instrument for advancing "Telugu national pride."[49]

In 1956, journalist Selig Harrison gave a dire assessment of India's condition. Echoing an old theme, Harrison described India as a composite of regions that could "properly be compared to the sovereign nations of Europe." Harrison believed that Nehru was struggling valiantly but fruitlessly to hold these parts together. The "centrifugal force" of regional self-interest, Harrison claimed, was tearing the country apart.[50]

Tensions between the center and regions were heightened by debate over India's official languages. The 1950 constitution stated that Hindi and English would be used for official business, but English could be discontinued after 1965. In 1963, Nehru's government introduced legislation that appeared to establish Hindi as the sole language for conducting the business of central government. The law triggered violent protests among non-Hindi speakers in south India. Some north Indian politicians accused southerners of subverting the union. Nehru's successor, Lal Bahadur Shastri, restored calm by promising that English would still be used at the center and that states could work in the language of their own choice.[51]

Another challenge for central government after the late 1950s was the intensification of political participation throughout the country. The decade of the 1960s has been described as the moment in which India transitioned from elite-dominated politics to mass politics.[52] There were thirty million more voters in the 1967 election than in 1962. Opposition parties were better organized, and election campaigns more sophisticated. Caste became an increasingly important factor in political mobilization, and demands on government were often expressed in terms of redress for caste disadvantages. Other forms of political action, such as riots, strikes, and student unrest, spiked dramatically between 1960 and 1970.[53]

Political upheavals were compounded by economic troubles. The policy of state-led industrialization produced promising results at first, but growth fell short of expectations in the 1960s.[54] The limitations of state control (lack of innovation, inefficiency, and corruption) became clear. Job creation in the manufacturing sector fell behind population growth. There was inadequate investment in people through primary education and healthcare as well. Agricultural production was compromised by policy failures and droughts. Many were humiliated when India sought emergency food aid from the United States.[55]

Nehru had expected that India's economic development would be carefully steered by technocrats within the Planning Commission. By the late 1960s, though, faith in the Planning Commission had faltered. Its work was upended by wars, droughts, and policy failures. The fourth five-year plan did not take effect on schedule in 1967: instead, central government announced a two-year "plan holiday." Experts lamented the "running crisis of Indian planning."[56] Five-year planning recommenced in 1969, but the status of the Planning Commission began a long decline.

This was only one aspect of a broader decay in decision-making capacity at the heart of government during the 1960s. The effectiveness of the regime since independence had depended heavily on Nehru himself. The strain on Nehru was immense and by the early 1960s his health was failing. Observers worried what might happen when Nehru died.[57] Nehru was succeeded after his death in 1964 by Shastri, who died eighteen months later. Nehru's daughter, Indira Gandhi, became India's third prime minister, but only after a fierce contest within the Congress party. Fractures within Congress widened over the next two years. Factionalism among Congress leaders was not the only problem: after the 1967 elections, Congress no longer controlled most state governments.[58] Since independence, the party had served as forum for brokering differences between importance constituencies, but its effectiveness in this role was declining.

By the early 1970s, it seemed that India was being overwhelmed by centrifugal forces. "What was noticeably absent," one writer said at the time, "was any sense of cohesion and resilience in the political life of the country as a whole."[59] Prime Minister Indira Gandhi responded to this crisis by reasserting central control over everyday life and radically reconfiguring the structure of leadership within the Indian regime. Some thought the country was on the path to dictatorship.[60]

National economic policy shifted sharply leftward under Gandhi. By 1975, central government had nationalized all major banks and insurance companies, as well as the oil and coal industries, many steel and textile mills, and the wholesale wheat trade. Industrial licensing rules were stiffened to restrain big businesses and favor small ones, and foreign investment was sharply restricted.[61] Central government introduced many programs to help the poor, especially in rural areas, including new government employment schemes, increased rations of essential goods, price controls, and promises of debt relief and free land.[62]

Political calculations drove this shift in economic policy. Gandhi called an early election in 1971, breaking from the practice of holding central and state polls at the same time. This reduced the likelihood that regional issues would influence the national vote. Gandhi campaigned relentlessly and her economic program proved to be immensely popular.[63] She was returned to the prime minister's office with a larger majority than Nehru ever obtained. This overwhelming success allowed Gandhi to crush rival factions within Congress, and the party apparatus ceased to have much independent influence after this time.[64] Gandhi had won power by a personal appeal to the mass electorate.

Gandhi combined her populist economic policy with a renewed emphasis on law and order. Another state of emergency was declared in 1971 during India's brief war with Pakistan. Gandhi's government adopted the Maintenance of Internal Security Act, which expanded powers for preventive detention, wiretapping, and warrantless searches. By 1972, more than twenty thousand people were detained without trial on the pretext of internal security.[65] Gandhi also used emergency provisions in the constitution to suspend state governments thirty-nine times between 1966 and 1977, typically when states were run by opposition parties. Critics complained that Gandhi sought "personal control" over the whole system.[66]

In June 1975, Gandhi went further. As protests grew larger, Gandhi declared another emergency and placed the entire country under martial law. Civil rights were suspended, tens of thousands of political opponents were jailed, and strict censorship was imposed on the press. The national election scheduled for 1976 was postponed. The constitution was hurriedly amended to prohibit courts from hearing challenges to the emergency and protect Gandhi from liability for her actions.[67] Central government promised more populist economic measures but also launched harsh programs of slum clearance and forced sterilization.[68]

Gandhi claimed that her actions were necessary to protect India against "forces of disintegration," and supporters praised her for imposing discipline on the "soft" Indian state.[69] But many wondered whether the democratic experiment in India had ended. Gandhi's true aim, one observer suggested in 1977, was to construct "a permanent regime of authoritarian rule."[70] Others said that Gandhi was building a personality cult: "Indira is India and India is Indira."[71] The larger question was whether this was the only way in which a country like India could be held together.

The Millennial Regime

Democracy in India may have been saved by miscalculation. In January 1977, Gandhi loosened restrictions on civil liberties and called a national election. She was facing domestic and international pressure to reverse course and believed she was likely to win the election.[72] Instead, Congress was trounced. A coalition of opposition parties took power but quickly collapsed because of internal divisions and inexperience. Gandhi was re-elected in 1980, followed by her son Rajiv in 1984. This was the last time that Congress would win a majority in the Lok Sabha. From 1989 until 2014, India was ruled by a succession of coalition governments.

The Indian regime changed substantially in the three decades following 1980. In many ways, central government loosened its control over Indian society. The structure of the central executive also changed markedly. Broadly speaking, power was diffused within the Indian polity. Until the early years of the new millennium, this new formula for governing seemed to work well. By the 2010s, however, old anxieties about centrifugal tendencies had resurfaced and a new effort to reconcentrate authority had been launched.

The shift in attitude about government regulation of the economy in the last years of the twentieth century was remarkable. Even in the 1980s, there were signs that Congress was ready to retreat from its policy of intensive control over the economy.[73] An economic crisis in 1991 pushed India more clearly onto the path of economic liberalization. Tariffs were lowered and import controls loosened. Some public sector monopolies were broken, and foreign investment was encouraged. Industrial licensing requirements, price controls, and restrictions on domestic investment were removed. This was seen as a "radical shift" toward free-market policies.[74]

Central control over lower levels of government also declined in the same period. Sometimes this was the result of deliberate choices by central government. Seven new states were created between 1987 and 2014. Central government modestly increased the share of tax revenues that was provided to state governments.[75] The constitution was amended in 1993 with the hope of strengthening local governments.[76] But deeper societal dynamics were also at play. State politics was becoming more vibrant and expressive of regional identities. A new generation of state-level leaders was more willing to resist directions from Delhi and better at playing center-state conflicts to political advantage.[77] Some states, prospering because of their new connection to global markets, were less inclined to follow directions from Delhi.[78]

At the same time, however, there were more pressures on central government because of the deepening of democratic norms. There was another "upsurge of the underprivileged" in the 1990s.[79] Unlike their counterparts in other democracies, India's poor were more likely to vote than the middle and upper classes. Disadvantaged sections of society looked to central government for measures that would remedy old inequalities and patterns of discrimination. Democratic competition also became more undisciplined after the 1990s. Controls on campaign finance weakened and criminal influence in elections became more extensive.[80]

Caste became an increasingly important basis of political mobilization, and conflict between castes over access to government benefits intensified. In 1980, a centrally established advisory body, the Mandal Commission, recommended an expansion of reservations for central government jobs and seats in public universities, to accommodate a broader range of disadvantaged castes. The recommendations led to violent protests from members of other castes when they were finally adopted a decade later. In following years, electoral competition was more sharply defined as a struggle between castes.[81]

The court system also put pressure on central government in this period. India's Supreme Court issued a string of decisions that interpreted individual rights in the constitution broadly and expanded government's responsibility for protecting those rights.[82] It sometimes provided detailed instructions about how these responsibilities should be fulfilled. Judicial activism, and the spread of rights-based thinking, limited the capacity of central government to chart its own course in domestic policy. In the early 2000s, it adopted a series of laws that promised to protect a range of fundamental rights.[83]

Meanwhile, the capacity of central government to manage relations between faith communities was in decline. Partly this was the result of rising consciousness about faith, especially among Hindus in northern India.[84] At the same time, however, the old formula for managing Hindu–Muslim relations was breaking down. British rulers had presented themselves as neutral arbiters between the two communities and Nehru's government had attempted to continue this role. But it was hard to maintain the pretense of neutrality as elections became more competitive. As Congress struggled to retain power in the 1980s and 1990s, it made concessions to Hindu and Muslim communities that undercut its claims to impartiality in managing communal relations.[85]

The ability of the central executive to manage the multiple pressures that were being placed upon it, and to pursue a clearly defined national agenda, was compromised after the late 1980s. No single party won a majority in the Lok Sabha in any election after 1984 and before 2014. Coalition government was the rule. Some coalitions were short-lived. The more durable coalitions were built on a carefully brokered settlement among the ruling parties.[86] The role of the senior bureaucracy also changed in this period. A small group of influential technocrats, many located within the Ministries of Finance and Commerce, played an important role in shaping the program of economic liberalization.[87] More generally, though, the effectiveness of the core civil service declined. Positions in government became less attractive as opportunities in the private sector expanded. Political interference and corruption in the bureaucracy increased.[88]

The Return of Fissiparous Pressures

Over the span of three decades – from 1980 to 2010 – central government loosened its grip on the marketplace, lower levels of government, and society more generally. The result was a society that was more prosperous, more vibrant, and more deeply democratic than in earlier decades. But this millennial regime had its defects, and, as years passed, these defects became more glaring. Anxieties about fissiparous pressures mounted once again.

Overall economic performance certainly improved in this era. Average annual GDP growth was over six percent between 1990 and 2010, compared to 3.5 percent in the 1960s and 1970s.[89] But gains from economic liberalization were not evenly shared. For example, foreign investment was mainly concentrated in six of India's twenty-nine states.[90] The economic gap between poorer and wealthier states, substantial even before reforms, grew larger. Thriving states in the south and west were in a better position to invest in infrastructure and social services, which intensified differences in living standards and prospects for further growth. The economic reform process, one analysis concluded, had unleashed new "centripetal forces."[91]

The number of Indians living in extreme poverty declined after the economic reforms.[92] But there was also a spectacular increase in wealth of India's upper classes. Economic inequality between individuals increased, especially in cities.[93] This growing inequality was easily observed. The rising middle class celebrated its good fortune through conspicuous consumption while journalists documented the lavish lifestyles of billionaires. Mounting resentment about inequality threatened social stability in urban areas.[94] Meanwhile some rural areas suffered badly, partly because of the removal of tariff protection and price supports for agricultural products. More than three hundred thousand farmers committed suicide between 1995 and 2012.[95]

In theory, government could take action to offset the effects of unequal growth. It could invest in services such as education and healthcare and provide income support and essential goods for the poorest. Competition for votes provided a strong incentive for parties to promise such benefits. The number of "centrally sponsored schemes" intended to aid the poor grew during the period of liberalization. But many of these centrally initiated programs were ill designed or badly executed. Delhi was far away from the frontline of service delivery, and its capacity to prevent corruption and assure proper implementation was limited. This was especially true of complex services like education and healthcare.[96] In 2009, one scholar described India as a "flailing state" whose "head is no longer reliably connected to its own limbs."[97] Some state governments were better than others at implementing central schemes. But this meant that the quality of services received by citizens depended heavily on where they lived.[98]

Even though economic growth after the 1980s was better than it had been before, it still fell short of expectations. The unflattering comparison was with China. In 1990, per capita income in India was about twenty percent higher than in China; but in 2010, Chinese per capita income was three hundred percent higher than in India.[99] A common Indian defense of slower growth was that its reforms were achieved through democratic rather than authoritarian methods, which meant more social stability. But the prosperity gap was so large by 2010 that this defense was becoming unpersuasive. India was not creating enough good jobs for a booming number of young workers. Youth unemployment became a source of social unrest.[100]

Faster growth in India was impeded because of the inability of central government to achieve deeper reforms in many areas.[101] Attempts to sell or shutter inefficient state-owned companies were stymied by political opposition. Laws that inhibited the reallocation of land, labor, and capital to more efficient uses were not easily revised. The electric power system and other forms of essential infrastructure such as highways and railroads were increasingly inadequate to support a growing economy. The agricultural sector was hobbled by price and marketing controls and wasteful subsidies. In many areas, reform was blocked by vested interests, or impeded because government could not develop plausible programs for compensating citizens who would bear the short-term costs of reform. Complaints grew about "policy paralysis" at the heart of Indian government.[102]

By 2014, there was a palpable sense of drift within the Indian polity. There was an echo of political conditions in the early 1970s, although the "crisis of governability" in 2014 was less intense than in 1974. Still, many believed that the country was being pulled apart by liberalization, regionalism, and caste and religious conflicts. The sense of national purpose, the "idea of India," had become muddied. And the central executive did not appear to be in charge. India had been ruled by coalition governments for more than twenty years, and the Congress-led coalition that governed in 2014 was tired and scandal-ridden. New Delhi, it seemed, was no longer "fully in control."[103] In surveys, many Indians said that they were ready for strong leadership even if it meant sacrificing democratic principles.[104]

Hindu Superglue

The 2014 national election was a turning point, the prelude to another reconstruction of the Indian regime.[105] For the first time since 1984, a single party, the Bharatiya Janata Party (BJP) led by Narendra Modi, won a majority in the Lok Sabha. Like Indira Gandhi, Modi practices a form of strongman populism. He has reconcentrated power and undermined liberal democratic institutions. But Modi has not tried to weld the country together through state-directed socialism, as Gandhi did. Instead, he practices a form of faith-based nationalism, applying what one observer has described as a sort of Hindu superglue.[106]

Hindu nationalism, Hindutva, is a creed that regards the Indian state as an instrument for the advancement of Indian civilization and identifies that civilization with the Hindu faith.[107] It is not a new phenomenon. The Rashtriya Swayamsevak Sangh (RSS), a disciplined social movement dedicated to Hindutva, was established almost a century ago. Some early Congress activists were sympathetic to the Hindu nationalist cause.[108] But Congress itself was committed to secularism, and Hindu extremism was regarded as a threat to survival of the Indian state. The nationalist movement was discredited when extremists assassinated Mahatma Gandhi in 1948. Dominated by upper castes, and generally hostile to socialism, the movement had little appeal to Indian voters in the first decades after independence.

The Hindutva movement gained new energy after the 1980s. The BJP itself was formed in 1980 and is closely tied to the RSS. A phalanx of other organizations, specializing in the propagation of Hinduism and mobilization of workers, students, women, Dalits, and aboriginal peoples, has grown up around the RSS.[109] This constellation of organizations, known as the Sangh Parivar, now reaches deeply into Indian society. The Parivar has become more sophisticated in bridging caste differences and has learned how to provide services such as education and welfare that the Indian state has failed to deliver competently.[110] And it has benefited from the decay of its main rival, the Congress party.

Narendra Modi grew up as an RSS activist and became the BJP chief minister of Gujarat in 2001. In 2002 his government was complicitous in anti-Muslim rioting that resulted in thousands of deaths across Gujarat.[111] The BJP won an easy majority in state elections a few months later, but many observers thought that Modi's role in the 2002 riots had destroyed his prospects for a career in national politics.[112] Modi, they argued, had transgressed the principles of secularism and communal accommodation, which were cornerstones of Indian politics.

These observers were mistaken. In Gujarat, Modi refined a style of governing that made Hindu nationalism a winning electoral formula.[113] He countered the old upper-caste reputation of the BJP by playing on his own modest origins. A sophisticated communications and electioneering apparatus promoted Modi as a defender of the common man. Modi promised to spur economic growth by courting investors and embracing market-friendly policies.

Modi pledged to share the benefits of economic growth more widely. In practice, though, Gujarat's spending on social services remained modest in comparison to other states.[114] Limited but well-promoted welfare schemes were crafted to fulfill the promise of "inclusive growth."[115] Modi compensated for this modest expenditure by using the state's powers to promote Hindu identity, while distancing himself from the most controversial elements of the nationalist community. Modi's formula produced renewed majorities in Gujarat in 2007 and 2012. And in 2014 it produced a majority in India's national elections.

Since 2014, Modi has guided a redesign of the Indian regime that responds to the feeling of drift and dissipation that prevailed in the last years of the Congress-led coalition. Following the Gujarat model, the BJP government in Delhi has attempted to move more forcefully on reforms such as tax harmonization, relaxation of land acquisition rules, streamlined bankruptcy procedures, and liberalization of foreign investment, which seemed essential to market-driven economic growth. At the same time, it has expanded the number of centrally sponsored schemes to allay complaints about inequalities. This is just one aspect of a broad reassertion of control over state governments. Modi has "re-empowered the center," dictating more about the design of state-delivered programs, reversing commitments on revenue sharing, and using emergency powers to intervene in states ruled by opposition parties.[116]

Modi's government has also intensified central control for the purpose of advancing the Hindutva agenda. To stop what it calls an "infiltration" of Indian society, Delhi has limited the ability of Muslim refugees to gain Indian citizenship and moved to deport some refugees who have lived in India for decades.[117] In 2019, Delhi imposed direct rule on the Muslim-majority territory of Jammu and Kashmir and restricted civil liberties there as well. The BJP has promised to remove the special status of Muslim personal law and encouraged the construction of a Hindu temple at Ayodhya, where a mosque was demolished by Hindu nationalists in 1992. Modi and other BJP leaders have incorporated Hindu practices into their everyday politicking and refused to condemn rising vigilantism and hate speech against Muslims.[118]

The Modi government has also cracked down on dissent. In 2021, Human Rights Watch complained that the Modi government had "increasingly harassed, arrested, and prosecuted rights defenders, activists, journalists, students, academics, and others critical of the government."[119] Thousands of people have been charged with sedition after challenging BJP policies.[120] Controls on universities have been tightened. The World Press Freedom Index has warned about pressure on media to "toe the Hindu nationalist line" and says that India has become one of the world's most dangerous countries for journalists.[121] The United Nations High Commissioner for Human Rights has worried that new laws regulating non-governmental organizations are being used to "stifle the voices" of Modi's critics.[122]

The structure of leadership within the Indian regime has also changed since 2014. In government and party messages, Modi is presented as a strong leader wielding a firm hand on the machinery of government. The *Indian Express* reported in 2015 that the Prime Minister's Office had become "the most powerful since Indira Gandhi's, virtually the command center for all ministries."[123] Modi has not hesitated to circumvent ministers and deal with bureaucrats directly. In 2017, the *Wall Street Journal* pronounced him the "Micromanager-in-Chief."[124]

At the same time, the power of institutions that might check the prime minister has declined. Cabinet has been excluded from important decisions, and legislation has been forced through the Lok Sabha without time for debate.[125] The Planning Commission was abolished in 2015.[126] The Modi government delayed the appointment of an anti-corruption commissioner, weakened the body that oversees India's open government law, and challenged the independence of the Reserve Bank of India.[127] The autonomy of the Supreme Court has been undermined by executive interference in the appointment of judges.[128] Like Gandhi, Modi clamped down on opposition within his own party, cultivating a "high command culture" within the BJP.[129]

The BJP increased its majority in the Lok Sabha in the 2019 national election. The election seemed to confirm that Modi had discovered a politically viable formula for governing India, and that changes to the Indian regime under his leadership were likely to persist. For advocates of liberal democracy this provoked profound concern. Freedom House concluded in 2021 that Modi was "driving India toward authoritarianism."[130] Another respected group said in 2021 that India should be classified as an "electoral autocracy" rather than a democracy.[131]

Whether the Modi formula will endure remains an open question. The formula has its weaknesses. One familiar problem is the strain that centralization puts on decision-makers at the very center of government. Modi does not have the temperament for long-term planning and has weakened institutions that can perform this function on his behalf.[132] His reliance on a small circle of advisors has resulted in serious miscalculations. The 2016 decision to demonetize banknotes failed to accomplish its anti-corruption goals and caused a major shock to the Indian economy.[133] Raghuram Rajan, Central Bank governor at the time, later criticized the government for ignoring warnings and failing to plan carefully.[134]

At the same time, the Modi government has struggled to overcome the problems of implementation that have always been associated with schemes designed and imposed by Delhi. Important initiatives like the 2018 plan to improve access to health services have been compromised by lack of cooperation from state governments, inadequacies in bureaucratic capacity at the local level, and corruption.[135]

The Modi government has also wrestled with the constraints of "electoral autocracy." Restrictions on civil liberties and democratic institutions since 2014 have been significant. Nevertheless, people retain substantial freedom to speak, organize and protest. Elections, although compromised, are still largely free. And state governments still have a significant degree of autonomy. Central government does not have the capacity or interest to pursue a more thorough project of political repression. But in this middle ground between democracy and autocracy, the adoption and execution of large-scale reforms is still difficult. Delhi cannot act as decisively as Beijing does. Measures that the Modi government has regarded as essential to economic growth, such as those on land acquisition or agricultural marketing, have been stymied by mass protests, while others, such as tax harmonization, have required long and complex negotiations with states.

In this middle ground, the Modi government also remains vulnerable to electoral upsets. Failure to deliver stronger economic growth or improved services, or missteps in managing caste and regional tensions, could result in a weakening of support for Modi and the BJP. Polling conducted in 2021 showed a decline in support for Modi, attributed in part to a flagging economy.[136] Support for Modi in south India was especially weak.[137] The party launched an internal stock-taking exercise in 2021 after a series of losses in state elections.[138] Discipline within the party apparatus has been undermined by internal frustration over top-down decision-making.[139] However, Modi's troubles should not be overstated. The BJP performed very well in state elections held in early 2022.

History Repeating

Sunil Khilnani describes Indian governance as "an extemporized performance" – a process of invention and reinvention in which leaders struggle to "hold together divergent considerations and interests."[140] Still, the performance has a theme. Worries about centrifugal pressures are always present but rise and fall in intensity. When these worries are most intense, authority is concentrated in Delhi, with the hope that some program of strong action from the center will hold the country together. Nehru followed this course in the 1950s, Gandhi did the same in the 1970s, and so has Modi since 2014.

Of course, these three responses to centrifugal pressures are not entirely alike. Nehru followed a model of elitist and technocratic centralism. India's ruling group in the 1950s and early 1960s consisted of a small, well-educated cadre that saw itself as the steward of the national interest. This cadre wanted to establish India as a liberal democracy, but its mentality contained traces of British-era paternalism. By contrast, Gandhi and Modi pursued forms of populist centralism. The concentration of power in the hands of the prime minister was justified as a way of exercising the will of the mass public, manifested in electoral majorities won by relentless campaigning.

Another difference between these three episodes relates to the character of the program pursued by the center. On one hand, there is the secular-socialist model pursued in slightly different ways by Nehru and Gandhi. On the other hand, there is the model pursued by Modi, which blends a market-friendly growth policy, a modest program of compensatory welfare policies, and promotion of Hindu nationalism.

Still, we can see a dangerous commonality in these three responses: the premise that intensification of central control, and the compromise of liberal democratic institutions, is necessary to overcome "fissiparous tendencies." Another commonality is an overestimation of Delhi's ability to execute its program effectively. Power is concentrated, but leaders are overloaded and cannot make sound decisions. Or the head is disconnected from the limbs, so policies set in Delhi are not properly implemented. Given these obstacles to effective central action that would bind the country together, there is a temptation to rely on other adhesives, like a national creed built on Hindu nationalism.

The dilemmas of leadership and control that have confronted India since independence are not new. As we have seen, these dilemmas have afflicted empires throughout history. And they are confronted by other superstates today. For example, we can see parallels between India and American politics. In the US as in India, deepening democracy has created pressure to expand the role of central government; central government has struggled to make decisions and implement policies competently; and leaders have recently turned to strongman populism and ethnic nationalism to preserve their authority.

There are other superstates that have adopted radically different formulas for governing at scale, as we shall see in the following chapters. China has gone one way, by repudiating "Western-style theories" entirely and refining its model of centralized rule. It seeks to avoid the pitfalls of electoral autocracy by persisting with full-bore authoritarianism. This formula has produced impressive results since 1980, but at the cost of fundamental rights.

Meanwhile the European Union has gone another way, following a model of decentralization so radical that there is some question about whether it should be counted as a state at all. The EU relies on member states, rather than central institutions, to perform most of the hard work of preserving order, providing services, and protecting rights. And, unlike China, the EU embraces Western liberal-democratic principles, although it applies these principles with varying degrees of rigor at different levels of the EU regime.

6

China
Authoritarian Dilemmas

Superstates are a hybrid form of polity that combines features of ancient empires and modern states. China might be the best example of a polity with this combination of features. The connections between past and present are evident. For centuries, a succession of empires ruled much of the territory now claimed by the People's Republic of China (PRC). Some observers consider the PRC simply as the latest Chinese empire.[1] Mao Zedong, the PRC's first paramount leader, was described by his colleagues as the first emperor of a new dynasty, while Xi Jinping, the current leader, has been counted as China's latest emperor.[2] Chinese leaders themselves see commonalities with their imperial predecessors.[3] Rulers of the PRC obsess about cohesion and stability, just as emperors did. The design of the PRC regime shares some essential features of earlier imperial regimes, including an emphasis on centralized control and autocratic leadership.

The comparison is imperfect, of course. The PRC is not an empire. It also has the ambitions and burdens of a modern state. From the start, the PRC's leaders were committed to a radical transformation of economic and social life. And in recent decades, the regime has been remarkably successful in this project of transformation. The country is more united and prosperous than ever before.

Still, the regime is not robust. It suffers from four dilemmas that require constant and adroit management. Two of these, relating to leadership and control, are inherited from the age of empires. Concentrated authority and an extensive bureaucracy enable the rapid mobilization of national resources, but also make China vulnerable to the old problems of bad emperors and bureaucratism. Two more dilemmas are distinctively modern. Like most modern states, the PRC has made a constitutional commitment to democracy and individual freedom. In practice, though, the regime denies political and civil rights as it seeks to maintain order within the core of its territories. The constitution also promises that the PRC will struggle against imperialism. In its own borderlands, however, the PRC pursues a familiar program of colonization. China is subject to withering international criticism for human rights abuses in the interior and on its frontiers.

Three Continuities

There are three clear continuities in statecraft between China's imperial age and the period of rule by the PRC. The first is a fixation among leaders with cohesion and stability. "Stemming the forces of disintegration," historian Yuri Pines has observed, was "the singularly important dictum" for rulers of China's earliest dynasties.[4] One of the great works of Chinese antiquity records a conversation between the emperor Hsiang and philosopher Mencius. The emperor asks: What will bring peace to our torn lands? Mencius answers that peace will come only by uniting the country under one good leader.[5]

China's rulers have always had good reason for worrying about disintegration. Like the empires that preceded it, the PRC encompasses a vast territory with borders that are long and hard to defend. Throughout history, the loyalties of peoples living in China's borderlands, who sometimes have more in common with peoples of neighboring territories than with the Han people of the heartland, have been questioned. And even in the heartland, rulers have wrestled with "powerful centrifugal forces."[6] China's current rulers emphasize commonalities within the Han ethnic group, but there are significant cultural differences between regions in the heartland.[7] One marker of diversity is language. Many dialects are spoken among the Han, some of which are mutually unintelligible. Perhaps thirty percent of the population cannot communicate in the dialect preferred by Beijing.[8] The heartland is divided in other ways too. There have always been divisions between poor interior provinces and coastal areas that are wealthier and more cosmopolitan.[9] Inequalities between interior and coastal areas have sharpened since 1980. Old gaps between cities and rural areas have widened as well.[10]

During the age of empires, China's rulers juggled a range of hazards, including invasions, economic collapses, peasant uprisings, and rebellions by provincial elites. Moreover, there was always the risk that these problems would cascade; for example, that provincial elites would rebel against a central authority weakened by invasion, or that foreign powers would seize the opportunity created by peasant uprisings. A cascade of hazards could easily become unmanageable and ultimately fatal to empire.

This is what happened to the Qing empire in the nineteenth and early twentieth centuries.[11] The empire was assaulted by foreign powers that used superior military capabilities to wrest concessions that weakened the Chinese economy and undermined the empire's capacity to assert authority throughout its territory. Economic decline and ethnic rivalries precipitated rebellions in the Chinese heartland. At the same time, minorities in western territories rose against Beijing. Internal conflicts became a pretext for more aggression by foreign powers. Given time, the Qing empire might have managed any one of these problems competently. But a sclerotic bureaucracy and faction-alized court could not manage all of them at once, and after a century of struggle the empire collapsed.

The collapse of the Qing empire in 1911–1912 was followed by a period of tumult lasting almost forty years. Initially, a weak repub-lican government in Beijing struggled to gain control over regional warlords. An American observer in Beijing, William Willoughby, compared conditions in China in 1916 to those in the last years of the Roman empire, when power "lay almost wholly in the hands of generals commanding the armies in the provinces." (Willoughby thought that the only way to restore order was for Western powers to put China into "receivership.")[12] Conflict among warlords mutated into a civil war between nationalists and communists that ended in 1949 with the establishment of the PRC.

There was little confidence in 1949 that the advent of a new regime would lead to quick restoration of stability. Shortly before the Communist Party took power, the intellectual Huang Yanpei warned Mao Zedong that a new regime would confront the same "vicious cycle" of growth and decay that had plagued empires.[13] Fears about the survival of the PRC persisted for years. Throughout the 1950s, the regime struggled to execute its ambitious plans and contain "contradic-tions among the people" when those plans failed to produce results.[14] In the early 1960s, Chinese leaders confronted an economic collapse, peasant uprisings, and discontent within the military.[15] In 1969, during the Cultural Revolution, political scientist Tang Tsou observed a system in "profound crisis."[16] Another political scientist reported in

1972 that the political situation in China was still "highly fluid and volatile."[17]

Only after the accession of Deng Xiaoping as paramount leader in the late 1970s did circumstances improve. But the concern for stability has scarcely diminished. Deng's maxim "stability overrides everything" has guided national policy for the last forty years.[18] In 2021, Xi Jinping re-emphasized that preserving "stability and harmony" was the foundation of CCP policy.[19]

The second continuity between past and present relates to the fundamental aspects of regime design. Stability and harmony are to be achieved through highly centralized and intensive control. Of course, the standard for judging intensity of control has ratcheted over time. Chinese empires before 1911 sought more control than many contemporaneous empires, and similarly the PRC seeks more control than many modern states. The constitution of the new republic, adopted in 1954, said that it would protect human rights, defined just as broadly as they were in the constitution of the Indian republic. But China's 1954 constitution went further, promising that the state would use its power to achieve the complete demolition of feudal and capitalist systems of exploitation.[20]

A constitution is supposed to provide operating rules for a regime that are not easily changed, and which constrain the actions of the political executive. But the constitution of the PRC has always been pliable. The document has been comprehensively overhauled three times, most recently in 1982, and frequently adjusted since then.[21] Constitutional flexibility follows from the CCP's commitment to another twentieth-century doctrine, Leninism. Lenin held that "centralized organization of force" was essential for communist revolution, and the Chinese constitution is designed on this principle.[22] Authority in the PRC is highly concentrated, as it was in empires. Although the country is divided into provinces and territories, these subdivisions have no real autonomy. China is a unitary rather than a federal state. Nor is there a true separation of powers. The court system is subordinate to the National People's Congress (NPC), which is dominated in turn by the State Council, the "highest state organ," led by the Premier.[23]

Members of NPC and lower-level assemblies are chosen through elections, but these elections are not free. According to the constitution, the defining feature of the regime is leadership by the CCP. The party apparatus determines who will be elected to legislative and executive bodies created under the constitution. The Chinese military is directly controlled by the party. The party also determines appointments to thousands of key positions within the government bureaucracy and supervises universities, labor unions, religious and ethnic organizations, and major media.

"The party leads everything," *The People's Daily* declared in 2022: "Party, government, military, civilian, and academic, east, west, south, north, and center."[24] The CCP itself is governed by a constitution that emphasizes centralized leadership and compliance with the party line. Authority within the party is concentrated in the hands of its General Secretary, presently Xi Jinping, who is supported by a small leadership group known as the Politburo Standing Committee.

The third and perhaps most surprising continuity relates to the creed that is used to justify the regime. Of course, the rhetoric of Marxist–Leninist revolution is alien to the age of empires. But the current leadership of the PRC also appeals to old Confucian ideals about the need for unity and harmony, the importance of respecting authority, and the reciprocal obligations of superiors and subordinates.[25] PRC leaders were initially ambivalent about Confucianism: amenable to its ideas about statecraft but repelled by its role in supporting a feudal social order. In the 1960s and early 1970s, the CCP launched virulent attacks on Confucian traditions.[26] However, Confucius has been rehabilitated over the last forty years. Today, CCP leaders including Xi Jinping often praise him.[27] Confucian ideals are said to work better than Western ideals in countries like China, which are harder to rule because of their size and diversity.[28]

Like many courtiers and intellectuals in the last decades of Qing rule, leaders of the PRC also emphasize their determination to restore national honor. The humiliation that was felt in China because of the predations of other empires in the nineteenth and early twentieth centuries was profound. In the late nineteenth century, this humiliation propelled a reform movement that aimed at restoring the Qing empire's "wealth and power" by adapting Western technologies and practices.[29] The movement borrowed this hallmark phrase from an ancient prescription for imperial survival: "If a wise ruler masters wealth and power, he can have whatever he desires."[30]

In the early years of the PRC, leaders expressed this ambition to restore national honor in the language of anti-imperial struggle. A 1949 party program promised to "abolish all the prerogatives of imperialist countries," and a commitment to oppose imperialism can still be found in the PRC constitution. In recent years, though, the PRC's leadership has also expressed this ambition in the ancient language of wealth and power. Xi Jinping played on the old refrain when he promised in 2014 to make "the people prosperous and the country strong" so that the country will never be bullied again.[31]

Four Dilemmas

Mao Zedong's theorizing about the governance of China was distinguished by his preoccupation with contradictions.[32] As CCP leaders set up a new government, they often wrestled with objectives and principles that collided with one another. Moreover, these contradictions seemed to be ineluctable: they could never be reconciled satisfactorily. Mao was using Marxist–Leninist vocabulary to describe dilemmas in regime design. The survival of the PRC has depended on the skillful management of four dilemmas. Two are inherited from the age of empires, and two are distinctly modern.

The dilemma of leadership. The critical feature of the current Chinese regime is concentration of power. Central government retains tight control over provinces, markets, and social groups. And authority is concentrated within central government too. The leadership structure provides for few checks or balances on the paramount leader. This sort of leadership structure can be effective in mobilizing societal resources rapidly and in executing painful reforms. Concentration of power in the hands of a small ruling group is one reason why China was able to reorient so quickly toward a market economy after 1980. But there is a dilemma: concentrated authority also creates potentially fatal vulnerabilities for the regime.

One danger is that leaders will perform incompetently because of personal weaknesses or lack of adequate support. This is the ancient problem of the bad emperor.[33] The early history of the PRC provided catastrophic evidence that this problem had survived into the modern age. Like Nehru, Mao was a charismatic and powerful leader. But Mao faced even fewer constraints on his actions than Nehru. In 1957, he ignored advisors and launched a rash plan to double agricultural and industrial output within three years. Known as the Great Leap Forward, the plan involved a radical reconstruction of rural life and resulted in one of the greatest man-made disasters in human history. Agricultural output plummeted and China suffered a devastating famine. Thirty million people died.[34]

A system that concentrates power so intensely cannot recover easily from such devastating mistakes. State propaganda emphasized the infallibility of Mao's judgment.[35] Evidence of failure was suppressed by subordinates who wanted to appease the leader. Mao also orchestrated campaigns to destroy critics throughout his rule. The biggest of these campaigns, known as the Cultural Revolution, was launched by Mao in 1966 and continued until his death in 1976. At its peak in 1967–1968, the country verged on civil war.[36] Almost two million people died, and millions more were detained and persecuted.[37] In 1981 the CCP acknowledged the Cultural Revolution was a "grave blunder."[38]

Some empires had a simple formula for succession: power passed on the death of an emperor to his eldest son. This formula was imperfect, because the heir might be incompetent, but at least the rule was clear and generally understood. The early PRC lacked any formula for succession that was equally straightforward. Although the PRC purported to be a thoroughly modern enterprise, Mao ruled until death just as emperors did. He periodically designated successors but denounced them when they grew too powerful. As Mao's health declined, a vicious factional struggle erupted. Deng Xiaoping only emerged as China's next paramount leader two years after Mao's death.[39]

Between 1980 and 2000, Deng and his allies attempted to renovate the leadership structure of the PRC to remedy problems of the Mao era. There were two important lines of reform. First, power was diffused within the ruling group. The Politburo Standing Committee (PSC) rose in prominence and a norm of consensual decision-making was encouraged within that body. The paramount leader came to be regarded as the "first among equals" within the PSC. Party and state decision-making bodies met more regularly.[40]

A second line of reform was aimed at refreshing the ruling group and reducing the turmoil of succession.[41] The party established age limits for senior posts and prohibited individuals from serving more than ten years in the same position. Procedures were established for identifying promising young leaders, with more emphasis placed on technical and professional expertise. The CCP managed the careers of party officials more carefully. Individuals were tracked through positions of increasing importance, with promotion tied to performance. At the apex of the party, leaders invented routines for identifying successors to the general secretary many years before he was scheduled to step down.

The CCP was applying a very old solution to the problem of bad emperors. The leadership structure was changed so that paramount leader was less consequential. The party itself said the reformed structure was designed "to prevent arbitrary decision-making by a single top leader."[42] In 1992, one expert suggested that the reformed structure had "fundamentally constrain[ed] leadership choice" and made the topmost position "not very important."[43] This was an overstatement. Deng showed that the new rules could be bent during critical moments like the 1989 Tiananmen Square crisis.[44] Still, it did seem by the end of the millennium that China had shifted to a more consensual and technocratic model of executive decision-making. In 2003 an American expert concluded that the new system was "increasingly stable" and that the PRC was demonstrating an unappreciated capacity to adapt and survive.[45]

A decade later, however, appraisals of the system were less generous. Weaknesses of the consensual and technocratic model became obvious. Ideological fervor waned as more senior posts were occupied by technocrats. Conflicts within the ruling group produced stalemates, compromises, and reversals in policy. Succession rules turned the "first among equals" into a lame duck in the last years of his service, making it harder for him to break deadlocks among party leaders.[46]

Added to this was a growing problem of corruption within senior ranks of the party. In a booming economy, there were many opportunities for party leaders to abuse power for personal gain. The CCP attempted to strengthen anti-corruption rules, but keeping peace within the ruling group sometimes meant turning a blind eye to misconduct. By 2012, public support for the regime was threatened by flagrant corruption within the party elite.[47]

There is an interesting parallel between events in India and China in the first fifteen years of the twenty-first century. In both countries, power within the leadership group was diffused at the start of the century. The causes of diffusion were different: the breakdown of the Congress Party in one case, and corrections to Mao-era excesses in the other. But the eventual result in both cases was a perception of malaise and corruption at the center of government. In India, the result was a reconcentration of power under Narendra Modi. A similar path was followed by Xi Jinping, who became China's paramount leader in 2012.

Xi reduced the size of the Politburo standing committee. He also established a series of high-level groups under his direct charge to steer policy in critical areas.[48] One observer joked that Xi had made himself the "Chairman of Everything."[49] (Recall that Modi was described at the same time as "Micromanager-in-Chief.") Xi also launched a vigorous anti-corruption campaign that targeted many senior party leaders. The campaign was intended to restore public confidence but also served as a tool for eliminating rivals.[50] The two-term limit for the PRC president that had been established in 1982 was removed in 2018, allowing Xi to rule indefinitely and eliminating his "lame duck" problem. Xi ignored the norm about identifying a successor at the end of his first term.

By 2021, the consensual-technocratic model of leadership had been consigned to history. After Xi's renovations, the PRC's leadership structure permitted firm action to address problems of the preceding two decades. This was a short-term benefit. But observers already speculate about the long-term viability of the Xi model. The old dangers of concentrated power cannot be escaped. Commentators worry about the re-emergence of a Mao-style cult of personality around Xi. Xi's philosophy of rule, "Xi Jinping Thought," has been added to the constitution as one of the country's guiding doctrines. There are already signs of overload at the center because all major decisions require Xi's approval.[51] In addition, there is a heightened danger of mistakes because critics are silenced. And there is the growing possibility of reaction by party insiders who have been punished or ostracized during Xi's rule.[52]

The dilemma of bureaucracy. Rulers of Chinese empires generally preferred to exercise tight control of everyday life throughout their territory. This meant that empires always had extensive bureaucracies. But this produced another dilemma: bureaucracies enabled imperial control over territory and populations, but generated control problems of their own. Officials in distant provinces ignored edicts from the center, sent false reports to the capital, refused to take risks, and discredited the regime through corruption and abusive behavior. Chinese empires developed sophisticated but expensive techniques for controlling these pathologies. These imperial-age problems of bureaucratic control persisted after the establishment of the PRC. As a twentieth-century state, and a revolutionary regime, the PRC had large ambitions for changing society. This meant more bureaucracy and thus more bureaupathologies too.

Bureaucratism, as Mao and other CCP leaders called it, was considered to be one of the main problems confronting the PRC in its early years.[53] Their main frustration was the failure of the state bureaucracy to move aggressively on economic and social reforms. A related problem was protectionism, roughly defined as the tendency of provincial and local officials to ignore Beijing and favor regional interests. A third was departmentalism, the fixation of ministries on their own goals and hostility toward collaboration. Transparency was yet another difficulty. During the Great Leap Forward, officials often falsified progress reports to avoid punishment from Beijing. Corruption was a common problem too, aggravated by market reforms after 1980.

In theory, the CCP itself served as a check on bureaucratism. Spread throughout the country, the party apparatus was supposed to monitor and prod the state bureaucracy. Important posts within the state bureaucracy were reserved for loyal party members. But this was an imperfect remedy. Party members sometimes lacked the expertise required to govern competently. Moreover, the CCP apparatus was itself a bureaucracy. Mao's complaints about bureaucratism were directed as much to the CCP as to the state apparatus. His two policy disasters, the Great Leap Forward and the Cultural Revolution, were provoked by frustration over the inability of these twin bureaucracies to act boldly. State and party bureaucratism preoccupied Mao's successors as well. One of Deng Xiaoping's top priorities was "disciplining the bureaucracy."[54] In 2000, Jiang Zemin warned a CCP conference that the PRC was still plagued by bureaucratic problems inherited from the imperial age: aversion to risk, deceitfulness, preoccupation with status, and corruption.[55]

After 1980, the PRC honed techniques for managing bureaucratism. It reduced the number of positions in the state bureaucracy that were reserved for party members and put more emphasis on technical qualifications for civil servants.[56] At the same time, it developed more sophisticated techniques for selecting and monitoring party members who are appointed to key posts in the state bureaucracy. This includes a performance-based control system that connects promotion to the achievement of targets specified by superiors. The system, based on principles that would be familiar to Qin-era Legalists, is powerful but crude. It encourages local officials to focus intensely on a small number of objectives that are easily monitored by higher levels.[57]

Another method for countering bureaucratism is reducing the intensity of state control and thus the need for bureaucracy at all. Under Deng's leadership, Beijing gradually reduced its role in managing the Chinese economy. Increasingly, decisions about production and distribution of goods and services were made in the marketplace rather than government offices.[58] This project of liberalization triggered an extraordinary boom. The size of the Chinese economy grew forty-fold between 1978 and 2020.[59] Prosperity bolstered the legitimacy of the regime.

But this tactic had its limitations as well. Deng justified the shift away from state planning as a purely pragmatic measure. "To get rich is no sin," he said in 1986.[60] However, the embrace of market-friendly policies contributed to a feeling of drift by the end of the century. The regime appeared to have lost its ideological anchor. "Party theory does not involve any discussion of theory," one critic complained in 2013, "it consists only of methods."[61] Under Xi Jinping, the regime has attempted to counter this drift by intensifying ideological training throughout the bureaucracy.[62]

Market expansion also led to the emergence of a powerful new class of companies and entrepreneurs whose loyalty to the regime was suspect. At the same time, private wealth fueled official corruption. To counter market power, the regime has expanded its anti-corruption bureaucracy and taken measures to extend control over the business class. In the 1990s, the PRC required large businesses to establish internal party cells, and under Xi these cells have been given a bigger role in management and personnel decisions.[63] The regime also makes a show of punishing wealthy entrepreneurs who challenge Beijing's authority.[64]

Beijing's approach to economic reform was careful and gradual. It did not follow the radical path that came to be known elsewhere as shock therapy. Limited experiments were approved by Beijing and then extended if they were successful. This was in keeping with Deng's emphasis on pragmatism. Observers suggest that Beijing has invented a technique of centrally guided experimentation that counters the usual conservatism of large bureaucracies.[65] But the effectiveness of this technique depends on the attention and motivation of authorities at the center of government. One study suggests that Beijing's interest in experimentation flags whenever economic and political uncertainty increases, and that central authorities are just "muddling through" rather than engaging in systematic learning.[66]

The Chinese bureaucracies, party and state, are more effective instruments for governing than they were under Mao. They have given Beijing an impressive capacity to mobilize resources at critical moments. But the state apparatus is highly complex. Officials wrestle with problems of coordination at all levels of the apparatus, and progress on reforms usually requires "enormous amounts of discussion and bargaining."[67] Local compliance with central edicts is uneven, especially when tasks are complex and results are hard to observe. The ancient contradictions of bureaucracy require constant attention.

The dilemma of democracy. In only a few decades, the PRC has engineered an economic miracle and restored China's global standing. In 1990, two-thirds of the Chinese population lived in extreme poverty; by 2015, less than one percent did.[68] No surprise, then, that public support for the regime is generally robust. A large majority of people say that they trust leaders in Beijing and are satisfied with their performance.[69] Leaders in Western democracies fare poorly in similar surveys.

However, satisfaction with Beijing is not universal or unqualified. Support for the regime is heavily contingent on rising prosperity. Moreover, economic progress has been uneven. Inequalities between regions, between cities and rural areas, and between classes in urban areas are large by international standards.[70] Many people lack adequate access to education, healthcare, and retirement plans. China has also suffered the side-effects of rapid industrialization: displacement of people from land, environmental degradation, tainted foods and drugs, dangerous workplaces, and petty corruption. China's family planning rules, although recently loosened, are still widely disliked.[71] And some people chafe against restrictions on civil liberties.

Mass disaffection was fatal for the Qing empire and is also a preoccupation of PRC leaders. In the abstract, the threat of mass action is greater today, because people are concentrated in cities, better educated, and more mobile and wired. Consequently, CCP leaders are fixated on the potential for popular unrest. Maintaining social stability is a "hard target" for local administrators.[72] For several years, Beijing publicly reported the number of "mass incidents" – protests, demonstrations, and riots – across the country. The tally increased from nine thousand in 1993 to 180,000 in 2010. Data on mass incidents are no longer released.[73]

In other superstates, citizens are allowed to select leaders through free elections, with the expectation that this will increase support for the regime. In the late 1990s, some Western observers thought that China might shift to the democratic model as well. But this was wishful thinking. Deng Xiaoping and his successors have rejected "Western-style" democracy. Deng said in 1979 that one of the regime's cardinal principles was preserving a proletarian dictatorship. Since then, the CCP has been consistent in repressing pro-democracy movements.[74] One of the central contradictions of the regime is that it persists in upholding dictatorship as part of its self-avowed "struggle for democracy and freedom."[75] Deng argued in 1986 that democratization would jeopardize stability by undermining the ability of the "structure of leadership" to act decisively.[76]

Because it has rejected democratization, the CCP must rely on other tactics for maintaining popular support. Maintaining economic growth is critical.[77] The party cannot depend on gratitude for past accomplishments: most Chinese reached adolescence after the 1990s and have no memory of Mao-era poverty. But matching growth of the 1990s and early 2000s is difficult, because China has exhausted the easy gains that came from loosening a centrally planned economy with a predominantly agricultural workforce.[78] At the same time, the regime has attempted over the last twenty years to improve the quality of public services. This, too, is a difficult assignment, because Beijing cannot easily guide or monitor the production of complex social services at the local level.[79]

In 2021, attempting to show seriousness about reducing inequality, Beijing launched a high-profile campaign against conspicuous consumption, tax avoidance, and marketplace abuses. And the regime has appealed to non-material factors as well. Its governing creed relies on the idea of national redemption, the recovery of honor and status after the humiliations of the nineteenth century. This is the CCP's "core mobilization," the promise to deliver "a rejuvenated, powerful, strong, proud country."[80] This message resonates with a population in which patriotic sentiments are strongly felt.[81]

To spread its messages, Beijing has built a system for propaganda and censorship that is powerful but fragile.[82] The system's objective, as Xi Jinping explained in 2016, is "correct guidance of public opinion."[83] It achieves this by broadcasting the party line on national policies and current events, restricting dissent, distracting attention away from controversial topics, and erasing history on sensitive topics like the Tiananmen Square protests. China's constitution says that citizens shall enjoy freedom of speech and freedom of the press; in practice, China limits these rights more severely than almost every other country in the world.[84]

This propaganda system is a "sprawling bureaucratic establishment" and suffers from the usual problems of bureaucratism.[85] Sclerosis is a particular danger. Methods of control must be updated constantly to deal with an evolving information environment. In the Mao era, guiding public opinion was simpler, because the propaganda system directly operated all major media. After Deng, the task became more complicated. Broadcast media remained under tight state control, but many newspapers and magazines became subject to market pressures, which encouraged editors to publish edgier stories about government failures and corruption. The growth of print media meant more work for censors who struggled to define the boundaries of acceptable criticism.[86]

The advent of the internet posed an even greater challenge for the propaganda system. The proportion of the Chinese population using the internet skyrocketed from five percent in 2002 to more than fifty percent in 2015.[87] Beijing responded with an overhaul of the bureaucracy responsible for controlling the internet. It has developed sophisticated techniques for monitoring and censoring activity on social media and websites, and pressured internet companies to police the behavior of customers on its behalf. All this work tests the boundaries of bureaucratic adaptability. Censors are engaged in a fast-paced game of cat-and-mouse with internet users who play with language and new technologies to evade Beijing's restrictions.[88]

The CCP also keeps a close watch on organizations that might serve as focal points for dissent. Major religious organizations and labor unions are controlled by the party, while other non-governmental organizations are subject to registration requirements and limits on political activity.[89] Under a 2017 law, foreign non-governmental organizations are banned if their work seems to threaten stability.[90] The CCP has tightened its hold on universities as well, prohibiting instruction on topics such as Western democracy and requiring the inculcation of Xi Jinping Thought.[91] The regime has punished lawyers who advocate for human rights.[92]

Other methods are used to preserve public order more generally. Spending on the internal security apparatus increased fourfold between 2007 and 2017, until it exceeded spending on national defense.[93] However, the regime has struggled to make this growing security bureaucracy perform well.[94] In cities, Beijing encourages the development of a form of intensive governance, known as grid management, that improves detection of potential unrest.[95] The regime is also deploying sophisticated technical methods of public surveillance, including face recognition technology.[96] In 2014, it proposed a "social credit" system that assigns scores to individuals based on good behavior and uses those scores to ration access to government services.[97] Critics complain that the PRC is constructing an Orwellian system of social control. In practice, though, the implementation of all these schemes has been fraught with technical and bureaucratic problems.

The dilemma of the borderlands. "Governing border areas," Xi Jinping said in 2015, "is the key for governing a country."[98] And, in the Chinese borderlands, a fourth contradiction in governance plays out. Since 1949, the PRC has presented itself as a leader in the global anti-colonial struggle.[99] The 1954 constitution promised that China itself would be constituted as "one great family of free and equal nations" and prohibited the "oppression of any nationality" within its borders.

Similar language is contained in the current constitution. In reality, however, the PRC is attempting to preserve unity on its frontiers by pursuing an old form of imperial control.

The continuity between imperial and contemporary preoccupations is clearest in the region of Xinjiang in northwest China. This region is vast, accounting for one-sixth of China's total territory, but thinly populated, with only twenty-five million inhabitants, or two percent of the total Chinese population. Most residents are Muslim and nearly half are Uyghurs, one of the Turkic peoples of central Asia. Uyghur separatists call the region East Turkestan.

The region was conquered by the Qing empire in 1759, late in the history of Chinese dynasties. It was named Xinjiang, "new frontier," in 1884. At first, a system of indirect rule known as the light-rein policy was applied in the territory. But policy changed in the nineteenth century as the empire confronted Muslim rebellions as well as interference from Russia. The territory was subjected to military rule in the 1870s. In the last years of the Qing empire, Beijing adopted a plan for Han colonization of Xinjiang modeled on European ideas about the civilizational duties of more advanced races.[100]

Xinjiang recovered some autonomy following the Qing collapse. The region was governed by warlords who were advantaged by remoteness and protected by the Soviet Union. The region was absorbed into the PRC in 1949, but CCP leaders gave it status as an autonomous region in 1955. In practice, though, Xinjiang's Uyghur population has never enjoyed significant freedom within the PRC. From the start, critical positions in the local party apparatus were reserved for Hans loyal to Beijing. Beijing also encouraged Han migration into the region. Uyghur resentment led to violent protests in the 1980s. Beijing responded with measures to suppress Uyghur activism and consolidate control under Han loyalists.[101]

Beijing's concern about Xinjiang increased in the 2000s. The region holds a large share of China's reserves of oil, gas, and coal and is critical to Beijing's plans to promote overland trade through central Asia. Tensions between Hans and Uyghurs led to riots in 2009 that attracted international attention. CCP leaders have also claimed that Islamist radicalism is gaining a foothold in Xinjiang and spreading elsewhere in China. They describe Xinjiang as their "main battlefield" against terrorism.[102]

The result has been a policy of severe repression in the region. Beijing has intensified policing, embedded watchdogs within Uyghur communities, and deployed intrusive new surveillance technologies. It has restricted the use of the Uyghur language and other expressions of Uyghur culture, as well as practice of the Muslim faith. Between one and three million people have been detained in re-education camps. Former detainees have reported torture, sexual abuse, and forced sterilization within these camps. Xinjiang, one critic says, has been transformed into a "neo-totalitarian security state."[103] Other countries and human rights organizations have charged the PRC with genocide against Uyghurs.[104]

Beijing's policy toward Tibet, the vast territory in China's southwest, has followed a similar course. Qing emperors paid little attention to Tibet until the end of the nineteenth century, when the Russian and British empires laid claims on the territory. The Qing court claimed sovereignty over Tibet in 1910 but its attempt at military occupation failed. Tibet enjoyed de facto independence until it was occupied by the People's Liberation Army in 1950. The PRC initially promised that Tibetans could retain their political and religious institutions. Faith in Beijing's promises quickly eroded and the Tibetan capital, Lhasa, witnessed an armed rebellion against Chinese rule in 1959. Beijing responded with a campaign against Tibetan independence.[105] It lightened control modestly in the 1980s. This was followed by a resurgence of the Tibetan movement for independence, this time with substantial international support. In 1989, Chinese leaders imposed martial law throughout Tibet.

Since 1989, Beijing has intensified efforts to impose its model of modernization on Tibet. It has invested heavily in extractive industries and forced Tibetans to abandon nomadism. As in Xinjiang, Beijing has increased policing and surveillance, imposed travel restrictions, and limited the practice of Buddhism and Tibetan-language education. Chinese leaders were embarrassed by protests in Lhasa on the eve of the 2008 Olympic games in Beijing. This resulted in a military occupation and further hardening of repression. Xi Jinping has promised "an unswerving anti-separatism battle" in Tibet.[106] Critics decry Beijing's policy as colonization.[107]

Hong Kong is yet another troublesome borderland. Britain wrested the territory from the Qing empire in the nineteenth century but held much of it on a lease that expired in 1997. In 1984, Britain and the PRC negotiated a treaty for the return of Hong Kong at the end of the lease. The PRC promised that Hong Kong would enjoy a "high degree of autonomy," that the territory's social and economic systems would remain unchanged until 2047, and that residents would retain fundamental rights.[108] The PRC said that its "ultimate aim" was to provide Hong Kong with a democratically elected local government. Beijing called this the principle of "one country, two systems."[109]

However, Beijing's tolerance for the two-systems principle declined quickly after the 1997 handover. The balance of economic power between Britain and China shifted dramatically, undermining Britain's ability to hold China accountable. And Hong Kong was no longer an essential bridge to global markets, as other commercial centers developed within China. In fact, the territory threatened to become a different sort of bridge, infecting mainland China with Western ideas. Protests erupted in Hong Kong as Beijing restricted civil liberties and delayed election reforms.

Beijing asserted "comprehensive jurisdiction" over Hong Kong in 2014 and three years later declared that it was no longer bound by the 1984 treaty.[110] The independence of Hong Kong courts has been restricted and loyalty tests have been required of government workers. In 2020, an onerous national security law was imposed on the territory. Rights of assembly and free speech have been trimmed and programs of patriotic education introduced in schools.[111] A human rights expert recently pronounced the death of the two-systems principle: "Hong Kong is now to be ruled like the rest of China."[112]

The PRC has taken a tough approach to Taiwan as well. Nationalist forces established their government there in the last years of China's civil war. For decades the island has lived in the grey areas of international law. The PRC constitution declares that it is the "sacred duty" of all Chinese people to reunify Taiwan with the motherland, and Beijing has obstructed actions by other states or international organizations that might support a claim to Taiwanese independence. Negotiations over reunification have been undermined by Taiwanese fears about the future of their system under PRC rule, given Beijing's behavior toward Hong Kong. Beijing has responded with shows of military force near Taiwan and affirmations of its "unshakeable commitment" to gaining control of the island.[113]

The Price of Survival

In the last forty years, the PRC has done what the Qing empire could not do in the nineteenth century, and what the nationalist government could not do in the early twentieth century. As Xi Jinping observed in 2021, it has achieved the "two miracles" of sustained economic development and social stability.[114] More fundamentally, the regime has kept China together, despite "fissiparous tendencies" and external threats.[115] In 2021, Xi boasted about the "sharp contrast between the order of China and the chaos of the West."[116] A senior diplomat said that China's advance was "unstoppable" and that history was leaving Western democracies behind.[117]

However, there are more skeptical views about China's prospects. Observers outside the country have enumerated the internal pressures that face Chinese leaders and speculated about whether the regime will survive.[118] Some suggest that China will eventually democratize; others, that the country might even break up.[119] In 2021, one author predicted that China would convert to democracy as the result of a coup d'état that would occur before the end of 2022. Such a complex society, Roger Garside argued, could only be run on liberal democratic principles.[120]

These observers dwell on China's fragility, but the country is not exceptional in this respect. Fragility is endemic to all superstates. The CCP has chosen to approach the problem of fragility by constructing a regime that allows centralized and tight control by a ruling group that is closed by the standards of other superstates but open by the standards of most empires. There is strong evidence that the ruling group is acutely conscious of fragility, notwithstanding its public statements about the durability of the regime. PRC leaders do not take survival for granted. Moreover, the ruling group has demonstrated its capacity to shift course in response to new circumstances. The Chinese regime is not what it was forty years ago, or even twenty years ago. Constitutional principles and governing ideals are highly flexible. Chinese rulers avow "scientific socialism" while experimenting with capitalism and appealing to the ancient philosophy of Confucianism.

Still, the system has several weaknesses. It puts an immense load on decision-makers at the center of government and requires that they manage public affairs with skill and nimbleness. A breakdown in leadership – a paramount leader whose bad behavior cannot be restrained, unmanageable factional conflicts, problems with succession, loss of focus, or weaknesses in support for executive decision-making – may have devastating consequences for the whole system. The regime is also heavily dependent on bureaucracy and thus unusually susceptible to the pathologies of bureaucratism. This, too, requires constant attention from the top. New technologies of surveillance and control can reduce but not eliminate old problems of bureaucratism.

The third weakness has to do with human rights. The workability of the system depends on the suppression of fundamental rights in the heartland and even more in the borderlands. Unlike empires, the PRC pursues this course of action in a world in which the concept of human rights is well established. Consequently, the regime is subject to unrelenting criticism from abroad and would be subject to criticism from within as well, if constraints on free speech and assembly were loosened. The Soviet Union was also criticized for human rights abuses by the West but found intellectual allies within the movement of world communism. There is no comparable global movement that is built around the Chinese model and ready to defend it.

China may be able to withstand criticism on human rights, especially if its economy and global power continue to grow. Comparisons will also be made to other superstates. For example, India and the United States pay more attention to democratic principles, but recent history shows that these regimes also struggle to contain centrifugal pressures, and even suggests that democratic principles can intensify those pressures if they are not carefully applied. China may show how a carefully designed authoritarian regime, augmented with new technologies of surveillance and control, can hold a superstate together for a very long time. But if the survival of a superstate requires the surrender of fundamental rights, why is its survival desirable at all?

7

The European Union
Cohesion without Coercion

The European Union (EU) is an unusual polity that consists of a complex of institutions connecting the governments of twenty-seven countries. It has evolved into its present form over seventy years. In 1951, six countries in western Europe created the European Coal and Steel Community to govern a new common market in coal and steel. In 1958, they agreed to build a broader common market through the European Economic Community. Gradually the project of collaboration included more countries and subjects, and the European Community was transformed into the European Union in 1993. The European Central Bank was established in 1998 and a common currency, the euro, was launched the next year. Many say that Brussels is the EU's capital. Typically for the EU, this is a matter of dispute.

The EU is the only one of the four polities in this book that is routinely described as a superstate. This has never been a compliment. In 1988, British prime minister Margaret Thatcher warned that the project of European cooperation threatened to produce "a European super-state exercising dominance from Brussels."[1] Many British eurosceptics echoed Thatcher. The United Kingdom, they claimed, was becoming a mere province within a centralized, unitary leviathan, a "nightmarish superstate of petty restrictions" led by a massive bureaucracy "intent on controlling every aspect of everyone's life." Comparisons to the Soviet Union, "the most powerful superstate the world has ever seen," were rife.[2]

EU officials struggled to repulse this assault. "The European Union is not a superstate," one of its leading officials, José Manuel Barroso, insisted in 2007.[3] But what is the EU, if not a superstate? Barroso grasped for an answer. He conceded that it was unlike simple alliances because countries had "pooled their sovereignties" within EU institutions. Barroso suggested that the EU might be a "union of states," but not a tight union like the United States. The EU also seemed to Barroso like an empire, because of its scale and diversity. But empires were held together by oppression, in Barroso's view, while the EU is not. He wondered whether the EU might count as a "non-imperial empire," or as a "unique construction," impossible to categorize at all.

When eurosceptics complain about the EU superstate, they are not using the word as I do in this book. I have defined superstates as hybrid polities, governing vast territories and diverse populations, and having important features of both empires and states. Certainly, the central institutions of a superstate could be domineering. China is an example of such a superstate, and the Soviet Union was too. But this is not inevitable. Some empires were loosely joined and so are superstates like the United States. The EU is nothing like the Soviet Union or China, and not even like the United States. It is the most loosely joined of all superstates. It is so loosely constructed that most people, far from viewing it as a leviathan, wonder whether it counts as any sort of state at all.

The EU is distinct among superstates because it seeks to govern at scale while minimizing coercion. At some point in history, every other superstate has resorted to violence to preserve unity and impose its creed. The EU has avoided this. Use of force is antithetical to one of the main aims of the EU project: avoiding bloodshed on a continent that has been wracked by war. The project of European integration is guided by the post-World War II doctrine of human rights. In 1973, member states of the European Community affirmed that respect for human rights is fundamental to the idea of Europe.[4] A creedal commitment to human rights constrains the use of violence as a governing instrument.

This distinctive feature of the EU project, governing at imperial scale while abjuring coercion, has produced a regime not easily categorized. It is complicated and changeable. Critics question the effectiveness and durability of the EU regime. But the real questions are whether it is any less effective or durable than other superstates, and whether effectiveness and durability could be improved without resort to coercion. Critics also complain about the inability of the regime to respond decisively to new hazards. But they discount the impressive track record of the EU system in responding to challenges.

So far, the EU has found a way to survive crises and achieve its aims while broadly respecting human rights.

A New Leviathan?

Strictly as a matter of law, the European Union consists only of those institutions that are created by the treaties that have been agreed by its twenty-seven member countries. From this point of view, a clear line can be drawn between the EU and its member states. For our purposes, however, it is helpful to think about the EU differently, as a regime that incorporates central institutions as well as governing institutions within member states.[5] This broader view allows us to think about the European polity just as we would about China, India, and the United States.

The EU differs from other superstates because responsibilities within the EU are radically decentralized. Member states have extensive civilian, police and military bureaucracies, which are engaged in a wide range of functions associated with modern statehood – from physical security to economic management to social services and protection of civil rights. Moreover, the structure of government varies substantially among member states. There is no common design as there is for American and Indian states and Chinese provinces. Six EU countries are constitutional monarchies, while twenty-one are republics; eighteen are unitary states, while nine are federal or quasi-federal; twenty-one have parliamentary governments while six have some form of presidential government. By international standards, EU member states are generally well run, stable, democratic, and respectful of human rights. But there is variation on these dimensions too. Since 2010, a few member states have wavered on democracy and human rights.

The EU system may be highly decentralized, but the role of central institutions is still substantial. As the European Court of Justice said in 1964, central bodies have "real powers stemming from a limitation of sovereignty" by member states.[6] On a few subjects, EU institutions have exclusive authority to make law. Bureaucrats working within EU institutions owe loyalty to the union and not home countries.[7] In some circumstances, laws created by EU institutions are binding on governments even if their representatives opposed them during deliberations within EU institutions.[8] Citizens of member states are also citizens of the EU itself, with rights under EU law that they can enforce through appeals to the European Court of Justice. The EU has a flag, an anthem, and a directly elected parliament. It has attempted, with some success, to cultivate a sense of European identity among EU citizens that exists alongside their sense of national identity.

Since the 1950s, EU laws have created a single market within Europe by removing barriers to the movement of goods, services, people, and money. The EU has established common tariffs and a common currency, and it monitors the fiscal policies of member countries too. It provides support for agriculture and regional economic development and promotes cooperation in education and research. Although law and order is primarily a responsibility of member countries, the EU promotes collaboration among national police services and coordinates national policies on border control and migration. EU leaders have pursued a common position on defense and foreign policy as well.

Clearly, the EU is more than a mere alliance among member countries. But how much more? Opinions differ dramatically. On one side are critics who fear that EU institutions are becoming so powerful that they will destroy the autonomy of member countries. Thatcher pioneered this way of thinking when she warned about a superstate that would "bury" member countries.[9] During the Eurozone crisis of 2008–2012, a Spanish eurosceptic complained that his country was being "choked to death" by a regime that allowed northern countries to impose their vision of "mercantile Europe" on southern countries.[10] Some Greeks complained at the same time that the EU had turned Greece into "an occupied country."[11] A few years later, prime minister Viktor Orbán urged fellow Hungarians to rise up against a "Brussels empire" that was bent on destroying the country's traditions.[12] Polish prime minister Mateusz Morawiecki warned in 2021 that the EU was becoming "a centrally administered organism" in which "European institutions can force their provinces to do as the central power wants."[13]

These criticisms of the EU have something in common. They are complaints from communities on the edges of the European project about attempts by communities at the center to impose their vision of economic and social order. Conservatives in eastern Europe complain about western Europe's project of promoting gender equality and the rights of LGBTIQ people. Progressives in Greece and Spain complain about northern Europe's ordoliberal fixation with monetary and fiscal discipline. Free-market Britons complained (until they departed) about the continental obsession with social and economic regulation. In every instance, there is resentment that peripheral territories are being civilized by the center. Eurosceptics protest that they are treated as "barbarians . . . [who] are not as advanced and civilized" as people at the core of the European project.[14]

Tensions between core and periphery were commonplace in empires and are commonplace in superstates as well. Eurosceptic frustration with Brussels is paralleled by the frustration of southern American states with Washington, southern Indian states with Delhi, and Chinese borderlands with Beijing. Moreover, the perception among eurosceptics that EU institutions are engaged in a civilizing mission has some foundation. The 1973 Declaration on European Identity affirms that the purpose of unification is "to ensure the survival of . . . a common European civilization." The essential elements of the EU creed – human rights, the rule of law, democracy, a well-ordered market, monetary and fiscal discipline – were reaffirmed when the EU prepared for admission of new countries in the 1990s.[15]

Although the EU has a *mission civilisatrice*, just as empires did, it does not use the same methods. This is the mistake of eurosceptics. Member states are not provinces subjugated by Brussels. The critical difference is the inability of central institutions to impose their vision by force. Brussels does not have an army that it can use to enforce its law in member countries, as Washington did in Arkansas in 1957. Brussels cannot dismiss a "morally corrupt" government, as Delhi did in Tamil Nadu in 1976. Nor can Brussels establish re-education camps in recalcitrant regions, as Beijing is doing in Xinjiang today. The tools for promoting conformity available to central institutions in the EU are more benign.

Perhaps the EU is a non-imperial empire, as José Manuel Barroso suggested in 2007. Countries choose whether to join the union. Every member state has a veto on significant changes to governing treaties. And member states may opt out of key EU policies. Only nineteen of twenty-seven member countries use the euro as their currency, while twenty-two participate fully in the Schengen policy, which removes border controls within the EU. (This practice of allowing opt-outs is sometimes referred to as differentiated or multi-speed integration.) In addition, member states also have the right to leave the union. Withdrawal is a painful but real option, as the United Kingdom demonstrated in 2020.

Is the EU in Control?

A more common criticism of the EU is that rather than being a leviathan, it is barely in control at all. The fact that the Treaty on European Union acknowledges a right of exit seems to confirm this fact. According to some experts, a polity should not be counted as a state if its leaders cannot prevent the secession of its parts.[16] A real state (again, according to some experts) can deploy armed forces to stop attempts at unilateral secession. Of course, this assumes that central authorities have armed forces at their disposal. Partly for this reason, the existence of armed forces under central control has also been considered a marker of statehood.

But there are no armed forces under the direct charge of the EU's central institutions. Plans to establish a European army failed because of French opposition in the 1950s. Since the 1990s, there have been attempts to integrate the military forces of member countries, but control over forces has never been surrendered to central institutions.[17] In 2015, the EU established its first uniformed service, Frontex, to improve control of EU borders. However, Frontex deploys personnel and equipment only with the consent of national authorities.[18] In 2021, Poland refused Frontex aid in dealing with an influx of migrants from Belarus.[19]

Even the civilian bureaucracy of the EU central institutions is modestly sized. It comprises just 60,000 people.[20] Seven times that number work for central government in the United Kingdom, while thirty times as many are employed by central government in the United States. Nor do the EU institutions have much capacity to influence national policy by dispensing money. In 2021 the EU budget was little more than one percent of GDP in the EU. The US federal budget is twenty times larger as a share of American GDP.

The EU mainly works by adopting laws that are put into effect by the governments of member states. These laws are enforced in two ways. Individuals and businesses who believe that member states are denying rights and benefits granted under EU law can seek remedies in national courts, with a right of appeal to the European Court of Justice. And if the European Commission itself believes that a member state is not respecting EU law, it may begin an "infringement proceeding" and attempt to negotiate a resolution with that country. The Commission's leverage comes from its ability to refer an infringement case to the European Court of Justice. If the Court concludes that EU law is not being followed, it can impose financial penalties on a member state.[21]

These methods of enforcement are imperfect and EU institutions themselves perceive a "compliance deficit" within the union.[22] The European Commission has limited resources for detecting infringements and pursuing remedies. The process for resolving infringement cases is cumbersome, and it may take years for a complicated case to be closed.[23] The EU has another tool for achieving compliance by member countries, but it has limitations too. Article 7 of the Treaty on European Union says that the European Council can suspend the voting rights of a member state that seriously breaches core EU values. But this is widely regarded as a "nuclear option," a remedy so draconian that it has never been applied.[24]

All of this suggests a regime in which central institutions are very weak indeed. However, the case can be overdrawn. For example, the explicit right of withdrawal from the union may be less consequential than we imagine. The trend of international law since World War II has been to acknowledge that communities have the right to choose independence, even when this right is not acknowledged by the regime in which they live. This is known as the principle of self-determination. A 1960 United Nations declaration condemns "armed action and repressive measures" to prevent self-determination as a violation of human rights.[25]

This principle of self-determination was first advanced in defense of colonized peoples, and for many years there was reluctance to acknowledge that it might apply to communities within established democratic states. Gradually, however, the principle has been applied more widely, because the idea of using force to block secession has become more repugnant. When the province of Quebec threatened to split from Canada in the 1990s, central authorities never seriously contemplated the use of force in response.[26] Similarly, the British government has renounced the use of force to block Scottish independence.[27]

If force cannot legitimately be used to quash secessionism, then it does not matter that EU institutions lack direct control over the armed forces that would be needed for that purpose. The other purpose for which armed forces are needed is defense against major external threats. But polities do not create standing forces under central control unless it is necessary to counter an imminent danger. For most of the first seventy years of its existence, the central government of the United States maintained a standing army of fewer than seven thousand men. A large, centrally controlled army was considered unnecessary and "dangerous to the safety of a republican form of government."[28] The idea of a large standing army under central control was only accepted in the United States after the late 1940s, when the country faced a prolonged and existential threat from the Soviet Union.

The European Union has never faced a comparable threat since its creation in 1993, and so the lack of a centrally controlled military force is not surprising. The strong response of EU leaders to the Russian invasion of Ukraine in 2022 suggests that their calculations about the need for such a force could change very quickly. In any case, twenty-one EU member states are also members of the NATO alliance, which could defend against external threats. In the absence of an existential danger that would require a large centrally controlled force, some Europeans worry about the side-effects of militarization, just as Americans did before 1941. They fear that the availability of a standing force would encourage the use of arms for problems that could be solved in other ways. American history shows that this is a real danger, illustrated by the ill-fated rush to war after the terror attacks of 2001.

The most critical question when judging whether a polity should be counted as a state is whether it has effective control over its territory and performs the essential functions that are required of a modern state. A common mistake is to assume that the burden of performing these functions lies with central authorities alone. There are many established states in which responsibility is constitutionally divided between central and subnational governments, and in these systems the proper question is whether the regime as a whole, combining all levels of government, governs to the necessary standard. We should think the same way about the European Union. From this point of view, there can be no doubt that the EU regime exercises effective control over its territory: there is no place where the authority of governing institutions is seriously contested. The least stable member country within the EU (Cyprus) is still more stable than most countries outside the EU.[29] The quality of governance throughout the EU is generally higher than in most other places, including other superstates.[30]

Moreover, the "compliance deficit" within the EU can be overstated. While the number of infringement cases handled by the European Commission increased steadily from the early 1990s to about 2008, it has declined since then. And the volume of cases must be put in context: there are now more EU laws and more member states. One study finds that the number of infringement cases relative to the number of "violative opportunities," a product of the number of laws times the number of countries, has declined steadily throughout the history of the EU. After a thorough study, one scholar has concluded that the EU does not suffer from chronic noncompliance, with a few important exceptions: "almost all member states comply with almost all EU law almost all the time."[31]

When judging the EU's compliance problems, we should also compare apples to apples. Compliance deficits are found in all super-states, just as they were found in all empires. Beijing struggles to overcome bureaucratism and local protectionism. In India, state and local governments often fail to implement centrally mandated schemes properly. Washington accommodates state governments by allowing deviations from national policy and ignoring flagrant violations of national law. Unfortunately, it is not easy to measure and compare these compliance deficits. But they are clearly substantial in every case. What may be unique about the European project is the extent to which the European Commission has systematized and publicized its process for pursuing infringements of EU law by member states.

Can the EU Decide?

A polity may be weak in another way. Even if it has mechanisms for enforcing law throughout its territory, a polity might lack the capacity to respond to events and make intelligent decisions about priorities and policies. Within the regime, there must be some apparatus for steering the ship. Experts have this in mind when they say that real states have a clearly defined ruling group, an "executive authority," that is responsible for exercising power.[32] The EU has been criticized for lacking a well-defined and effective ruling group. But this criticism is also overdrawn.

The leadership structure of the EU is undoubtedly complicated. There is a central bureaucracy, the European Commission, that is responsible for overseeing EU laws and proposing new laws. It is led by a twenty-seven-member College of Commissioners, with one commissioner drawn from each member country, headed by a Commission president. There is also a European Parliament, directly elected every five years, which has its own president. The Parliament approves legislative proposals from the Commission but cannot initiate new laws. A third body is the Council of the European Union, also known as the Council of Ministers, which approves new laws as well. It is made up of government ministers from member countries: which minister attends a meeting of this Council depends on the subject being discussed. The presidency of the Council of Ministers rotates among member states every six months. A fourth body is the European Council, comprised of the heads of government of member countries, which provides strategic direction for the whole enterprise. The European Council has a president too. It appoints the Commission president and College of Commissioners, with consent of Parliament.

The leadership structure of the European Union is so complex that most EU citizens admit ignorance about how it works.[33] Even statesmen have expressed confusion. "The European Union, the European Commission, the European Council – sometimes I get them mixed up," US president Barack Obama conceded in 2014.[34] At a much earlier stage in European integration, US Secretary of State Henry Kissinger asked: "If I want to talk to Europe who do I call?"[35] Kissinger's question is often repeated by American critics of the European project. "As we all know," a *Wall Street Journal* columnist explained in 2010, "The EU has three presidents . . . competing to see who's the most presidential."[36] In fact, not everyone knows this: some American experts say that the EU has two presidents, while another *Wall Street Journal* columnist claimed in 2016 that it had four.[37]

Whatever the number, the EU's leadership structure has seemed to American observers to lack two essential characteristics: a clear locus of authority and the capacity to act decisively. Especially during the first years of the millennium, as the United States responded vigorously to terrorist threats following the attacks of September 11, 2001, European leaders were chastised for dithering and inaction in the face of grave danger.[38] The decision-making process in EU institutions was routinely dismissed as slow and cumbersome.

Twenty years after September 11, the relative virtues of the American system are not so clear. The American president certainly enjoyed more freedom of maneuver in the aftermath of the 2001 terror attacks: many experts complained about the passivity of Congress and resurgence of an "imperial presidency" in the United States. But the result of presidential assertiveness was two wars that are now counted among the worst foreign-policy decisions in American history.[39] And the recent performance of the American system in the sphere of domestic policy is unimpressive as well. As I observed in Chapter 4, the United States has become more deeply divided in recent decades. But the leadership structure of the American regime is not built to manage these divisions well, and the results have been gridlock and rancor. The EU system, by contrast, takes the management of internal divisions as a central problem of governance.

In fact, there are parallels between the EU system and the American regime of the pre-New Deal era, the period in which Frederick Jackson Turner described the United States as a set of "rival societies" like the nations of Europe. In that period, the role of American central institutions was limited, just as the role of EU central institutions is limited today. In the pre-New Deal United States, democratic principles were applied cautiously at the apex of the regime. The president was weak and the Senate was strong. The leadership structure was designed to encourage sectional accommodation, but one result was confusion about who was in charge. Anticipating Kissinger's complaint, the British writer Walter Bagehot lamented in the 1870s that the American regime lacked a clear "deciding power."[40] Another British writer, James Bryce, concurred: the American system seemed to work, but there was no one person who could be described as its head.[41]

The leadership structure of the EU has changed over time. At first, the European Commission and Council of Ministers were the critical institutions. These two bodies trace their history back to the establishment of a common market in coal and steel in 1951. The mode of decision-making within these two institutions can be described as a blend of technocracy and diplomacy. Experts working within the Commission were responsible for drafting policies to create a European common market. Meanwhile, ministers and ambassadors worked within the Council of Ministers to protect national interests and approve Commission proposals.

This technocratic-diplomatic machinery had two limitations. First, it was not effective in maintaining public support as the Community's role expanded. Reformers insisted from the start that the European project could not be treated simply as a technical enterprise and that an "injection of democracy" was necessary to preserve its legitimacy.[42] However, national leaders have always measured this injection carefully. A European Parliament was established in 1962 but its members were not directly elected until 1979. Its powers are limited in comparison to most national parliaments. The parliament only acquired the ability to veto proposed EU laws in the 1990s, and even today it cannot initiate new laws. Its role in determining the composition of the College of Commissioners and selecting the Commission president is also constrained.

The second limitation of the technocratic-diplomatic machinery was its inability to manage questions of statecraft relating to the European project: whether its objectives should be extended, its structure amended, or new members added. Neither bureaucrats within the Commission nor the functional ministers who participated in meetings of the Council of Ministers had the breadth of view or authority to resolve these "basic questions" about the nature of the union.[43] Heads of national governments had to address them, but there was no forum in which this could be done routinely. This deficiency was remedied by establishment of the European Council in 1973. The Council now meets four times a year to set "general political directions and priorities" for the EU.[44]

Critics who complain about the EU's inability to respond decisively to events overlook the most important bit of contrary evidence: the extent to which the European project has transformed in response to new challenges over seventy years. This includes innovations in leadership structure such as the European Parliament and the European Council, the reworking of the European Communities of the 1950s into the more ambitious European Union, and the adjustment of EU institutions to accommodate many more countries after 1993. The treaty law that serves as the constitution for the European project has been substantially revised six times since the mid-1960s.[45]

The process of treaty reform has not always been easy. This was especially true after the 1980s, as complaints mounted about the secretiveness of EU decision-making and lack of opportunities for public influence. In some countries, people were unwilling to accept treaty reforms without a national referendum. In a 1992 referendum, Danish voters rejected the Maastricht Treaty establishing the European Union. At the time, this was perceived as a crisis that might bring the European project to a "dead end."[46] These fears were overblown. Denmark was allowed to opt out of some treaty provisions, voters endorsed the treaty in a second referendum, and the European project rolled on.

Another attempt at treaty reform failed in 2005 after defeats in French and Dutch referenda. This was interpreted as a "cataclysmic" setback that signaled "the death of the continental dream."[47] But European leaders regrouped once again and proposed more modest treaty reforms. Voters in one country, Ireland, initially balked at these reforms, but endorsed them after the European Council gave assurances on key Irish concerns. Overall, European leaders have become more sophisticated in navigating the shoals of treaty reform since the 1980s. This is another sign of adaptability within the system.

Muddling Through

Perhaps more than any other superstate, the EU is a protean entity, whose architecture has been renovated repeatedly in response to new challenges. This suggests that the EU leadership structure can perform its most essential task, that of anticipating and managing hazards, even if that structure is so unlike those of other superstates. As Deng Xiaoping once said: "It does not matter whether a cat is black or white, as long as it catches mice." The workability of the EU leadership structure has been further tested by three significant challenges over the last fifteen years. Its response has not always been elegant. On balance, though, it has performed better than critics have suggested.

The financial and debt crises. The first of these challenges arose because of the collision of two experiments, one peculiar to the European Union, the other not. The latter experiment, financial liberalization, was launched in the United States in the 1970s and pursued aggressively in that country for the next quarter-century. The United Kingdom, and other members of the European Economic Community, followed in the early 1980s. Liberalization was expected to spur growth by removing constraints on innovation and cross-border activity by financial institutions. Within the European Community, and then the European Union, liberalization was closely tied to the project of building a single European market.

Eventually, it would be realized that European policymakers made two mistakes as they loosened restrictions on financial institutions. National financial systems were now deeply integrated, but there was inadequate consideration of how an EU-wide financial crisis might be handled by national regulators.[48] When the European Central Bank was established in 1998, its role in crisis management was neglected as well. In fact, few people on either side of the Atlantic anticipated a financial crisis at that time. The expert consensus of the early 2000s was that financial liberalization was an overwhelming success: improved access to credit had boosted growth, and financial institutions had become much more sophisticated in managing risks.[49]

In 2007, it became clear that the experts were wrong. As in the past, loose credit had encouraged unwise speculation in real estate and other assets. Major financial institutions realized suddenly that they had gambled badly and were insolvent. Panic led to a constriction of credit and more institutional failures. In the United States, the Treasury and Federal Reserve took dramatic action to prevent a catastrophic collapse of the financial system. In Europe, however, the response was more muddled. There was no EU equivalent to the US Treasury and powers of the ECB were limited. European governments sometimes failed to coordinate as they struggled to save financial institutions that had ballooned in size because of liberalization.

Europe's financial crisis transmuted into a sovereign debt crisis. Governments had borrowed heavily to save financial institutions and keep their economies afloat. Meanwhile, an economic slowdown caused a decline in government revenues. As lenders questioned whether some governments could repay their loans, the cost of additional borrowing escalated. By 2010, several European governments – Greece, Italy,

Spain, Portugal, and Ireland – faced the prospect of defaulting on their debts.

Now the effect of a second policy experiment was realized. In 1993, most EU member states had agreed to replace their own currencies with the euro. Before the euro, governments could mitigate debt crises by devaluing their currencies. But governments were now borrowing in euros and devaluation was not possible. As governments teetered on insolvency, EU leaders argued about providing aid. A legal impediment was a provision in the EU treaties, the "no-bailout clause," which said that member states would not be responsible for the debts of other member states. There were political impediments too. Some Germans had little sympathy for Greece, especially after it was revealed that Greek leaders had evaded EU debt rules before the crisis by hiding some government borrowing.[50] Greeks protested in turn about fiscal and monetary rules that were designed to favor German interests.

Some American experts were sharply critical of the European response to the financial and sovereign debt crises. One compared the EU to a riderless horse.[51] Another said that the EU was dying for want of leadership.[52] An appreciation of American history might have chastened these critics. The policy tools that were available to American decision-makers after 2007 were not recent inventions. They had emerged over more than a century, in response to a succession of crises that usually placed sections of the American union in virulent opposition to one another. During one of these crises, in the mid-nineteenth century, one-third of American states, mainly in the west and south, defaulted on debt after the national government refused assistance. Political and social upheaval in the United States was so profound at that time that the country was dismissed by European observers as an "ungovernable anarchy."[53]

EU leaders responded vigorously, if imperfectly, to the threats confronting their union after 2007. A new forum, the Euro summit, was created in 2008 so that the heads of Eurozone governments could negotiate a response to events. EU leaders then executed several about-turns in EU policy. Sidestepping treaty prohibitions, leaders found a way of providing support to Ireland, Portugal, and Greece, using money that was borrowed on the credit of all Eurozone countries. EU treaties were amended in 2012 to create a permanent mechanism for helping distressed member states. This mechanism was used to support Spain and Cyprus in 2013 and Greece again in 2015.[54]

At the same time, the European Central Bank redefined its role.[55] Before the crisis, the bank fixated on inflation control and followed a strict rule against buying government debt. This pre-crisis policy conformed to the trans-Atlantic consensus among experts about the proper role of a central bank. But ECB policy was amended during the euro crisis. In 2010, it started buying government debt from distressed countries. This policy was extended two years later, as bank president Mario Draghi promised to "do whatever it takes" to save the euro.

EU leaders also created new regulatory bodies to rationalize oversight of financial institutions across the EU and reduce the risk of another crisis. And mechanisms for coordinating fiscal policy were overhauled as well. In a 2013 treaty, twenty-five member states promised to adopt national balanced-budget laws and set up independent organizations to monitor their spending and taxing. The European Commission designed a process for scrutinizing national budgets and became responsible for drafting an EU-wide macroeconomic policy. New procedures allowed the EU to impose financial sanctions on countries that violate deficit and debt targets or pursue other policies that threaten economic stability within the union.[56]

The reforms that EU leaders made in response to the financial and debt crises were comprehensive. One observer says that they amounted to a "constitutional transformation" within the EU, a fundamental change in its legal order, which was motivated by the shared determination of leaders to keep the union alive.[57] In the end, the twin crises gave evidence of the polity's ability to adapt and survive.

Migration crisis. The EU's performance during the migration crisis of 2015–2018 was less impressive. Still, it was not as catastrophic as critics suggested. The crisis was triggered by a surge of immigration into the EU in 2015. Civil war in Syria displaced millions of people, many of whom traveled through Turkey into Greece, an EU member state. At the same time, people fled from upheavals in north Africa by crossing the Mediterranean to Italy. The number of illegal crossings detected at the EU's external borders jumped from 100,000 in 2013 to more than 1.8 million in 2015.[58] Four thousand people drowned while trying to reach Europe that year.[59] Once in the EU, migrants continued moving north to richer countries that seemed more likely to grant asylum. By mid-2015, EU member states were receiving more than 150,000 new requests for asylum every month.[60]

The migration surge put pressure on the EU in three ways. Because border control is primarily a responsibility of member states, the burden of managing the surge fell heavily on Italy and Greece, and leaders in those countries complained about the unfairness of this. The surge also threatened freedom of movement within the union.

Following the 1985 Schengen treaty, many EU member states had removed internal border controls, which meant that refugees could travel easily throughout the EU after they arrived in Italy and Greece. But the treaty allowed reimposition of controls in extraordinary circumstances, and in 2015 several countries did this.

The third challenge related to asylum requests. All EU member states have ratified the 1951 Geneva convention that allows refugees to seek asylum in other countries. The convention is a cornerstone of international human rights law. Under a 1997 policy, the Dublin Regulation, EU countries agreed that individuals should only be allowed to request asylum in the country where they first entered the EU. Refugees who moved elsewhere in the EU would be returned to the country where they entered. The intention was to discourage refugees from pursuing multiple claims. But the effect in 2015 was to intensify the burden on frontline countries. Courts also intervened, blocking governments from returning refugees to member states that appeared to be mishandling asylum requests. In August 2015, Chancellor Angela Merkel announced that Germany would no longer return Syrian refugees as required by the Dublin Regulation.[61]

By autumn 2015, the EU seemed to be overwhelmed by the migrant crisis. One news outlet catalogued "apocalyptic warnings of the EU's demise."[62] But these assessments were off the mark. EU leaders moved quickly to renovate EU policy on border control and migration. The EU expanded its joint search-and-rescue operations in the Mediterranean, increased the powers and resources of its border control agency, Frontex, and launched a reform of the EU agency responsible for coordinating the asylum procedures of member states. It also struck agreements under which the governments of Turkey, Libya, and other countries promised to curb the flow of migrants. These agreements were effective, but strongly and justly criticized for abandoning people to inhumane treatment by other governments.[63]

However, the EU failed to find a way of sharing responsibility for migrants who succeeded in reaching Europe. In May 2015, the European Commission proposed a two-year plan under which all member states would be required to receive a share of migrants arriving in Greece and Italy. After a fierce reaction, especially from countries in central and eastern Europe, this was replaced by a plan for voluntary relocation, which was adopted by a large majority of member states in September 2015.

But several countries dragged their heels in complying with the policy and only a fraction of migrants were relocated. The Commission launched infringement cases against three laggards, Hungary, Poland, and the Czech Republic, which were upheld by the European Court of Justice in 2020. Meanwhile, pressure to resolve the relocation question ebbed. In 2017, the number of detected illegal border crossings was one-tenth of what it had been in 2015.[64] The Commission has continued with negotiations on a new pact for handling migrants.

The EU did not manage the migration crisis elegantly. But elegance is too high a standard. No superstate manages mass migrations well. More than eleven million illegal immigrants now live in the United States.[65] The country is deeply divided on border control and immigration policy, and state and local governments have impeded attempts by Washington to enforce existing law. Measures taken by the Modi government in response to the migration of millions of Bangladeshis into eastern India have proved equally divisive.[66] And China has struggled for decades to regulate mass migration from the countryside to cities. Its policies have been condemned as a system of urban–rural apartheid.[67] What we can say about the European Union case is that its leadership recognized and responded to the challenge posed by migration in 2015, even if it did this very roughly, and that the regime again confounded critics who predicted an end to the union.

The rule of law crisis. The last fifteen years have been marked by a surge of popular unrest across the European Union. During the financial and debt crises, there were massive protests against austerity measures that were a condition of emergency aid from the EU and other sources. Over the next decade, right-wing nationalist parties gained enough strength to sway governmental decision-making in several countries. And in a 2016 referendum, British voters chose to "take back control" by leaving the EU. Some European politicians feared that Brexit would trigger the collapse of the entire union.[68] There were similar fears when a conservative eurosceptic, Marine Le Pen, advanced to the final round of the French presidential election in 2017.[69]

This prolonged bout of discontent should not have been surprising. Throughout history, financial crises have usually generated social and political shockwaves. In Europe, conditions were aggravated by the collision of other events, such as the failed attempt at treaty reform in 2005 and the migrant crisis of 2015. European leaders faced the old imperial nightmare: a cascade of hazards. European Commission president Jean-Claude Juncker called it a "polycrisis."[70]

But the European Union stumbled through these troubles. In the second round of France's 2017 presidential election, pro-Europe voters delivered a decisive defeat to Le Pen. (This drama was reprised, with the same result, in the 2022 election.) Negotiations over Britain's departure were prolonged and painful, but no other dominoes have fallen so far. And public support for the union has rebounded in countries that were hit hardest by austerity measures. In a 2021 survey, large majorities in Spain, Portugal and Italy expressed optimism about the EU and support for the euro. Even in Greece, more people had a favorable opinion of the EU than a negative one, and three-quarters of respondents wanted to keep the euro.[71]

The EU confronted a more stubborn problem after conservative parties won control of governments in Hungary in 2010 and Poland in 2015. Prime Minister Viktor Orbán, leader of Hungary's Fidesz party, vowed to challenge "western European dogmas" and build "an illiberal state" that renounced "liberal methods and principles of organizing a society."[72] This project of "regime change," as Orbán called it, has included assaults on courts, the media, universities, religious groups, and other non-governmental organizations.[73] The Law and Justice party that gained power in Poland in 2015 pursued a similar but less aggressive agenda, tightening control over the judiciary and promising to protect "traditional values" with laws limiting LGBTIQ and reproductive rights.[74]

Many of the measures adopted in Hungary and Poland clashed with EU law, and the European Commission responded with its standard compliance tool, an infringement proceeding. In the past, this tool had been effective in fixing occasional problems of non-compliance by generally well-intentioned governments. But the tool was less effective in countering systematic revolts against "Western dogma." Hungary became artful in crafting responses to infringement proceedings that avoided fines while preserving the substance of its misbehavior.[75] In any case, a government that had taken a stand on high principle was unlikely to reverse itself because of a fine.[76] In 2021, the biggest fine in EU history was levied on Poland after it failed to reverse measures undermining judicial independence. The Polish government dismissed the penalty as "blackmail."[77]

In 2014 the European Commission devised another approach for countering illiberal regime change. It instituted a new process for "structured dialogue" with member states in which there were "systemic threats to the rule of law."[78] If dialogue was fruitless, the Commission said that it would recommend that the European Council use its authority under Article 7 of the Treaty of European Union to suspend the member state's voting rights in the Council. The

Commission complemented this process of dialogue with a "justice scoreboard" rating the integrity of national judicial systems. Later, the Commission added another innovation – an annual report on "checks and balances" within all member states.[79] Meanwhile, the Council of Ministers launched its own series of "dialogues" among member states on the rule of law.

This intensified scrutiny did not deter Hungary and Poland from adopting more policies that clashed with EU laws and values. Formal proceedings to penalize Poland under Article 7 were begun in 2017, followed by proceedings against Hungary in 2018. But this had no deterrent effect either, because Article 7 has a serious flaw: any penalty requires approval of all states except the one being sanctioned.[80] Hungary protected Poland from punishment, and vice versa. Consequently, EU leaders have tried to invent other methods of discouraging systemic abuses. In 2020, a new EU law, adopted over the objection of Hungary and Poland, gave the Commission authority to withhold EU funds from countries in which breaches of the rule of law were likely to result in the misuse of that money.[81] Poland and Hungary challenged the validity of the law, and the Commission promised not to apply it until the challenge was resolved. The European Court of Justice upheld the new law in February 2022. Immediate enforcement was complicated by Brussels' need for Polish and Hungarian cooperation in responding to the Russian invasion of Ukraine. However, there were also signs that the invasion might be driving a wedge between Poland and Hungary on questions of collaboration with Brussels.

The EU has innovated in response to the challenges posed by Hungary and Poland, but there are experts who argue that European leaders ought to press even harder on the two countries. The EU, these experts say, confronts a moral crisis that must be resolved by a "militant" affirmation of the European creed.[82] Militancy would include even tougher enforcement mechanisms, such as an independent watchdog with authority to withhold payments to member states when EU values have been breached.[83]

However, there is a good case against militancy. A powerful independent watchdog would be a technocratic solution to what is essentially a problem of statecraft, involving delicate judgments about ends and means. Respect for national identities and self-determination are also important EU values. Hungary and Poland are still functioning, if flawed, democracies, and it would be better if governments changed course because of domestic electoral pressures.[84] There is still popular support for the EU in both countries, but history has shown how nationalist governments can use hard measures from Brussels to break down that support.[85] And the rule of law crisis may need more time to ripen. EU institutions have laid down more markers about their creedal commitments, and if there is a fundamental breakdown in judicial or democratic institutions in Hungary or Poland, a firm response would be essential to avoid hypocrisy. Even if the EU itself does not act, governments and courts in other member states may stop cooperating with Hungary and Poland if they believe that EU law is not respected there.[86]

The European Paradox

"Europe is awash in crisis," Leonard Seabrooke and Eleni Tsingou observed in 2018: "Crisis talk is part of everyday life" within the union.[87] Over the years, many other scholars have agreed with this view. The EU, they say, is rent by "powerful centrifugal forces" that give the regime a "contingent and fragile" quality.[88] European citizens also perceive the EU to be "in a perpetual state of crisis."[89]

The invasion of Ukraine by Russia in February 2022 might seem to reinforce this sense of never-ending distress. We could adopt Jean-Claude Juncker's phrase and call the events of early 2022 a polycrisis, because of the many ways in which EU leaders have been challenged: by a massive inflow of refugees, fears about aggression against EU member states directly, painful choices about importation of Russian oil and gas, and pressures for admission of Ukraine into the union. Still, this crisis was distinctive because it was not immediately accompanied by the predictions of EU collapse. On the contrary, the crisis seemed in its first months to bolster cohesion. Leaders and citizens were unified not only by shared concern for security, but by common disgust about the Russian assault on values that were core to the EU creed.

Looking backward, though, we must agree that the European project has always been afflicted by a sense of imminent catastrophe. In 1965, political scientist Leon Lindberg observed that the European Economic Community was constantly enveloped in an "atmosphere of bickering and hostility" and that the decision-making process within the Community was little more than a crisis management system.[90] In the late 1970s, experts still despaired about the future of the Community.[91] Later, there were doubts that the European Union would survive treaty reform efforts of the 1990s and early 2000s. "The future of European integration is in jeopardy," historian John Gillingham warned in 2003.[92] Almost twenty years later, the EU lumbers on.

Scholars who look only at the European Union may think that it is unique in suffering from persistent crises and a continuing pall of despair. As we have seen, though, anxieties about centrifugal forces are felt in every superstate. And they were felt in every empire too. Fragility is endemic to these large-scale forms of governance. If fragility seems more pronounced in the EU, it may be the result of a deliberate decision to limit the coercive capacity of central institutions, that is, to deny leaders at the center the capacity to maintain unity by force. There are good reasons why the core of the EU regime is denied this capacity. Peaceful coexistence and respect for human rights are cornerstones of the EU creed.

Also, we should keep crisis talk in perspective. The system seems perpetually in disarray, and yet it stumbles its way through and even thrives. This paradox was noted by Lindberg in 1965: "How can we reconcile repeated newspaper stories about [the Community's] imminent collapse because of one crisis or another with its persistence and seemingly ever more impressive accomplishments?"[93] A half century later, Erik Jones agreed that the European project "has a tremendous track record for resilience even under the worst circumstances."[94] Another group of scholars concluded in 2019 that the EU has demonstrated its ability to "constantly adapt to sudden disruptions and social and political changes."[95]

Perhaps the EU survives crises because its leaders appreciate the fragility of the system. As with American leaders in the nineteenth century, preserving the union is foremost in their minds. Sectional accommodation, as the Americans once called it, is the style of EU statecraft, and central institutions are built to facilitate it.

There are other ways in which the regime is designed to promote cohesion. For example, the role of the center is circumscribed. This reduces the range of subjects that must be negotiated and the burden of monitoring compliance with negotiated settlements. Rigorous rules about accession – who is allowed to join the club – reduce the risk of unmanageable differences between member states. By allowing opt-outs from key policies, the system makes it possible to defer some disagreements for another day.

Democratic ideals are applied carefully within this regime. The European Parliament plays a significant but limited role in EU governance. Some topics are reserved for technocrats, "depoliticized," while others are negotiated by diplomats and ministers behind closed doors. These restrictions improve the capacity of the system to manage fragility. By contrast, democratic practices are well established within member states. Generally, political freedom is well respected. National elections and referenda have become the main channels through which citizens express their approval or disapproval of the path being taken in the European project and their willingness to continue participating in it.[96]

In 2007, José Manuel Barroso suggested that the European Union should be counted as a UPO: an Unidentified Political Object. But it is not so exceptional. The EU is a superstate, albeit a loosely joined one. Broadly conceived, the EU regime governs its territory closely and well, performing all the functions associated with modern statehood. However, the EU also has features that were associated with empires. The regime has an uneven and ramshackle quality. It articulates its creed in high-flown language but often governs through compromise and accommodation. And the structure and reach of the regime changes constantly. In early days, advocates of the European project suggested that it was following a clear path to a definite goal, an "ever-closer union."[97] In reality, the goal is always being renegotiated and the path is uncertain. In the short run, the EU does what all empires once did. It wrestles with the crisis of the moment, extemporizes and temporizes, and aims to survive another day.

8

The COVID Test

The COVID-19 pandemic, says Peter Baldwin, "was like a visitor from a forgotten and neglected past."[1] The COVID virus moved so quickly around the world that we could almost think of it as something that emerged simultaneously in all four superstates. The first cases of the disease were identified in Wuhan, China in December 2019. The first case in the United States was confirmed on January 19, 2020, the first in Europe on January 24, the first in India on January 27. The stage was set for the reprise of a grim experiment. Pandemics had been one of the ancient scourges of empire. Now a pandemic would test the resilience of superstates. How would each react, and what would the response tell us about the strengths and weaknesses of its distinctive approach to governance?

This experiment came with measures of performance: the number of deaths caused by COVID-19, the number of people vaccinated, and the effect on economic growth. By the end of 2021, the official results were as shown in Table 1.

Experts looked askance at some of these figures, suspecting that governments were not counting all COVID-19 deaths. Still, there was general agreement that China suffered less than the EU and the United States in 2020 and 2021, while the EU suffered fewer deaths but more short-term economic losses than the United States. Official data from India were viewed with the greatest suspicion. According to non-governmental estimates, the true number of deaths in that country was between three and five million in 2020 and 2021.[2] In terms of deaths per million, this suggests that India

Table 1. Results from the Covid Test, 2020–2021

	Deaths	Deaths per million people	Persons fully vaccinated per 100 people	% Real GDP growth 2020/2021
China	6,000	4	74	2.3/8.1
India	476,000	340	35	–7.3/9.0
EU	876,000	1,990	67	–6.4/5.2
US	793,000	2,403	59	–3.4/5.6

Source: COVID-19 data for China, India, and the United States from COVID-19. who.int. EU data from www.ecdc.europa.eu. GDP data from International Monetary Fund, *World Economic Outlook* (January 2022). GDP data is for the Eurozone only.

performed no better than the EU and the United States, and probably worse.

As usual, there were fears that the pandemic might be the crisis that finally broke the European Union. The EU survived after all. But the pandemic provided more evidence of the general fragility of superstates, aggravating old problems and undermining stability in several of them. China's superior performance in 2020 to 2021 also raised questions about the relative competence of democratic systems in moments of crisis. However, this was not the only aspect of regime design that proved to be important in pandemic response. Another critical factor was the allocation of powers between central and sub-central governments. In the United States and India, central institutions took on a bigger role than they could handle competently.

Beijing Mobilizes

The first confirmed outbreak of COVID-19 happened in Wuhan, a city of eleven million in the central Chinese province of Hubei, in December 2019.[3] Between December 24 and 30, several government and private laboratories in Wuhan attempted to identify the illness. On December 30, Wuhan's Municipal Health Commission warned hospitals about the arrival of a new disease. Within a few days, scientists at the Wuhan Institute of Virology had fully sequenced the genome of the COVID-19 virus. A test to detect the COVID virus was developed by Chinese researchers on January 10. The genomic sequence was made public one day later.

There was still much that remained unknown about the disease: whether it could be transmitted between humans, how easily it could be transmitted, whether an individual could transmit disease before symptoms appeared, and how often infection led to serious illness or death. The first death of a confirmed COVID-19 patient happened in Wuhan on January 9. On January 20, China's central health authorities publicly confirmed cases of human-to-human transmission and recommended travel restrictions in Wuhan, while Xi Jinping promised that the outbreak would be "resolutely curbed." A national health emergency was declared on January 23 and a travel ban was imposed on Hubei province. Within six days, all Chinese provinces were adopting emergency measures.[4]

Some critics have argued that China is responsible for the global pandemic because of missteps in December 2019 and January 2020: that more transparency and an earlier shutdown might have stopped the spread of disease to other countries and given other governments more time to respond.[5] There is some evidence that three long-standing vulnerabilities of the Chinese regime – over-centralization, bureaucratism, and obsession with information control – compromised its initial response to the COVID-19 outbreak in Wuhan.[6] Medical professionals who spoke to the media in December about suspicious cases, or posted messages on social media, were warned by police to keep silent. Beijing may have begun censoring social media as early as December 31. Municipal leaders downplayed risks as they prepared for meetings of local legislatures in early January, and failed to take steps that would disrupt celebrations for China's new year. Local officials later claimed that they lacked authority to adopt emergency measures without approval from higher levels. In Beijing, health officials had recognized the possibility of a pandemic by January 14 but said nothing publicly.

Critics said that China had repeated the mistakes made after the outbreak of another disease, SARS, in November 2002. Chinese authorities suppressed information about SARS for months, only notifying the World Health Organization in February 2003. The Chinese regime fell into deep crisis in Spring 2003 as international and domestic criticism mounted over its bungled management of the SARS epidemic.[7]

However, the comparison between COVID-19 and SARS was inapt. By 2019, China's leaders were chastened by experience. Overall, the Chinese regime collected and disclosed information more quickly in 2019 and 2020, largely because of reforms undertaken after the SARS debacle, and because suppressing information was harder than twenty years earlier. Experts outside China were aware of an outbreak, and officials from Beijing were in Wuhan, by the last week of December.

Taiwan started screening airline passengers from Wuhan on December 31, and Thailand adopted similar measures on January 3.

An even faster response by Chinese officials might have slowed the spread of disease but would not have stopped it. Researchers have discovered that the COVID-19 virus was already present in the United States and Europe by mid-December 2019, when investigations began in Wuhan. And, while authoritarian impulses certainly caused some delay in sounding the alarm, the behavior of Chinese officials was not substantially worse than that of officials in several democratic states. Chinese authorities were acting on fragmentary information, at the height of a severe flu season, and the delay in imposing a lockdown in Wuhan was perhaps ten or fifteen days.[8] Other governments armed with better information performed more poorly. The United States did not declare a national emergency until March 18, 2020, two months after its first confirmed case in Washington state. By then, there were confirmed cases in forty-six other American states.

Once Beijing had declared an emergency, it acted decisively. Stringent measures were imposed in hundreds of cities, including some in which no cases had been reported.[9] These measures included the suspension of public transportation, closure of schools and workplaces, mask requirements, temperature checks at transportation centers, and isolation of suspected and confirmed cases. In Wuhan alone, more than ten thousand people were employed in contact tracing. More than forty thousand healthcare workers and tons of equipment were moved from other parts of China to Hubei province. Two new hospitals capable of treating 2,500 patients were constructed in Wuhan within two weeks. A team of international observers said in February 2020 that China had executed "the most ambitious, agile and aggressive disease containment effort in history."[10]

While doing this, Beijing had little regard for local or individual autonomy. Watchdog organizations outside China reported cases of forced testing and isolation, discrimination against minorities, intensified surveillance, and punishment of individuals who reported on the outbreak.[11] But the response was unambiguously effective in containing the disease. Research showed a rapid reduction in the rate of spread and number of COVID-19 cases across China.[12] By the time that the World Health Organization declared a pandemic in March 2020, the disease had been largely contained in China. The country began easing restrictions and reviving economic activity in early April. China's economy grew in 2020, while other major economies shrank. People who had criticized China's handling of the outbreak in January 2020 now acknowledged the advantages of the "China model" for control of the disease, especially in contrast to the bungling of the United States.[13]

Washington Stumbles

Decision-makers in Washington could not have duplicated China's measures even if they had wanted to. The American constitution gives state governments the primary responsibility for controlling the spread of disease and limits the ability of government at any level to infringe individual rights. But federal authorities were not powerless, and their response to the emerging crisis was slow and confused, especially in the critical first weeks when the disease was spreading – in the words of a February 2020 report from the World Health Organization – "with astonishing speed."[14]

President Donald Trump has rightly received much blame for the bungled federal response. The United States had the misfortune of confronting the pandemic with a president who is ranked as one of the least competent in the country's history. The bill of indictment against Trump is extensive. He reassured Americans that everything was "just fine" while privately acknowledging the danger posed by COVID-19.[15] The White House delayed the declaration of a national emergency to avoid an adverse effect on the stock market.[16] Trump denigrated experts within federal government – "Fauci and all those idiots" – and pressured agencies to withhold information about the pandemic.[17] Trump himself refused to wear a mask, encouraged armed protests of stay-at-home orders issued by governors, and promoted unapproved drugs that were useless in treating COVID-19.[18]

It was not by mere chance that the United States had a president like Trump when COVID-19 arrived in the United States. For years, the country had been roiled in debate about the American creed and the role of the federal government. Trump won office in 2016 as a tribune for voters in America's red states who were skeptical about the competence and trustworthiness of the federal bureaucracy. In 2017, a key advisor to Trump, Stephen Bannon, said that the new administration would "deconstruct" a federal establishment that was "innately hostile" to the American people.[19] During the pandemic, Trump behaved much as he had promised during the 2016 election. Trump supporters reciprocated in 2020 with overwhelming support for his handling of the crisis.[20]

It was inevitable, in a deeply polarized political environment, that aspects of pandemic response would become entangled in the broader debate about the American creed and the role of government. A 2020 survey found that Democrats were twice as likely as Republicans to wear a mask when they left home.[21] Democratic governors were more likely than Republican governors to impose lockdowns during the first phase of the pandemic.[22] A 2021 study found that the vaccination rate among Democrats was over ninety percent, and less than sixty percent for Republicans.[23] Decisions about public health were rarely construed as being just about public health. Every choice became an opportunity for citizens to express allegiances in the broader struggle between red and blue.

Here was a good illustration of an old problem of empire: one hazard (pandemic) compounding another (sectionalism). The pandemic widened other divisions as well. African Americans and other minorities were more likely to be infected by the COVID virus, more likely to be hospitalized and die after infection, and more likely to suffer financially during lockdowns.[24] The disease provided more evidence of structural racism in American society, adding fuel to protests about police violence against the black community in the summer of 2020.

President Trump did not bear sole responsibility for federal missteps in the response to COVID-19. Federal interest in pandemic preparedness had waxed and waned over the preceding twenty years, despite multiple warnings that the country was vulnerable to new diseases. Offices to improve preparedness were established, relocated, and eliminated as one president succeeded another.[25] The budget of the lead federal agency, the Centers for Disease Control (CDC), declined by ten percent in real terms in the decade before the pandemic.[26] Federal assistance to state and local governments for public health preparedness declined by thirty percent between 2002 and 2019.[27] The Strategic National Stockpile – a reserve of medical equipment likely to be needed in emergencies – was mismanaged and fell short of needs during the pandemic.[28]

The federal bureaucracy also fumbled at key moments. President Trump was not alone in downplaying dangers in January and February 2020. The day after the Wuhan lockdown, a senior federal official, Anthony Fauci, assured a Senate committee that the risk to the United States was "very low."[29] A month later, Fauci still thought that spread within the country was "extraordinarily unlikely."[30] On February 26, a top CDC official, Nancy Messonnier, said containment strategies had been "largely successful" and that there were "very few cases" of

COVID-19 in the country.[31] "The risk at this time is low," CDC head Robert Redfield confirmed on February 29. "The American public needs to go on with their normal lives."[32]

Federal officials made these statements because they overestimated their ability to track the spread of COVID-19.[33] There was no widely available test for COVID-19 in February 2020. In New York City, which became an epicenter of the pandemic, only thirty-two COVID-19 tests were administered by the end of February.[34] Without widespread testing, federal officials had to draw inferences about the spread of COVID-19 from data about the kinds of medical treatment that people were receiving and tests for related diseases across the country. Interpreting these data was difficult. The data – collected from state and local agencies as well as private healthcare providers – were incomplete and often weeks old. In January and February 2020, this imperfect surveillance system failed badly. In fact, there may have been more than one hundred thousand cases of COVID-19 in the United States by early March.[35]

More testing would have given a better sense of how fast COVID-19 was spreading and enabled local authorities to isolate cases and track contacts. But federal authorities impeded the development of tests in the early phase of the pandemic.[36] Federal law enabled the CDC to claim an exclusive role in performing COVID-19 tests and manufacturing test kits for broader distribution. However, the CDC's own capacity to conduct tests was limited, so it restricted eligibility for testing. Meanwhile, CDC test kits proved to be almost useless because of defects in design and manufacturing. Public health agencies in state and local government were not allowed to substitute a simpler test already in use in Europe. Universities that developed their own tests were denied permission to use them except for research. Businesses hesitated to enter the test kit market so long as the federal government asserted the exclusive right to design and manufacture kits. The United States did not begin to acquire the capacity for mass testing until late March. By this time, parts of the country were overwhelmed with COVID-19.

The federal government's initial approach to testing contrasted with its approach to vaccine development. The federal government did not dictate how a COVID-19 vaccine should be designed or attempt to manufacture the vaccine itself. Instead, it provided grants and advance-purchase contracts to private manufacturers and streamlined procedures for approving vaccines. This federal initiative – known as Operation Warp Speed – was a spectacular success. Vaccines were developed in record time, using new and more effective technologies. By contrast, the main Chinese vaccines, produced by older methods, were less effective in preventing disease.[37] However, this success was tainted by the refusal of many Americans to get vaccinated. At the end of 2021, the US vaccination rate was still lower than in China and the European Union.[38]

The CDC also struggled to provide consistent guidance on public health measures during the pandemic. Federal officials initially recommended against mask-wearing, citing a lack of evidence about the effectiveness of masks in reducing transmission of disease. The CDC reversed its position in April 2020, and made another confusing turnabout in May 2021.[39] Experts also questioned the reasoning behind the CDC's guidance that individuals should stay six feet apart to avoid transmission, and its revision of that recommendation to three feet inside schools in March 2021.[40] The CDC offered detailed advice on how schools should operate during the pandemic, but critics said that it lacked the practical knowledge of school operations that was necessary to give sound advice.[41]

Most Americans operated on the assumption that federal government had the main responsibility for crafting a response to the pandemic.[42] Citizens and experts alike looked to Washington for guidance on public health decisions that could only be taken by state and local governments.[43] This focus on Washington was not unusual: it is part of a broader trend of nationalization in the realm of domestic policy – and especially in the area of disaster response – over the last half century.[44] The fixation on Washington was encouraged by President Trump, who asserted – wrongly – that he had "total" authority to set policy about the closure of businesses and schools during the pandemic.[45]

In April 2020, a former CDC director condemned the federal government for "epic failures" in responding to the pandemic.[46] Some frustrated governors responded by claiming a bigger role for state government in pandemic response. But the ability of states to play a bigger role was hindered by limitations in their own administrative capabilities.[47] Workers in state and local public health bodies are poorly paid, poorly trained, and poorly equipped. Most local public health organizations – and many state organizations – have not met national accreditation standards. Almost fifty thousand jobs – one-fifth of the workforce – were eliminated within state and local public health agencies in the decade before the pandemic. Leaders of these organizations often suffer from a lack of authority and status. Many were fired, harassed, or threatened with violence during the pandemic.[48]

Americans were left in a predicament: neither the federal government nor state governments were prepared to handle the COVID shock. Some reformers thought that the way out of this predicament was more centralization: expanding federal authority and bolstering federal agencies so that they can forge a unified national public health system. This has been a standard recipe for policy reform in many areas in the United States since World War II. It assumes that experts in federal agencies will have freedom to exercise professional judgment, that they can collect the information needed for sound decisions, and that those decisions will be respected by the public.

The pandemic challenges these assumptions. In a divided country, decisions made in Washington are always likely to be received with skepticism by a large part of the population. Decisions about public health are more likely to become entangled in the bigger red-blue debate about national priorities. The intensity of political struggle also means that political leaders will find it hard to resist interfering in decisions by experts within the federal bureaucracy. The whole nation would become more vulnerable to miscalculations by unseasoned leaders like Donald Trump. The scale of the country and complexity of the health system means that decisions made in Washington are likely to be delayed, misguided, or impracticable.

Given these realities, the better way of improving resilience might be through decentralization: by building up the capacity of state governments to assume a leadership role during pandemics. The country would have a network of public health systems rather than a unified national system. Obviously, there are limits to how far this can be done: some tasks can only be performed by federal government. But decisions taken at the state level – assuming a substantial improvement in state capabilities – might be quicker and better tailored to local conditions. Of course, some states also suffered from internal divisions during the pandemic. Sometimes these divisions were reverberations from the ongoing red-blue fight in Washington. In general, though, state-level decisions might be better respected than decisions coming from Washington. And in a regime that abjures Chinese-style coercion to ensure compliance, respect for government decisions is a crucial commodity.

Hubris in Delhi

COVID-19 is especially dangerous for people with pre-existing conditions. This is true for countries too. India was not well-prepared for a pandemic.[49] Its public health and healthcare systems are badly underfunded, and many key positions within those systems are vacant. Weaknesses in reporting mean that central authorities often lack a good picture about the prevalence of disease. Many Indians live in crowded settings where isolation is difficult. And many were unprepared to deal with the economic consequences of a shutdown: they lacked savings, were self-employed, or worked for small businesses in the grey economy. The social safety net is weakened by gaps and corruption, so that it is difficult for government to dispense emergency assistance. Moreover, central and state governments are constrained in their ability to finance large-scale relief programs.

Indian governments do have the advantage of extensive legal powers. State governments have broad authority granted under the Epidemic Diseases Act, which was adopted by imperial administrators to control bubonic plague in the 1890s. And the Disaster Management Act (DMA), adopted in 2005, allows central government to assume an expansive role in responding to emergencies, including the right to give directions to state and local governments.[50] Donald Trump merely imagined that he had "total authority" over lockdowns during the pandemic: under the DMA, Narendra Modi had it in fact.

Modi used this law to impose a complete country-wide lockdown on March 24, 2020. On paper, the lockdown was judged to be the most stringent in the world – even more rigorous than controls imposed by China.[51] A few days later, central government also announced an economic relief package that included cash transfers and free food grains for poor families, along with orders for employers to pay wages and for landlords to stop rent collections. The nationwide lockdown continued for two months. After May, stringent restrictions were maintained for districts with extensive infection, but gradually reduced elsewhere. The process of unwinding central controls continued in phases for the rest of 2020.[52]

The Modi government won praise internationally for responding vigorously to the pandemic.[53] But the first phase of the lockdown was delayed, poorly planned, and brutal. In early 2020, Indian authorities tested even less intensively than their American counterparts and also underestimated the spread of disease.[54] State governments complained about a lack of consultation before the nation-wide lockdown was announced with only four hours' notice.[55] The lockdown announcement was followed by a welter of orders that were sometimes enforced arbitrarily or not at all.[56] Employers ignored orders to continue paying wages, and perimeter controls for designated "hot zones" were sporadically enforced.[57] The lockdown was especially hard on millions of migrant workers who were unable to get food or medical care in the cities where they worked, and unable to return home. In December 2020, one critic called this the greatest humanitarian crisis in the history of the Indian republic.[58]

Despite all this, many observers thought that the lockdown had been effective in achieving its main aim: protecting India from a devastating wave of disease. In October 2020, a panel of experts appointed by central government concluded that the worst of the pandemic had passed. India had "fare[d] better than many other countries," the panel said, with a fatality rate that was ninety percent lower than in the United States and Europe. Only 200,000 Indians had died, according to government data; without the lockdown, it might have been more than two million.[59] Even at this time, there were skeptics who questioned the accuracy of India's official statistics. But many considered the numbers to be roughly correct. They speculated that India had fared well because people were generally younger and had stronger immune systems – and because the Modi government had acted so decisively.[60]

A defect of centralized regimes is that they are vulnerable to miscalculations by top leaders. This was India's predicament after December 2020. Relief at dodging a cataclysm turned into hubris. At the World Economic Forum in Davos in January 2021, Modi said that India had "saved humanity from a big disaster by containing corona effectively."[61] The next month, leaders of Modi's Bharatiya Janata Party (BJP) declared that COVID-19 had been "defeated" and lauded Modi for "introducing India to the world as a proud and victorious nation in the fight" against the disease.[62] The national scientific taskforce on COVID-19 did not meet for three months in early 2021.[63] Modi's health minister affirmed in early March 2021 that India was "in the end game of the pandemic."[64]

The Modi government had made a fatal miscalculation. COVID-19 had not been defeated in India. On the contrary, the country was about to be hit by a devastating second wave of disease. The number of confirmed COVID-19 cases tripled between mid-February and mid-March 2021 and then increased ten-fold by the last week of April.[65] By early May, the country was recording nearly three million new cases a week. No country had experienced such an explosion in the number of new cases.[66]

This second wave gained force because of the emergence of a more contagious and deadly version of the COVID virus known as the Delta variant. But it was also amplified by missteps of the Modi government.

An aggressive vaccination program might have slowed the resurgence of disease in 2021. However, central government ignored warnings and failed to make investments in vaccine production capacity in 2020.[67] It also placed orders for vaccines later than other governments.[68] In Davos, Modi even boasted that India was exporting vaccine supplies to less fortunate countries. At home, the public's interest in vaccination was dulled by its perception that crisis had passed. By the time the second wave hit in March 2021, only one percent of the Indian population had been vaccinated.[69]

Meanwhile the Modi government refused to acknowledge the severity of the emerging crisis. On March 30, Modi's health minister assured the country that "the situation is under control."[70] On April 9, Modi himself rejected another national lockdown, insisting that the country had the "resources and experience" to contain the pandemic with less draconian measures. Modi told states to impose localized controls on COVID-19 hotspots instead.[71] As the second wave intensified throughout April and early May, Modi still resisted appeals from experts for a national lockdown.

Modi might have wanted to avoid the harsh effects of a national lockdown that had been observed in 2020. But his government was also caught by its own rhetoric. It could not impose a lockdown without conceding that its boasting in January and February had been unwarranted. And there were immediate political considerations. The BJP was contesting important state and local elections in March and April. A national lockdown would have compromised the party's ability to campaign.

The Modi government encouraged mass gatherings even as the second wave of COVID-19 gained force. In mid-March, more than one hundred thousand people crowded into the newly christened Narendra Modi Stadium in Gujarat to watch a high-profile cricket competition between India and England.[72] In late March, Modi appeared in national advertisements encouraging attendance at the Kumbh Mela, a Hindu festival planned for April 2021 in the state of Uttarakhand.[73] Experts had warned that health risks posed by the pilgrimage were "enormous."[74] Eventually, on April 17, Modi reversed himself and urged organizers of the festival to discourage large crowds. But his reversal came too late. Attendance at the 2021 Kumbh Mela was estimated to be in the millions. As predicted, the gathering turned into a "massive super-spreader event."[75]

Modi also spoke – often without a mask – at more than twenty rallies in the four states that were scheduled for elections in April.[76]

One of these rallies, held in West Bengal in March, drew more than half a million people. On April 15, India's Election Commission tried to restrict campaigning in West Bengal, expressing concern about "blatant" disregard for the public health guidelines that it had established at the start of the election season.[77] The warning was ignored. Two days later, Modi spoke at another rally in West Bengal, congratulating followers for "showing their power" by gathering in "huge crowds."[78] A representative of the Indian Medical Association said that Modi himself had become a COVID-19 super-spreader.[79]

In April and May 2021, India realized the worst-case scenario that had been apprehended at the very start of the pandemic. The country's fragile health system broke down. The country was not ready, as Modi had assured on April 9. Even though a parliamentary committee warned in November 2020 that the number of hospital beds was "grossly inadequate" during the first wave, many temporary hospitals were dismantled in January and February 2021.[80] Central government was also slow to build up the country's capacity for producing oxygen, despite shortages during the first wave.[81] In fact, exports of oxygen doubled between April 2020 and January 2021.[82] During the second wave, Indians searched desperately for oxygen to save their parents and children. Morgues and crematoria were overwhelmed. The official estimate was that 250,000 people died between March and June 2021, but this was now recognized as a massive undercounting.[83]

The second wave, one report concluded in July 2021, was India's worst human tragedy since independence.[84] Modi dismissed his health minister and other officials that same month, trying to shed blame for the debacle. But blame was hard to avoid entirely. Modi's standing in public opinion polls slumped in late 2021. A critic compared Modi to "British colonial overlords who went hunting while Indians starved in mass famines."[85] India styled itself as the world's largest democracy, but it had not entirely escaped the old problem of the bad emperor.

Mortal Danger in Brussels

In three superstates, central authorities bore heavy responsibility for pandemic response, and whether that response went well or badly turned largely on their attentiveness and competence. In the European Union, a different story played out. As disease spread throughout Europe in early 2020, the fear was that central authorities were too weak to help in any significant way, and that the EU would collapse as member states scrambled to save themselves. The European project, former European Commission president Jacques Delors warned in March 2020, was in "mortal danger."[86] But the resilience of the European project was again underestimated.

The COVID virus arrived in Europe in December 2020 but went undetected for a month. As in the United States and India, the rapid spread of disease was not initially recognized because of weaknesses in testing and reporting. But it was clear to Italian authorities by late February that COVID-19 was spreading rapidly throughout their country. Within days, the confirmed case count was escalating in other countries as well. On March 13 the World Health Organization said that Europe had become "the epicenter of the pandemic."[87]

Responsibility for responding to the pandemic fell largely on national governments. Central institutions within the European Union have no direct responsibility for protection of public health or delivery of healthcare, although they are permitted to take actions that "complement national policies."[88] The European Centre for Disease Prevention and Control had been set up in 2005, after the SARS crisis, but it lacked the resources and status of its American counterpart.[89] Certainly there was no EU authority to impose lockdowns. The Italian government was the first to act in this way, by imposing a regional quarantine on February 22 that transformed into a nationwide lockdown over the next three weeks.[90] Other European countries adopted restrictions in March, and by early April most had imposed nationwide lockdowns as well.[91]

National governments followed different paths as they dealt with the pandemic, and some made serious mistakes. In Sweden, national policy was guided by experts in the national Public Health Agency who were skeptical about the effectiveness of lockdowns. The price paid for Sweden's less stringent policy was quickly observed. Adjusting for population, Sweden suffered more COVID cases and deaths in 2020 than other Nordic countries, all of which acted more firmly.[92] An independent investigation concluded that Sweden's initial response had been inadequate. Swedish authorities reversed course and tightened restrictions as the pandemic continued.[93]

Countries within the European Union were criticized for pursuing a "confusing patchwork" of responses to the pandemic.[94] But the Swedish reversal illustrated an advantage of the EU regime. Decentralization allowed experimentation, which was useful given uncertainty about which policies were likely to work. And it was easy in an open society to compare these experiments. Dire results from Sweden were contrasted with better results from Norway and Denmark.[95] Portugal's success in the early months of the pandemic was contrasted with the lacklustre performance of neighboring Spain.[96] The above-par results of Germany's decentralized response were contrasted with the below-par results of France's centralized response.[97] National leaders could not escape accountability for policies that were seen to be less effective than those applied elsewhere in the EU.

However, national initiatives had an unintended side-effect in the first weeks of the pandemic. As member states rushed to protect their people, they seemed to abandon the ideal of European integration. The union was built on the principles of solidarity and a single market, but in the first weeks of March 2020, Germany and France restricted the export of medical supplies to other EU member states.[98] In Italy, public anger mounted over the failure of other EU countries to provide aid in the first days of the pandemic.[99] Countries also jostled for access to new vaccines.[100] Meanwhile, the principle of free movement between member states was jeopardized as governments closed national borders. Economic coordination seemed to break down as governments abandoned EU deficit guidelines and introduced massive stimulus programs.[101] Hungary's Orbán government used the pandemic as a pretext to further consolidate its power, feeding concerns about erosion of the rule of law within the EU.[102]

Debate within Europe about pandemic response was soon accompanied by fears that COVID-19 might be the "final straw" for the EU.[103] In March 2020, Italian prime minister Giuseppe Conte warned EU leaders that they were in danger of making "tragic mistakes" that would destroy the union.[104] Spanish prime minister Pedro Sánchez cautioned that "Europe itself" would be in jeopardy if the EU did not formulate a quick and effective response to the crisis.[105] The philanthropist George Soros told Europeans to prepare for the "tragic reality" that the union might not survive the pandemic.[106]

EU institutions did stumble during the first weeks of the pandemic. Central authorities failed to anticipate the strains that would be put upon the union by the COVID shock. But EU institutions quickly recovered their footing as the threat to the union became clear.[107] By late March, European leaders had agreed on travel restrictions with non-EU countries and Brussels had launched a unified effort to repatriate EU citizens stranded abroad. National restrictions on the export of medical supplies were lifted and the European Commission introduced a joint procurement exercise for fresh supplies. At the same time, the Commission coordinated national policies to maintain the flow of freight and essential workers between countries.

EU institutions also moved quickly to support the economy. In mid-March 2020, the European Central Bank (ECB) promised to support member states by renewing its program for purchasing government debt. "Extraordinary times," ECB president Christine Lagarde said on March 18, "require extraordinary action."[108] Two days later, the president of the European Commission, Ursula von der Leyen, told member states that they were released from deficit spending rules during the pandemic and should "pump [money] into the economy as much as they need" to support their economies.[109] A few weeks later, the EU promised financial support for healthcare and unemployment insurance programs in struggling economies.[110]

In July 2020, leaders of the EU member states went a step further. For years, there had been debate about whether the European Commission should be permitted to finance its expenditures by borrowing on its own account. Some member states from northern Europe had opposed the idea, but in the face of this crisis they gave way. The Commission was empowered to sell bonds and assigned new sources of revenue to repay this debt.[111] EU spending on pandemic relief was doubled in July 2020. Advocates of European integration compared this to the historic moment in 1790 when the US federal government assumed state debts from the revolutionary war, thereby consolidating its place as keystone of the nascent American regime. The comparison between 1790 and 2020 was overwrought.[112] Still, the EU had executed a substantial reform which had seemed infeasible only a year earlier.[113]

EU leaders launched a second experiment in June 2020, by giving the European Commission responsibility for procuring vaccines on behalf of all member states. Earlier attempts by member states to make deals with manufacturers were abandoned. This centralized project did not go smoothly because of the Commission's inexperience with large-scale emergency procurements.[114] Commission staff were criticized for fixating on pricing and safety concerns when time was of the essence. By the end of March 2021, only eight percent of EU adults were fully vaccinated, compared to seventeen percent of US adults. *New York Times* columnist Paul Krugman – one of many EU critics in March and April 2021 – declared that the European procurement effort was a "debacle" that revealed the "fundamental flaws in the continent's institutions and attitudes."[115] Another *New York Times* writer called the effort "disastrous."[116]

The condemnations were premature. Certainly, the Commission mismanaged the early phases of its procurement effort. In February

2021 Ursula von der Leyen conceded that the commission had dragged its heels. "A country might be a speedboat," she said, "and the EU more a tanker."[117] But the Commission regrouped, and performance improved as the year progressed. By early July, the adult vaccination rate in the EU was the same as in the United States; by the end of August, it was seventeen percent higher. The Commission achieved its January 2021 target of vaccinating seventy percent of the adult population within eight months.[118]

Overall, the EU performed better during the first two years of the pandemic than the other liberal-democratic superstates. The United States and India each suffered higher death rates. Of course, the EU had advantages: it is wealthier than India, and its investment in public health systems is higher than in the United States. But the EU also performed better because of its more decentralized structure. Member states had the capacity to act vigorously, and voters held the leaders of member states accountable for action. Confronted by an existential risk to the union itself, national leaders also demonstrated their ability to collaborate and adjust EU institutions and policies. During the pandemic, the EU reinvented itself once again.[119]

As the crisis ebbed, the European Commission proposed further reforms that would strengthen the role of central institutions in responding to pandemics.[120] At minimum, the EU needs to do better in showing solidarity and coordinating national actions in the initial stages of such disasters. The Commission's proposals drew two types of criticism. Some said that the EU ought to go much further, addressing inequalities in healthcare across the union that have been exposed during the pandemic.[121] Others worried that the Commission might go too far, undermining the ability of member states to take initiative in the face of danger.[122] An age-old threat – pandemic – has revived an age-old question of empire: whether it was better to manage hazards by consolidating or distributing power.

Sen's Mistake?

In 1999, the Nobel-winning economist Amartya Sen challenged the widely held view that it is necessary to sacrifice political and civil rights to promote development in poor countries. Sen insisted that there was no tradeoff between democracy and development, and that on the contrary freedom improved the likelihood that people would be better off materially. Democracy, Sen said, "can even help to prevent famines and other disasters." Democratic leaders are compelled to answer critics and win votes, and therefore have "strong incentives to undertake measures to avert famines and other such catastrophes."[123]

People remember Sen's argument as one focused on the inverse relationship between democracy and famine. But we can see from Sen's own words that the argument was pitched more broadly, to disasters and catastrophes in general. The COVID-19 pandemic certainly fits in that category. Should it cause us to question Sen's argument? Millions of people died in the three superstates that take democratic ideals seriously, while thousands died in authoritarian China.

Since 2020, a growing body of research has examined the link between regime type – democratic or authoritarian – and response to the COVID-19 pandemic. Findings so far have been mixed. Some researchers have found that democratic regimes did worse than authoritarian regimes.[124] And some have found that democracies did better, just as Sen predicted.[125] But even Sen is proved eventually right in general, we might need a caveat for superstates. Within this category, democracy does not seem to have performed better, based on the results from 2020 and 2021. If China had the same COVID mortality rate as the United States in that period, an additional three million people would have died.

In fact, the democratic/authoritarian dichotomy is too simplistic as a model for explaining pandemic response. Democratic principles can be applied in different ways – and with varying rigor – at different levels of government within a superstate. An additional and critical question is how responsibilities are divided between central and subordinate governments. History also plays a role. Experience with past crises can make leaders more attentive to hazards of a particular kind – and stability in general – and it can shape their views about the best way of responding to those hazards.

China, as a highly centralized authoritarian regime, would ordinarily be vulnerable to problems such as weak leadership and bureaucratism. But in 2020 it happened to be well placed to manage these vulnerabilities. The regime had spent decades cultivating a skilled leadership group and improving its control capabilities. China's leaders were unimpeded by Western-style constitutional rules, and Xi's power was not seriously contested. Chinese leaders were also scarred by the SARS debacle. This was an authoritarian regime of a distinctive type, operating in distinctive circumstances. It was ready, both intellectually and practically, to act decisively when the COVID virus arrived. In other conditions – if SARS had never happened, if the bureaucracy had not been recently reformed, or if the leadership group had been more factionalized – the Chinese experience with COVID-19 might have been dramatically worse.

Central authorities in the United States and India could not act as decisively as those in China. In the first place there were constitutional constraints, more so in the United States than in India, that limited the ability of central authorities to dictate the behavior of states, businesses, and individuals. And American and Indian leaders were hobbled by problems of bureaucratism too. Sometimes, central agencies did not know what was happening on the frontline, did not make timely and sound decisions, or failed to execute those decisions properly.

Democratic politics also complicated the central response in the United States and India. It was a particular form of democratic government, after all, that placed the incompetent Donald Trump in such a critical position at the time of the pandemic. Trump hoped to retain the presidency by responding to voter expectations, which is exactly what Amartya Sen predicted that democratically elected leaders would do. But Trump's voter base comprised only half of a sharply divided electorate, and a large part of that base was skeptical about science, regulation, and the federal establishment. In this case, the play of democratic politics impeded the vigorous use of federal powers, even though the other half of the voting population wanted it – and to some extent was dependent upon it, because of the diminished capabilities of their own state governments.

Democratic politics – of a particular configuration – also compli-cated pandemic response in India. The system placed great power in the hands of Narendra Modi and created incentives for him to play the role of strongman in 2020, by imposing a tough but ill-planned lockdown. The system also encouraged blunders in 2021, as Modi sought credit on the campaign trail for defeating COVID-19, while a deadly second wave gained force.

After every crisis, there is an inclination to wish that there had been a more orderly and coherent response, and a temptation to bolster the authority of central institutions to achieve that result during the next crisis. We want better planning and more systematization. This is the trend of reform in the European Union. However, there are risks to centralization within a superstate that wants to honor liberal democratic ideals. It makes an entire system vulnerable to bureaucratic failures at the center, and vulnerable to gridlock if different populations have starkly different views about how central authorities should respond to crisis. Too much centralization also stymies experimentation in the face of uncertainty. An alternative approach would recognize the need for coordination at the top. But it would also stress the development of robust administrative capabilities and electoral accountability at lower levels, so that sub-central leaders have the ability and incentive to respond to crises in a timely way, as Sen suggests they should.

9

How to Rule a Superstate

The world changes quickly. Only a century ago, in 1922, the age of empires had not yet run its course. No one anticipated that by the end of the century, the world of empires would be divided into almost two hundred states. And no one imagined that two of these states would each contain 1.4 billion people. That was almost all the people on the planet in 1922. An expert assured in 1925 that the entire world population would not exceed two billion by 2020.[1]

Admittedly, the futurist H.G. Wells, writing around 1922, had predicted the emergence of some new form of supersized state. He nominated Russia, China, Europe, India, and the United States as likely candidates. But Wells did not contemplate the possibility of a state with a half-billion or billion people. He considered the United States, with 100 million people in 1922, to be exceptional. And the United States was not expected to have many more people – perhaps 150 million – by 2022.[2]

Moreover, Wells was engaged in loose speculation about the emergence of superstates. The facts of 1922 gave little reason for confidence about the emergence of stable regimes in most places he identified as candidates for superstate status. Russia was seized by economic collapse and civil disorder, China was fractured among warlords, Europe was recovering from a devastating continental conflict, and India (according to its British rulers) was kept together solely by force of arms.

Only the United States seemed to enjoy stability in 1922. But this should not be overstated. Sectional differences were profound, as Frederick Jackson Turner noted at the time. There were still tens of thousands of living veterans of the American Civil War. And in any case, the United States was an easy country to rule in 1922, by today's standards. The capacity of the population to organize and make demands on government was more constrained. The population was dispersed, with almost half still living on farms or in small towns. Most people lived without telephones, radio, or automobiles. Only a minority had a high-school education. Many adults could not vote. Few expected the national government to do much on their behalf.

Only ten decades later, four superstates are together responsible for the welfare of 3.6 billion people – most of them urbanized, affluent by historical standards, literate, wired, mobile, and rights-conscious. Even under favorable conditions, governing such large and diverse polities would be hard work. And we know that conditions for the remainder of the twenty-first century are unlikely to be favorable. Think of the profound effects that just one of several hazards – climate change – will have on everyday life. Polities that are more populous and complex than any in recorded history will confront a threat bigger and more deadly than anything in recorded history. What will be the outcome of this collision? Will all four superstates still exist, in something like their present form, a century from now?

The answer from history must be: Almost certainly not. Ignore the cheerful words of leaders who promise their regimes will endure forever. Leaders are expected to engage in this sort of bluster. Nothing in the historical record gives confidence that all four polities will survive the next century without major changes. The borders of a superstate may change substantially. The architecture of a regime may be radically altered. Or a superstate may break completely into pieces. We cannot predict exactly what the change will be. Historian J.B. Bury wrote in 1923 that empires collapsed as "the consequence of a series of contingent events."[3] Future historians will say the same when they write about the transformation or collapse of superstates in 2123.

A Fatal Path

We can speculate about one potentially fatal path that leaders of super-states might follow. We have already seen how leaders tend to alter regimes in particular ways when hazards accumulate. Control over sub-central governments, society, and the marketplace is intensified and centralized. Leadership structures are altered so that power is concentrated within the central executive. Consultative and countervailing institutions are weakened. And leaders rely more heavily on "creedal passions" to promote loyalty to central authorities.[4] Tolerance for non-conforming ways of life declines.

There are many reasons why leaders are tempted to govern this way during times of stress. Confronted with uncertainties, their reaction is to get a "handle on the situation" by tightening control. In addition, crisis response often requires the rapid mobilization of societal resources, which encourages centralization of authority too. There is evidence in some democracies that voters themselves expect government to provide more protection against an ever-expanding range of risks.[5] Central responsibilities may expand as politicians bid for the support of these voters in polity-wide elections.

As for creedal passions: imperial rulers throughout history have recognized that calls to rally in defense of collective honor, faith, and culture are one of the easier ways of uniting a fractured polity, at least for a short time. The temptation to stoke creedal passions is stronger when leaders lack the administrative capabilities that are necessary to ameliorate problems by crafting and implementing policy competently.

The result of prolonged stress within a superstate may be a regime that is more autocratic, controlling, and intolerant. Obviously, this is an undesirable outcome from the point of view of human rights. Civil and political liberties would be restricted in the drive to preserve stability and unity. But the goals of stability and unity might be unintentionally sabotaged as well. Within this sort of regime, leaders at the center are more likely to be overwhelmed with difficult decisions, and more likely to make poor choices as a result. More central control also means a bigger and more complicated bureaucracy, and therefore more problems of bureaucratism, such as disorganization, incoordination, noncompliance, inefficiency, and corruption. A bigger central role also provides leaders of subcentral governments and citizens with more cause for resentment about interference from the center. The regime's ability to manage internal divisions and popular unrest may decline as power shifts to the central executive and away from more inclusive legislative bodies.

The Case for Devolution

Superstates can be designed in ways that reduce these problems. One important step is to limit central control by devolving governmental responsibilities so far as possible. Robust administrative capacities would be built up within sub-central governments, and these governments would bear more responsibility for mobilizing resources and protecting the public when threats arise. Admittedly, this prescription goes against the conventional wisdom that some problems – climate change, pandemics, defense – are "too big [for sub-central governments] to handle" by themselves.[6] But conventional wisdom fails to recognize that centralization comes with problems too. As we have seen, the simultaneous centralization of responsibilities in many domains of policy may result in overload, bureaucratism, intensified sectional conflict, and popular discontent. In practice, decision-making by sub-central governments may be the better of two flawed options.

Leadership Structure

It is necessary to think carefully about the design of leadership structures within superstates. Certainly, we should aim for a robust application of democratic ideals within the leadership structures of sub-central governments. Leaders of these governments should be accountable to citizens through free and fair elections. This is desirable on its own account, as a realization of fundamental human rights, but also as a practical matter of superstate governance, so that these leaders can participate in higher level negotiations about sectional differences and membership in the polity with a clear mandate from their people.

How democratic principles should be applied in the design of leadership structures at the center of a superstate is a more complicated question. There is sometimes a tendency to think that leadership structures at the center and sub-central levels of government within a superstate must mirror one another. If sub-central governments are led by a strong executive who is chosen through direct popular election or by the vote of a legislative assembly, then central government should have the same sort of executive; and if elections are decided and laws are passed based on simple majorities at the sub-central level, then the same principle of majority rule should apply at the central level too. Any deviation from subcentral practice at the highest level of government seems to provide evidence of a "democratic deficit," to use a phrase often invoked by critics of EU institutions.

In fact, institutional mimesis of this sort can be dangerous within a superstate. The drive for consistency proceeds from a failure to appreciate how politics may differ at the center of the regime. At the sub-central level, executive dominance and majority rule might make sense, because the governed population is more likely to share values and interests. It is more reasonable to assume that the governed population constitutes a single people or public, that election results express a mandate from that public, and that voters on the losing side of an election are unlikely to be profoundly alienated after their defeat.

Circumstances are likely to differ at the central level within a superstate. Differences across the whole superstate might be so substantial that it makes little sense to talk about a single public. (In the United States, the notion of a solitary "American public" is largely an invention of the mid-twentieth century.)[7] It might be more accurate to imagine multiple publics instead. Under these circumstances, an electoral or legislative majority may not reflect a popular mandate: rather, it may simply reflect the dominance of one public over another. Segments of the population that fall in the minority might be profoundly alienated after an electoral or legislative loss, especially if it happens routinely. Elections for powerful offices at the center of government that are decided on the principle of majority rule are more likely to be perceived by different publics as contests for the continuation of one way of life rather than another.

In superstates, the main aim of governance at the center may not be identifying and executing popular mandates, because such mandates may not exist. More often, the critical task may be making a peace among multiple publics. Leadership structures must be designed so important publics are represented and conciliation between these publics is encouraged. Winner-takes-all institutions, such as a powerful executive chosen on the principle of majority rule, must be avoided. Authority might be shifted to technocrats or diplomats within central institutions to reduce the intensity of conflict and improve the odds of negotiated settlements. To create space for negotiation, ideals like transparency in decision-making may not be so strictly observed.

Measures like this may seem to make a regime undemocratic. This would be the wrong conclusion. Democracy is not a light switch; there is no single way to realize it in practice. Understandings about what democracy requires – or how much democracy can be tolerated – have varied substantially between countries and over time within countries. It is a question of crafting forms of democratic rule that will be durable given circumstances. In superstates, the formula most likely to succeed may be robust democracy below, and more tempered democracy above.

Central institutions that are designed to reconcile sectional differences may be slow in responding to new threats. Negotiation takes time. This is another reason why it is important for sub-central governments to have robust administrative capabilities. *Crises of mobilization* – that is, crises that demand the rapid mobilization of societal resources in response to new threats – ought to be handled at the sub-central level where possible, because differences of opinion about the right course of action are likely to be less intense at the sub-central level, and the concentration of authority that is necessary for timely mobilization is less likely to be objectionable. Central institutions can focus on *crises of cohesion* – that is, challenges to unity and stability that arise because of conflicts between publics, which can be resolved only through decision-making processes in which power is dispersed, and which allow settlements to be negotiated.

Accepting Fragility

The survival of superstates may require a different way of thinking about the character of leadership at the center of government. Scholars have used many different terms to describe the bundle of ideas that guide elite decision-making. During the Cold War, for example, American political scientists tried to describe the "operational code" of the Soviet elite, which they defined as the set of beliefs about history and strategy that guided elite decision-making within the Soviet Union.[8] Similarly, historians have described the "official mind" of the elite that ran the British empire, a composite of "beliefs about morals and politics, about the duties of government, [and] the ordering of society."[9] Followers of philosopher Michel Foucault have labeled this bundle of beliefs the "mentality of rule."[10]

We have encountered different operational codes throughout this book. American leaders from the pre-New Deal era, who obsessed about the health of the union and celebrated compromise, followed one kind of operational code. They shared an understanding about the major challenges confronting the United States and how to deal with them. Post-World War II American leaders who declared the death of sectionalism and pursued an aggressive project of nation-building were following a different operational code. Modern-day Indian leaders who manage "centrifugal pressures" by centralizing power and restricting liberties are following a distinctive code as well, with some roots in the era of British rule. Chinese leaders who constantly invent new bureaucratic techniques of "stability maintenance" follow yet another code. So do European leaders who meet fresh crises with another round of summits.

The operational codes of leaders in these four superstates differ substantially on questions of how to govern, but they have generally been consistent on one point – an appreciation that disunion and instability are ever-present dangers. The possibility that things might fall apart through the clumsy management of events has been foremost on leaders' minds. Jawarharlal Nehru gave evidence of this mindset in 1951:

> We live at a time of great danger in the world. No man can say what the next few months or the next year may bring. And when a country is face to face with grave problems and questions of life and death and survival, then there is a certain priority and a certain preference in the way of doing things.[11]

So did Xi Jinping sixty years later, when he quoted an ancient text: "One should be mindful of possible danger in times of peace, downfall in times of survival, and chaos in times of stability."[12] The attitude of American leaders from the 1950s until the 1980s might be the exception to this widely felt concern about fragility, but this period of complacency appears to have passed. Preserving the union, to use the old American phrase, is now a central concern for leaders in the capitals of all superstates – just as preservation of empire was the central preoccupation of rulers in past centuries.

Most people in the developed world – that small club of wealthy, democratized countries – are not accustomed to thinking about fragility as an immediate problem in governance. Political stability is usually taken for granted. "Fragile statehood" is construed as a pathology suffered by developing countries. It is contrasted with "successful modern statehood," found in countries like Denmark.[13] One of the reasons that American commentators have so often disparaged the project of European integration might be their assumption that no healthy polity should beset by recurring crises, as the European Union has been. However, we must abandon this way of thinking when we consider superstates. The essential characteristics of superstates – size, diversity, complexity – mean that fragility is inescapable, and recurrent crises are unavoidable. In superstates, an effective leader is one who accepts and prepares for this reality.

Proceed With Caution

The mentality of rule in superstates may also be distinctive in other ways. In some democratic states, leaders are often expected to have a clearly defined program which they pursue aggressively once in office. Former US president George H.W. Bush called this "the vision thing."[14] Bush's defeat in the 1992 presidential election was attributed to his inability to articulate a bold agenda that would lure voters to polling stations. Modern American presidents are routinely judged on their success in articulating and implementing an ambitious agenda within their first hundred days in office. The benchmark for appraising presidential performance is Franklin Roosevelt, who achieved sweeping reforms soon after his election in 1932.

This expectation about how presidents should behave might be reasonable when there is broad consensus within a polity on national priorities – as in 1932, when Roosevelt won in a landslide, or perhaps in 1960, when candidates Kennedy and Nixon agreed that the election was largely about means rather than ends. But this expectation is unreasonable, even dangerous, when polities are divided about national priorities. As a practical matter, the likelihood of quick progress on legislation is dramatically reduced when a country is divided. More importantly, the strategy of crowding the legislative agenda with contentious proposals, and insisting on rapid action on these proposals, will inflame divisions. This is exactly the wrong formula for governing a diverse and complex polity. Leadership in a superstate requires a more nuanced approach, driven by an understanding that there may be limits on the load that central institutions can bear at a particular moment, and consequently that there may need to be difficult choices about overall priorities for the center.

The rhetoric of governance in superstates sometimes imagines a steady march toward a well-defined end – "an ever-closer union" or a "more perfect union" – but the practice of governance is more often concerned with tacking and jibing as winds shift, or adjusting sails as storms blow through. As Deng Xiaoping suggested, leaders must be pragmatic about tactics, and prepared to bend doctrine for the sake of unity and stability. This is especially true in superstates because they are subject to a broader range of hazards and a greater risk of cascading hazards.

Similarly, the constitutional apparatus of a superstate must be flexible enough to allow adaptation and accommodation of differences. Rigid constitutionalism – manifested in the sacralization of constitutional texts, dogmatism about the application of constitutional principles, an unworkable amending formula, and enforcement of constitutional rules by a cloistered judiciary that is insensible to considerations of statecraft – may be especially dangerous in superstates. Different parts of the polity may need to be governed in different ways, and the whole apparatus may require adjustment as circumstances change. Of course, the process of adaptation cannot be left to a central executive alone: usually this results in further concentration of power. There must be mechanisms that allow important communities within the superstate to negotiate and assent to basic changes in the regime.

Creedal Commitments

However, there must be a limit to pragmatism and doctrinal pliability. A regime must be seen to stand for something if it wants to maintain the loyalty of subcentral governments and the general population. That is, it must have a coherent creed. Admittedly, there are other ways of maintaining cohesion – by making powerful constituencies better off materially, or by threatening to use force in cases of disloyalty. But material inducement and coercion by themselves are not adequate buttresses for central authority. Often it will be impossible to make everyone better off: sacrifices might be required instead. And coercion is a crude instrument. A well-crafted creed promotes cohesion while economizing on the use of treasure and force.

Leaders often craft creeds out of the cultural resources at hand – playing on ideas and values already familiar to people within the superstate. The task is to devise a creed that is effective in attracting loyalty but morally defensible too. A creed that plays too heavily on the defense of collective honor runs the risk of degrading into jingoism and encouraging aggression against outsiders. A creed that plays too heavily on the defense of faith or culture will stoke intolerance and persecution of minorities. We want a creed that avoids such extremes. A creed that is consistent with the doctrine of human rights must allow space for diversity in lifestyle, significant autonomy for individuals and communities within the superstate, and even freedom to dissent against the creed itself.

Imperial rulers sometimes showed a grudging tolerance of heterodoxy, usually because it was infeasible at a particular moment to stamp it out. Rulers of superstates must do something more. Any creed that is consistent with the doctrine of human rights must acknowledge the legitimacy of argument against the creed, and against the continued existence of the superstate as well. This is another sense in which superstates, if they are to remain morally defensible, are unavoidably fragile. Doubts about the need for these vast and complex structures can never be staunched.

Nor should they be. If a superstate cannot survive except by extinguishing human rights, then it ought to collapse. Most pieces of a shattered superstate would still be more substantial – more expansive and populous, and maybe more wealthy – than many other states existing today. They might be freer as well.

Acknowledgments

This is my tenth book, and like all the others it could not have been completed without the support of my wife Sandra and children John and Constance. Thanks also to my mother, Nancy McQuillan Roberts, whose love of learning inspired my scholarly career. A note as well in remembrance of my father, James Law Roberts, who passed away in 2018.

It has been a pleasure to work again with my editor at Polity Books, Louise Knight, and editorial assistant Inès Boxman. And appreciation to Susan Beer for her careful work in copyediting.

Notes

Epigraphs

"Barroso: European Union Is 'Non-Imperial Empire,'" Euractiv, July 10, 2007.

"PM Modi Townhall with Mark Zuckerberg at Facebook Headquarters," NDTV, September 27, 2015.

Xi Jinping, *The Governance of China, Volume 1* (Beijing: Foreign Languages Press, 2014), 304.

Joseph Biden Inaugural Address, January 20, 2021.

1 The Experiment

1 Lant Pritchett and Michael Woolcock, "Solutions When the Solution Is the Problem: Arraying the Disarray in Development." *World Development* 32.2 (2004): 191–212.

2 "Centralisation, c'est l'apoplexie au centre et la paralysie dans les extrémités": Félicité de Lamennais, 1848.

3 Charles-Louis Montesquieu, *Oeuvres De Montesquieu* (Paris: Belin, 1817), 105.

4 Alasdair Roberts, *Strategies for Governing: Reinventing Public Administration for a Dangerous Century* (Ithaca, NY: Cornell University Press, 2019), 27–28.

5 Malcolm Shaw, *International Law* (Cambridge University Press, 2008), ch. 20.

6 Alfred Stepan et al., *Crafting State-Nations* (Baltimore, MD: Johns Hopkins University Press, 2010), ch. 1.

7 Some students of empire define them as systems of domination.

If domination simply means control by a central authority, then we cannot distinguish between some unitary states and empires. Alternatively, we might define empires as systems in which one people dominates other peoples. But not all empires satisfy this definition. Some empires were ruled by monarchs who did not regard themselves as agents for any of the peoples they ruled, and minorities in some empires regarded central authorities as a check against oppression by provincial elites.

8 Joseph Tainter, *The Collapse of Complex Societies* (Cambridge University Press, 1988).

9 Stephen Howe, *Empire: A Very Short Introduction* (Oxford University Press, 2002), 16, 54, 102.

10 Josep Colomer, *The European Empire* (CreateSpace, 2016), 9.

11 Paul Strathern, *Empire: A New History of the World* (New York: Pegasus Books, 2020), 19.

12 Krishan Kumar, *Visions of Empire: How Five Imperial Regimes Shaped the World* (Princeton University Press, 2017), 385.

13 Ernest Barker, *The Ideas and Ideals of the British Empire* (Cambridge University Press, 1941).

14 Peter Crooks and Timothy Parsons, *Empires and Bureaucracy in World History: From Late Antiquity to the Twentieth Century* (Cambridge University Press, 2016), 3 and 105.

15 Krishan Kumar, *Empires: A Historical and Political Sociology*, (Cambridge, UK: Polity Press, 2020), 91; Howe, *Empire*, 15.

16 Irwin S. Tucker, *A History of Imperialism* (New York: Rand School of Social Science, 1920), 5.

17 John Darwin, *After Tamerlane: The Rise and Fall of Global Empires, 1400–2000* (London: Penguin, 2008), 23.

18 Strathern, *Empire*, 28.

19 Rein Taagepera, "Size and Duration of Empires: Systematics of Size," *Social Science Research* 7 (1978): 108–127, Table 2.

20 Excluding Antarctica: Philip Hoffman, *Why Did Europe Conquer the World?* (Princeton University Press, 2015), 2.

21 Japan began by annexing Korea in 1910. It occupied Manchuria in 1931.

22 John Campbell and John Hall, *The World of States* (London: Bloomsbury, 2015).

23 Ken Booth, *International Relations* (London: Hodder & Stoughton, 2014), ch. 2.

24 See the description of empires provided in the *Encyclopedia Britannica*, 1911, Volume IX.

25 Joe Painter and Alexander Jeffrey, *Political Geography: An Introduction to Space and Power* (London: Sage Publications, 2009), 20.

26 Paul Combes, "Social Evolution," *Literary Digest* 3.25 (1891): 678–679, 678.

27 Micheal Clodfelter, *Warfare and Armed Conflicts: A Statistical Encyclopedia of Casualty and Other Figures*, 4th edn. (Jefferson, NC: McFarland & Company, 2017), 184.

28 Strictly, against Prussia. Ibid., 182.

29 Walter Bagehot, "The Gains of the World by the Two Last Wars in Europe," *The Economist*, August 18, 1866, 966.

30 Friedrich List, *The National System of Political Economy* (London: Longmans, Green, 1885), 175–176.

31 Bagehot, "The Gains of the World by the Two Last Wars in Europe," 966.

32 Ibid.

33 John Acton, *The History of Freedom and Other Essays* (London: Macmillan, 1907), 295.

34 List, *National System*, 176.

35 George Grey, "The Federation of the Anglo-Saxon Race," *Public Opinion* 17.22 (1894): 521–522, 522.

36 Gustav Cohn, *Grundlegung Der Nationaloekonomie* (Stuttgart: F. Ente, 1885), 449.

37 John Seeley, *The Expansion of England* (Boston, MA: Roberts Brothers, 1883), 88–89, 301.

38 H.G. Wells, *A Short History of the World* (New York: Macmillan, 1922), chs. LX and LXVII.

39 There is debate about the threshold for small states: Tom Crowards, "Defining the Category of 'Small' States," *Journal of International Development* 14.2 (2002): 143–179.

40 Barry Bartmann, "Microstates in the International System" (1997), 10–11.

41 James Sheehan, *Where Have All the Soldiers Gone? The Transformation of Modern Europe* (Boston: Mariner Books, 2009), 3–21.

42 Shaw, *International Law*, ch. 8.

43 Inis Claude, "The Tension between Principle and Pragmatism in International Relations," *Review of International Studies* 19.3 (1993): 215–226, 220–221.

44 Lee Kuan Yew, *From Third World to First: The Singapore Story* (New York: HarperCollins Publishers, 2000), xiv–xv.

45 Generally, see: Jeffrey Frieden, *Global Capitalism: Its Fall and Rise in the Twentieth Century* (New York: W.W. Norton, 2020).

46 World Trade Organization, *World Trade Report 2011*, 124; *World Trade Report 2013*, 55–56.

47 Adrian Hastings, *The Construction of Nationhood: Ethnicity, Religion and Nationalism* (Cambridge University Press, 1997), 3.

48 Generally, see: Graham Robb, *The Discovery of France* (New York: W.W. Norton, 2007).

49 J.G. Herder, *J.G. Herder on Social and Political Culture* (Cambridge University Press, 1969), 324.

50 John Stuart Mill, *Considerations on Representative Government* (London: Parker, Son, and Bourn, 1861), 289–291.

51 Philippe Sands, *East West Street: On the Origins of Genocide and Crimes against Humanity* (London: Weidenfeld & Nicolson, 2017).

52 Daniel Yergin and Joseph Stanislaw, *The Commanding Heights* (New York: Simon & Schuster, 1998).

53 Thomas Piketty, *Capital in the Twenty-First Century* (Cambridge, MA: The Belknap Press, 2014), 27–33. John Judis, *The Populist Explosion* (New York: Columbia Global Reports, 2016).

54 Norman Angell, *The Great Illusion*, 4th edn. (London: G. P. Putnam's Sons, 1913), 322.

55 James Thomson Jr., "How Could Vietnam Happen?," *The Atlantic*, April, 1968, 47–53.

56 Robert Strayer, *Why Did the Soviet Union Collapse?* (Armonk, NY: M.E. Sharpe, 1998), 14.

57 Zygmunt Bauman, *Globalization: The Human Consequences* (New York: Columbia University Press, 1998), 56–57.

58 Kenichi Ohmae, *The End of the Nation State* (New York: Free Press, 1995), 11–12.

59 Jean-Marie Guéhenno, *The End of the Nation-State* (Minneapolis: University of Minnesota Press, 1995), 3 and 12.

60 Anthony Giddens, *Runaway World: How Globalisation Is Reshaping Our Lives*, 2nd edn. (New York: Routledge, 2003), xxiii and 3.

61 Alasdair Roberts, "The Nation-State: Not Dead Yet," *Wilson Quarterly*, Summer 2015.

62 "Italy Announces Tough New Measures as Coronavirus Death Toll Spikes," *ITV News*, March 22, 2020.

63 Michael Mandelbaum, *The Case for Goliath: How America Acts as the World's Government in the 21st Century* (New York, NY: Public Affairs, 2005), 3.

64 Katie Rogers and Nicholas Fandos, "Trump Tells Congresswomen to 'Go Back' to the Countries They Came From," *New York Times*, July 14, 2019.

65 By GDP (current US dollars): World Bank, World Development Indicators databank.
66 If GDP is calculated based on purchasing power parity. International Monetary Fund estimates, 2020.
67 Manmohan Singh, Address at the Meeting of National Development Council, December 9, 2006.
68 John Keay, *India: A History* (London: HarperPress, 2010), 509.
69 "An Economist's Guide to the World in 2050," *Bloomberg Businessweek*, November 12, 2020.
70 Luuk van Middelaar, *Alarums & Excursions: Improvising Politics on the European Stage* (Newcastle upon Tyne: Agenda Publishing, 2019), ch. 4.
71 Paul Dukes, *The Superpowers: A Short History* (London: Routledge, 2000), 1.
72 Derek Leebaert, *Grand Improvisation: America Confronts the British Superpower, 1945–1957* (New York: Farrar, Straus and Giroux, 2018), 482–483.
73 "Barroso: European Union Is 'Non-Imperial Empire,'" Euractiv, July 10, 2007.
74 Sunil Khilnani, *The Idea of India* (New York: Penguin Books, 2003), 179.
75 Robin Okey, *The Habsburg Monarchy* (New York: St. Martin's Press, 2001), 269.

2 Empires Always Die

1 Yuan Chen, "Legitimation Discourse and the Theory of the Five Elements in Imperial China," *Journal of Song-Yuan Studies* 44 (2014): 325–364, 327–328.
2 Evelyn Shuckburgh, *The Histories of Polybius*, 2 vols. (London: Macmillan, 1889), v.1:460–466 and v.2:529–530.
3 Ibn Khaldūn, *The Muqaddimah*, 3 vols. (New York: Pantheon Books, 1958), v.1:332–333 and 342–344.
4 Guanzhong Luo, *The Romance of the Three Kingdoms* (London: Penguin Books, 2018), 1.
5 Bernard Lewis, "Ottoman Observers of Ottoman Decline," *Islamic Studies* 1.1 (1962): 71–87, 79.
6 Bernard Lewis, *Islam in History: Ideas, People, and Events in the Middle East* (Chicago: Open Court, 1993), 233–238.
7 George Horne, *The Providence of God Manifested in the Rise and Fall of Empires* (Oxford: Daniel Prince, 1775).
8 C.F. Volney, *The Ruins* (New York: Peter Eckler, 1926), 13, 29, 36–37.

9 Emil Reich, *Success Among Nations* (New York: Harper & Brothers, 1904), 74.

10 C.V. Woodward, *The Burden of Southern History* (Baton Rouge, LA: Louisiana State University Press, 1960), 169.

11 *Hansard*, November 5, 1929.

12 For example: Piers Brendon, *The Decline and Fall of the British Empire, 1781–1997* (London: Jonathan Cape, 2007).

13 Rein Taagepera, "Size and Duration of Empires: Systematics of Size," *Social Science Research* 7 (1978): 108–127; "Size and Duration of Empires: Growth-Decline Curves, 3000 to 600 B.C.," *Social Science Research* 7 (1978): 180–196; "Size and Duration of Empires: Growth-Decline Curves, 600 B.C. To 600 A.D.," *Social Science History* 3.3/4 (1979): 115–138; "Expansion and Contraction Patterns of Large Polities: Context for Russia," *International Studies Quarterly* 41.3 (1997): 475–504.

14 Michael Doyle, *Empires* (Ithaca, NY: Cornell University Press, 1986), 137.

15 Timothy Parsons, *The Rule of Empires* (Oxford University Press, 2010), 4.

16 Charles Maier, *Among Empires: American Ascendancy and Its Predecessors* (Cambridge, MA: Harvard University Press, 2006), 76.

17 John Keay, *China: A History* (New York: Basic Books, 2009), 356 and 417–420; Christopher I. Beckwith, *Empires of the Silk Road* (Princeton University Press, 2009), 193–194.

18 A.W. Mitchell, *The Grand Strategy of the Habsburg Empire* (Princeton University Press, 2018), ix–x, 35–40, 320 and 337.

19 John Richards, *The Mughal Empire* (Cambridge University Press, 1993), 132–138.

20 C.R. Boxer, *The Portuguese Seaborne Empire, 1415–1825* (New York: Knopf, 1969), 111–137.

21 The United States also counted as an imperial power. It did not surrender sovereignty over the Philippines until 1946.

22 John Darwin, *Unfinished Empire: The Global Expansion of Britain* (New York: Bloomsbury Press, 2013), ch. 8.

23 See generally: Andrew Newman, *Safavid Iran: Rebirth of a Persian Empire* (London: I.B. Tauris, 2009).

24 Yitzchak Jaffe et al., "Improving Integration in Societal Consequences to Climate Change," *Proceedings of the National Academy of Sciences* 116.11 (2019): 4755.

25 Greg Woolf, *Rome: An Empire's Story* (Oxford University Press,

2012), 216; Kyle Harper, *The Fate of Rome: Climate, Disease, and the End of an Empire* (Princeton University Press, 2017), 129–136 and 188–198; Walter Scheidel, *The Science of Roman History: Biology, Climate, and the Future of the Past* (Princeton University Press, 2018), ch. 1.

26 Douglas Streusand, *Islamic Gunpowder Empires: Ottomans, Safavids, and Mughals* (Boulder, CO: Westview Press, 2011), 17–18; Ka-wai Fan, "Climatic Change and Dynastic Cycles in Chinese History: A Review Essay," *Climatic Change* 101.3 (2010): 565–573.

27 David Fischer, *The Great Wave: Price Revolutions and the Rhythm of History* (Oxford University Press, 1999), 265–267; Beckwith, *Empires of the Silk Road*, 221.

28 Geoffrey Parker, *Global Crisis: War, Climate Change and Catastrophe in the Seventeenth Century* (New Haven, CT: Yale University Press, 2017), 42–43, 270, 412, 507.

29 David Zhang et al., "Climatic Change, Wars and Dynastic Cycles in China over the Last Millennium," *Climatic Change* 76.3 (2006): 459–477.

30 Mike Davis, *Late Victorian Holocausts: El Niño Famines and the Making of the Third World* (New York: Verso, 2017), 59–65, 119, 153, 158, 163.

31 Harper, *Fate of Rome*, 4 and 15.

32 A.H.M. Jones, *The Later Roman Empire, 284–602* (Baltimore, MD: Johns Hopkins University Press, 1986), 287, 818, and 1043.

33 Lawrence Gunderson, "A Reassessment of the Decline of the Khmer Empire," *International Journal of Culture and History* 1.1 (2015): 63–66, 65.

34 William McNeill, *Plagues and Peoples* (New York: Anchor Books, 1989), 207.

35 C.R. Boxer, *Four Centuries of Portuguese Expansion, 1415–1825* (Berkeley: University of California Press, 1969), 27.

36 Glenn Trewartha, "Recent Thought on the Problem of White Acclimatization in the Wet Tropics," *Geographical Review* 16.3 (1926): 467–478, 467.

37 Bernard Lewis, *The Emergence of Modern Turkey* (Oxford University Press, 1961), 27–28.

38 Newman, *Safavid Iran*, 122.

39 Geoffrey Parker, *The Geopolitics of Domination* (New York: Routledge, 1988), 149–151.

40 Ray Huang, *China: A Macro History* (Armonk: M.E. Sharpe, 1997), 180–181.

41 William Maltby, *The Rise and Fall of the Spanish Empire* (New York: Palgrave Macmillan, 2009), 104, 125 and 141.

42 Krishan Kumar, *Visions of Empire: How Five Imperial Regimes Shaped the World* (Princeton University Press, 2017), 466.

43 C.R. Boxer, *The Dutch Seaborne Empire, 1600–1800* (New York: Knopf, 1965), 22.

44 Geoffrey Parker refers to these combinations as "fatal synergies": *Global Crisis*, xxi–xxii.

45 J.B. Bury, *History of the Later Roman Empire*, 2 vols. (London: Macmillan, 1923), v.1:311.

46 For a similar framework, see Kenneth Lieberthal's description of China's "imperial system": *Governing China: From Revolution through Reform*, 2nd edn. (New York: W.W. Norton, 2004), 6. Comparable concepts have been introduced by other students of empire. For example, "patterns of rule": Darwin, *Unfinished Empire*, 194. And "repertoires of rule": Jane Burbank and Frederick Cooper, *Empires in World History: Power and the Politics of Difference* (Princeton University Press, 2010), 3.

47 For similar categorizations, see: Parker, *Geopolitics of Domination*, 5; Michael Mann, *The Sources of Social Power, Vol. 1* (Cambridge University Press, 1986), 7. And the older concept of "political and administrative penetration": Martin Doornbos, "Concept-Making: The Case of Political Penetration," *Development and Change* 2.2 (1971): 98–106.

48 Yuri Pines, *The Book of Lord Shang: Apologetics of State Power in Early China* (New York: Columbia University Press, 2019), 64.

49 Dingxin Zhao, *The Confucian-Legalist State: A New Theory of Chinese History* (Oxford University Press, 2015), 199.

50 Gérard Chaliand et al., *A Global History of War* (Oakland: University of California Press, 2014), 48–54.

51 A.H.M. Jones, *The Decline of the Ancient World* (London: Longmans, 1966), ch. 3; J.H. Elliott, *Imperial Spain, 1469–1716* (Harmondsworth: Penguin, 1970), ch. 9.

52 A good example is the Spanish empire's attempt to control trade with its possessions in the New World: J.H. Elliott, *Empires of the Atlantic World: Britain and Spain in America, 1492–1830* (New Haven, CT: Yale University Press, 2006), 224–227.

53 Yuri Pines, *The Everlasting Empire: The Political Culture of Ancient China and Its Imperial Legacy* (Princeton University Press, 2012), 22 and 149.

54 Mann, *Sources of Social Power*, 237.

55 Pieter Judson, *The Habsburg Empire: A New History* (Cambridge, MA: Belknap Press, 2016), 82.

56 See John Fairbank and Merle Goldman, *China: A New History*, 2nd edn. (Cambridge, MA: Belknap Press, 2006), 179–182.

57 Boxer, *The Dutch Seaborne Empire*, 108. The same mentality prevailed in other empires. Within the Spanish empire, it was expressed in the principle, "Se obedece pero no se cumple": Maltby, *Rise and Fall of the Spanish Empire*, 76. A Chinese proverb says: "The mountains are high and the emperor far away": David Eimer, *The Emperor Far Away: Travels at the Edge of China* (London: Bloomsbury, 2014). In the 1930s, a Soviet official in Turkestan observed: "Moscow is so very far away, so we do what seems right to us": Alf Brun, *Troublous Times: Experiences in Bolshevik Russia and Turkestan* (London: Constable, 1931), 78.

58 As Istvan Kristó-Nagy observes: "The administrative systems of the Islamicate states consisted of parallel hierarchies of innumerable bureaus that complemented and supervised one another. The overlapping machinery promised a form of control, but . . . did not always result in efficiency": "Conflict and Cooperation between Arab Rulers and Persian Administrators in the Formative Period of Islamdom," in *Empires and Bureaucracy in World History*, ed. Peter Crooks and Timothy Parsons (Cambridge University Press, 2016), 54–80, 70.

59 Carlo Cipolla, "Introduction," in *The Economic Decline of Empires*, ed. Carlo Cipolla (London: Methuen, 1970), 1–15, 5–7.

60 Huang, *China: A Macro History*, 65–66; Keay, *China: A History*, 179–183.

61 Bernard Lewis, "The Arabs in Decline," in *The Economic Decline of Empires*, ed. Carlo Cipolla (London: Methuen, 1970), 102–120, 102.

62 Patrick Kinross, *The Ottoman Centuries: The Rise and Fall of the Turkish Empire* (New York: Morrow, 1977).

63 "All-under-heaven is a sacred vessel . . . Who grasps it will lose it": Lao Tzu, *Tao Te Ching: The Classic Book of Integrity and the Way* (New York: Bantam Books, 1990), 73.

64 Zhao, *Confucian-Legalist State*, 269–274.

65 Pines, *Everlasting Empire*, 21–25 and 86–87.

66 Mann, *Sources of Social Power*, 273; Michael Loewe, *The Government of the Qin and Han Empires* (Indianapolis: Hackett, 2006), 62.

67 S.E. Finer, *The History of Government from the Earliest Times*

(Oxford University Press, 1997), v.1:479; Mann, *Sources of Social Power*, 273; Loewe, *Government of the Qin and Han Empires*, 84.

68 Michael Whitby, "'The Late Roman Empire Was before All Things a Bureaucratic State,'" in *Empires and Bureaucracy in World History*, ed. Peter Crooks and Timothy Parsons (Cambridge University Press, 2016), 129–146, 131–132.

69 Darwin, *Unfinished Empire*, 194.

70 Frederick Lugard, *The Dual Mandate in British Tropical Africa* (Edinburgh: W. Blackwood and Sons, 1922), chs. 10 and 11.

71 Jan Morris, *Pax Britannica: The Climax of an Empire* (London: Faber, 1968), 269; Brendon, *Decline and Fall of the British Empire*, 230–333.

72 J.H. Parry, *Trade and Dominion: The European Oversea Empires in the Eighteenth Century* (London: Weidenfeld and Nicolson, 1971), 305–306.

73 Friedrich Naumann and Christabel M. Meredith, *Central Europe* (New York: Knopf, 1917), 183–184.

74 See Marsha Rozenblit's description of how Jews within the Habsburg empire viewed Emperor Franz Joseph: *Reconstructing a National Identity: The Jews of Habsburg Austria During World War I* (Oxford University Press, 2001), 28–29.

75 Cassius Dio, *Dio's Roman History* (New York: Macmillan, 1914), VI.115–117; Khaldūn, *The Muqaddimah*, v1: 337.

76 Richard Pipes, *Russian Conservatism and Its Critics: A Study in Political Culture* (New Haven, CT: Yale University Press, 2005), 71. The Russian statesman Sergei Witte argued similarly for autocracy and "strict centralization" a century later.

77 Herbert Storing and Murray Dry, *The Complete Anti-Federalist* (University of Chicago Press, 1985), 153, 167, 256.

78 About the Portuguese empire, C.R. Boxer observes: "Everything depended . . . upon the personal decision of the king. . . [Decisions] often involved delays of anything from two to ten years": Boxer, *Four Centuries of Portuguese Expansion*, 81.

79 Sam Whimster, "Empires and Bureaucracy: Means of Appropriation and Communication," in *Empires and Bureaucracy in World History*, ed. Peter Crooks and Timothy Parsons (Cambridge University Press, 2016), 437–456, 453.

80 Geoffrey Parker, *The Grand Strategy of Philip II* (New Haven, CT: Yale University Press, 1998), ch. 1.

81 Karl Deutsch argued that the "limited capacity of centralized decision-making" was one of the vulnerabilities of totalitarian

systems: "Cracks in the Monolith," in *Totalitarianism*, ed. Carl Friedrich (Cambridge, MA: Harvard University Press, 1954), 308–333, 318.

82 John Fairbank and Ssŭ-yü Têng, *Ch'ing Administration: Three Studies* (Cambridge, MA: Harvard University Press, 1960), 69.

83 Bury, *History of the Later Roman Empire*, 311–312.

84 Bernard Lewis, *The Middle East: A Brief History of the Last 2,000 Years* (New York, NY: Scribner, 1995), 129; Streusand, *Islamic Gunpowder Empires*, 51–56.

85 Mike Paterson, *Nicholas II, the Last Tsar* (London: Robinson, 2017), 8 and 19.

86 Streusand, *Islamic Gunpowder Empires*, 73; Newman, *Safavid Iran*, 175–176.

87 Jones, *Later Roman Empire*, 38–42.

88 Burbank and Cooper, *Empires in World History*, 104–114.

89 Boxer, *Dutch Seaborne Empire*, 329–330.

90 Denis Twitchett and John Fairbank, *The Cambridge History of China* (Cambridge University Press, 1978), 179–180.

91 Pines, *Everlasting Empire*, 66.

92 The Spanish system of council decision-making became more risk-averse over time and "often seemed interminable": *Rise and Fall of the Spanish Empire*, 79.

93 Edward Gibbon emphasized the role of self-absorption and moral dissipation in the collapse of the Roman empire: *The Decline and Fall of the Roman Empire* (New York: Modern Library, 2003).

94 Scholars have used different terms to describe the imperial creed. "Providential vision": Parker, *Grand Strategy of Philip II*, 286. "Mission or purpose": Kumar, *Visions of Empire*, 385. "Master narrative" or "civilizational gestalt": Mir Tamim Ansary, *The Invention of Yesterday* (New York: PublicAffairs, 2019), 54.

95 Krishan Kumar, *Empires: A Historical and Political Sociology* (Cambridge: Polity Press, 2020), 6–13.

96 Khaldūn, *Muqaddimah*, v1:320.

97 Kinross, *Ottoman Centuries*, 170–171, 205–206, 549–552.

98 J.B. Trend, *The Civilization of Spain* (Oxford University Press, 1944), 52 and 82.

99 Douglas Boin, *Alaric the Goth: An Outsider's History of the Fall of Rome* (New York: W.W. Norton, 2020), 7.

100 Zhao, *Confucian-Legalist State*, 15.

101 Michael Broers, "'Les Enfants Du Siècle': An Empire of Young Professionals and the Creation of a Bureaucratic, Imperial Ethos

in Napoleonic Europe," in *Empires and Bureaucracy in World History*, ed. Peter Crooks and Timothy Parsons (Cambridge University Press, 2016), 344–363, 357–358.

102 Gerrit Gong, *The Standard of "Civilization" in International Society* (Oxford: Clarendon Press, 1984), 14–15.

103 Generally, see: Mann, *Sources of Social Power*, chs. 8 and 9.

104 The glue metaphor is provided by Amy Chua: *Day of Empire: How Hyperpowers Rise to Global Dominance* (New York: Doubleday, 2007), ch. 12.

105 Ernest Gellner, *Nations and Nationalism* (Ithaca, NY: Cornell University Press, 1983), ch. 1.

106 Jones, *Later Roman Empire*, 71–76.

107 John Keay, *India: A History* (London: HarperPress, 2010), 342–363.

108 For example, see: Kristó-Nagy, "Conflict and Cooperation," 66 and 76.

109 Regarding the Inquisition: Maltby, *Rise and Fall of the Spanish Empire*, 93–94.

110 Whitby, "The Late Roman Empire," 138–139.

111 Boxer, *Dutch Seaborne Empire*, 138–139 and 150–160.

112 Karen Barkey, *Empire of Difference: The Ottomans in Comparative Perspective* (Cambridge University Press, 2008), 130–132 and 143–146.

113 Geoffrey Hosking, *Russia: People and Empire, 1552–1917* (Cambridge, MA: Harvard University Press, 1997), ch. 3.

114 Jawaharlal Nehru, *The Unity of India*, 2nd edn. (London: Drummond, 1942), 30–31.

115 Kumar, *Visions of Empire*. By contrast, Parsons says empires were never "humane, liberal or tolerant": *Rule of Empires*, 4.

116 "Tolerance was indispensable to the achievement of hegemony": Chua, *Day of Empire*, xxi.

117 Richards, *Mughal Empire*, 36.

118 Jawaharlal Nehru, *Glimpses of World History*, 4th edn. (London: Drummond, 1949), 773–774.

119 Steven Beller, *A Concise History of Austria* (Cambridge University Press, 2006), 152.

120 Edward Gibbon, *The Decline and Fall of the Roman Empire* (New York: Putnam, 1962), 230.

121 Huang, *China: A Macro History*, 256.

122 The British empire "was a kind of fiction, or bluff, in that it implied a far stronger power at the centre than really existed": Morris, *Pax Britannica*, 177.

123 J.M. Coetzee, *Waiting for the Barbarians* (New York: Penguin Books, 2010), 133.
124 Darwin, *Unfinished Empire*, xiii.
125 See Arnold Toynbee on the dangers of "idolizing" techniques and institutions: *A Study of History* (Oxford University Press, 1987), ch. 16.
126 "We know that . . . nothing is eternal, particularly in the institutions of man; yet, by a sort of fiction in language, . . . what is known to be temporary is considered as perpetual": William Playfair, *An Inquiry into the Permanent Causes of the Decline and Fall of Powerful and Wealthy Nations* (London: Greenland & Norris, 1805), 6–7.

3 Are Superstates More Durable?

1 Timothy Parsons, *The Rule of Empires* (Oxford University Press, 2010), 8–9.
2 Xi Jinping, "Speech to the Fifth Plenary Session of the Nineteenth Central Committee," QSTheory.cn, January 11, 2021.
3 John Keay, *China: A History* (New York: Basic Books, 2009), 404.
4 United Nations, *Growth of the World's Urban and Rural Population, 1920–2000* (New York, 1969), Table 8.
5 United Nations, World Urbanization Prospects, 2019 Revision.
6 World Bank estimates of slum populations: data.worldbank.org/indicator/.
7 Organisation for Economic Co-operation and Development, *How Was Life? Global Well-Being since 1820* (Paris, 2014), 93.
8 UNESCO, *World Illiteracy at Mid-Century: A Statistical Study* (Paris, 1957), Table 2.
9 World Bank data on literacy rates: data.worldbank.org/indicator/.
10 Fernand Braudel, *The Mediterranean and the Mediterranean World in the Age of Philip II* (New York: HarperCollins, 1992), 355–372.
11 J.G. Bartholomew, *An Atlas of Economic Geography* (Oxford University Press, 1914), Table 12b.
12 Federal Highway Administration, *2009 National Household Travel Survey: Summary of Travel Trends* (Washington, 2011), Table 12.
13 Ministry of Finance, *Economic Survey 2016–17* (Delhi, 2017), 265.
14 Hugh Morris, "The Largest Human Migration on the Planet," *The Telegraph*, January 16, 2017.
15 W.H. Gunston, "Telephonic Development of the World," *Telegraph and Telephone Journal* 11.118 (1925): 60–62, 62.

16 McKinsey India, *Digital India* (Delhi: McKinsey Global institute, 2019), 2. Historic data on fixed lines: data.worldbank.org/indicator.

17 Jörg Raab and H.B. Milward, "Dark Networks as Problems," *Journal of Public Administration Research and Theory* 13.4 (2003): 413–439.

18 Secretary General of the United Nations, *Report on Small Arms and Light Weapons* (New York, 2019).

19 Parsons, *The Rule of Empires*, 12 and 44.

20 John Gaddis, *The Long Peace: Inquiries into the History of the Cold War* (Oxford University Press, 1987), ch. 8.

21 Scott Gordon, *Controlling the State: Constitutionalism from Ancient Athens to Today* (Cambridge, MA: Harvard University Press, 1999), 295.

22 Edmund Fawcett, *Liberalism: The Life of an Idea* (Princeton University Press, 2014).

23 Universal Declaration of Human Rights, Article 21.

24 Francis Fukuyama, *The End of History and the Last Man* (New York: Free Press, 1992).

25 Martin Ravallion, *The Economics of Poverty: History, Measurement, and Policy* (Oxford University Press, 2016), 80–81.

26 Arnold Toynbee, *A Study of History* (Oxford University Press, 1987), 1.287.

27 Estimates from the Groningen Growth and Development Centre: www.rug.nl/ggdc/.

28 World Bank data on trade volume relative to GDP: data.worldbank. org/indicator/.

29 Ding Yi, "China's Mobile Payments Grew More Than 70 Percent in Q4," *CX Tech*, March 18, 2020.

30 OECD, *Tackling Vulnerability in the Informal Economy* (Paris, 2019), ch. 1.

31 Joseph Schumpeter, *Capitalism, Socialism, and Democracy* (London: Allen and Unwin, 1976), 77 and 83.

32 Thomas Piketty, *Capital in the Twenty-First Century* (Cambridge, MA: Belknap Press, 2014).

33 Charles Kindleberger, *Manias, Panics and Crashes*, 5th edn. (Hoboken, NJ: John Wiley & Sons, 2005).

34 Intergovernmental Panel on Climate Change, *Climate Change 2014: Synthesis Report* (Geneva, 2014), 2–6.

35 Ibid., 13–16; Intergovernmental Panel on Climate Change, *Climate Change 2014: Impacts, Adaptation and Vulnerability* (Geneva, 2014), 4–20.

36 Intergovernmental Panel on Climate Change, *Climate Change 2014: Mitigation of Climate Change* (Geneva, 2014), 10.

37 United Nations Environment Programme, *Emissions Gap Report 2020* (Nairobi, 2020), xiii–xxv.

38 Notoriously by Robert Angell: *The Great Illusion*, 4th edn. (London: G.P. Putnam's Sons, 1913), ix–xiii.

39 About 1.3 million for India, 1.4 million for the United States and European Union, and India, and 2.3 million for China, based on reports for 2016–2020.

40 Generally, see: Taylor Owen, *Disruptive Power: The Crisis of the State in the Digital Age* (Oxford University Press, 2015).

41 National Intelligence Council, *Global Trends 2040* (Washington, 2021), 40–41.

42 Nancy Stepan, *Eradication: Ridding the World of Diseases Forever?* (London: Reaktion Books, 2016), ch. 6.

43 F.M. Burnet and D.O. White, *Natural History of Infectious Disease*, 4th edn. (Cambridge University Press, 1972), 263.

44 Mark Honigsbaum, *The Pandemic Century* (London: W.H. Allen, 2020).

45 William McNeill, *Plagues and Peoples* (New York: Anchor Books, 1989), 152–153.

46 Samuel P. Huntington, "Dead Souls: The Denationalization of the American Elite," *The National Interest*, 75 (2004): 5–18; Harsh Gupta and Rajeev Mantri, *A New Idea of India* (Chennai: Westland, 2020), 23–28.

47 Alasdair Roberts, *The End of Protest: How Free-Market Capitalism Learned to Control Dissent* (Ithaca, NY: Cornell University Press, 2013), ch. 3.

48 Financial Times, "The World Should Beware a Technology Cold War," *Financial Times*, December 11, 2019.

49 *Government Finance Statistics: Summary Tables, Data 1995–2019* (Luxembourg: Eurostat, 2020); Yuen Yuen Ang, "Counting Cadres: A Comparative View of the Size of China's Public Employment," *The China Quarterly* 211 (2012): 676–696; S.K. Das, *The Civil Services in India* (Oxford University Press, 2013), 24; Federal Reserve, fred.stlouisfed.org/series/USGOVT.

50 Paul Light, *Fact Sheet on the New True Size of Government* (New York: Wagner School of Public Service, September 5, 2003).

51 Richard Rose, "Ungovernability: Is There Fire Behind the Smoke?," *Political Studies* 27.3 (1979): 351–370.

52 Daniel Yergin and Joseph Stanislaw, *The Commanding Heights* (New York: Simon & Schuster, 1998).

53 Donald Kettl, *The Global Public Management Revolution* (Washington, DC: Brookings Institution, 2005).

54 Alasdair Roberts, "The Third and Fatal Shock: How Pandemic Killed the Millennial Paradigm," *Public Administration Review* 80.4 (2020): 603–609.

55 Arthur M. Schlesinger, *The Imperial Presidency* (Boston: Houghton Mifflin, 1973).

56 Sanjay Ruparelia, "Modi's Saffron Democracy," *Dissent* 66.2 (2019): 94–106, 97.

57 Katja Drinhausen et al., *The CCP's Next Century* (Berlin: MERICS, 2021), 7.

58 New York Times, "Mrs. Gandhi's Speech," *New York Times*, June 27, 1975, 12; Xinmin Zhou, *Xi Jinping's Governance and the Future of China* (New York: Skyhorse Publishing, 2017), ch. 1.

59 Michael Ignatieff, "The Burden," *New York Times*, January 5, 2003.

60 Todd Purdum, "Washington, We Have a Problem," *Vanity Fair*, September, 2010, 291.

61 Barack Obama, *A Promised Land* (New York: Crown, 2020), 642.

62 Matea Gold et al., "Thousands Protest Trump in Rallies across the US," *Washington Post*, November 11, 2016.

63 Emma Anderson, "Orbán Slams Brussels Elite Who've 'Lost Touch with Reality,'" *Politico*, March 24, 2019.

64 Sudheendra Kulkarni, "India under Modi," in *Making Sense of Modi's India*, ed. M. Desai (Delhi: HarperCollins, 2016), 120–137, 131.

65 Anthony Pagden, *The Idea of Europe: From Antiquity to the European Union* (Cambridge University Press, 2002), 20.

66 American Academy of Arts and Sciences, *Our Common Purpose: Reinventing American Democracy for the 21st Century* (Cambridge MA, 2020), 18–19; George Packer, *Last Best Hope: America in Crisis and Renewal* (New York: Farrar, Straus and Giroux, 2021), 84.

67 Kerry Brown, *China's Dream: The Culture of Chinese Communism and the Secret Sources of Its Power* (Cambridge, UK: Polity, 2018), 45–52.

68 Marc Thiessen, "Trump's Defense of Western Civilization Is Not Alt-Right," *Washington Post*, July 12, 2017.

69 Christopher Coker, *The Rise of the Civilizational State* (Cambridge, UK: Polity Press, 2019).

70 Jan-Werner Müller, *Constitutional Patriotism* (Princeton University Press, 2007).

71 Alfred Stepan et al., *Crafting State-Nations: India and Other Multinational Democracies* (Baltimore, MD: Johns Hopkins University Press, 2010), 13.

72 Aakash Rathore and Ashis Nandy, eds., *Vision for a Nation* (Gurgaon: Vintage India, 2019), xviii–xix; Ivan Krastev and Stephen Holmes, *The Light That Failed: A Reckoning* (London: Allen Lane, 2019), 62–66.

73 E.B. Cromer, *Ancient and Modern Imperialism* (London: Murray, 1910), 113.

74 S.R. Sen, "Heartland and Borderland," *Economic and Political Weekly* 26.20 (1991): 1271–1273.

75 M.E. Sarotte, "China's Fear of Contagion: Tiananmen Square and the Power of the European Example," *International Security* 37.2 (2012): 156–182, 166.

76 Martin Dimitrov, "European Lessons for China: Tiananmen 1989 and Beyond," in *The Long 1989*, ed. P. Kosicki and K. Kunakhovich (Central European University Press, 2019), 61–88, 74.

77 Brown, *China's Dream*, 127.

78 Sebastian Rosato, "Europe's Troubles: Power Politics and the State of the European Project," *International Security* 35.4 (2011): 45–86, 47.

79 Joni Virkkunen, "Post-Socialist Borderland: Promoting or Challenging the Enlarged European Union?," *Geografiska Annaler: Series B* 83.3 (2001): 141–151.

80 Ian Traynor, "Hungary Prime Minister Hits out at EU Interference in National Day Speech," *Guardian*, March 15, 2012.

81 "Martin Helme: Nothing Scandalous About Comparing EU to Soviet Union," *Eesti Rahvusringhääling*, July 24, 2019.

82 George Soros, "Europe, Please Wake Up," *Project Syndicate*, February 11, 2019.

83 George Kennan, *Around the Cragged Hill: A Personal and Political Philosophy* (New York: W.W. Norton, 1993), 147.

84 Daniel Moynihan, *Pandaemonium: Ethnicity in International Politics* (Oxford University Press, 1993), 168–174.

85 Robert Kaplan, *The Coming Anarchy: Shattering the Dreams of the Post Cold War* (New York: Random House, 2000), 60.

86 Inaugural Address, January 20, 2021.

4 The United States: An Old Hazard Returns

1 Associated Press, "Southern Novelist Adjudged Winner of Pulitzer Award," *Dallas Morning News*, May 5, 1933, 3.

2 For following quotations, see: Frederick Jackson Turner, *The Significance of Sections in American History* (New York: H. Holt and Company, 1932), 23, 27, 37, 45, 51, and 289.

3 Barbara Walter, *How Civil Wars Start* (New York: Crown, 2022), 159.

4 Karen Treverton and Gregory Treverton. "Civil War Is Coming," *The Article*, December 14, 2021.

5 George Bancroft, *History of the Formation of the Constitution of the United States* (New York: Appleton, 1885), v.1:311 and 443.

6 Markus Hünemörder, *The Society of the Cincinnati* (New York: Berghahn Books, 2006), 18.

7 George Washington, *Last Will and Testament of Gen. George Washington* (Boston: John Russell, 1800), 6.

8 Alexander Hamilton, James Madison, and John Jay, *The Federalist* (New York: The Colonial Press, 1901).

9 Letter from Thomas Jefferson to James Madison, April 27, 1809.

10 "American Policy," *Boston Courier*, November 30, 1840, 3.

11 George Washington, *The Writings of George Washington*, 14 vols. (New York: G.P. Putnam's sons, 1889), v.9.58.

12 Alexander Hamilton, *The Works of Alexander Hamilton*, 7 vols. (New York: J.F. Trow, 1851), v.7.184.

13 Frederick Jackson Turner, *Rise of the New West, 1819–1829* (New York: Harper and Brothers, 1906), 74.

14 Roxanne Dunbar-Ortiz, *An Indigenous Peoples' History of the United States* (Boston: Beacon Press, 2014), ch. 5.

15 Remini, *A Short History of the United States* (New York: HarperCollins, 2008), 46–47.

16 *American Insurance Company v. Canter*, 26 US (1 Pet.) 511 (1828).

17 Waldemar Westergaard, "Senator Thomas R. Bard and the Arizona-New Mexico Statehood Controversy," *Annual Publications of the Historical Society of Southern California* 11 (1919): 9–17, 11.

18 Alpheus Snow, *The Administration of Dependencies* (New York: G.P. Putnam's Sons, 1902), 545, 578 and 603.

19 Hamilton, Madison, and Jay, *The Federalist*, 22–33.

20 Donald Hickey, *The War of 1812: A Forgotten Conflict* (Champaign: University of Illinois Press, 2012), ch. 10.

21 Benjamin Park, "The Angel of Nullification: Imagining Disunion

in an Era before Secession," *Journal of the Early Republic* 37.3 (2017): 507–536.

22 Joseph Story, *A Familiar Exposition of the Constitution of the United States* (Boston: Webb, 1842), 39.

23 Stanley Engerman and Robert Gallman, *The Cambridge Economic History of the United States, Vol.* 2 (Cambridge University Press, 2000), chs. 8 and 12.

24 Michael Greve, "Federalism," in *Oxford Handbook of the Constitution*, ed. M. Tushnet et al. (Oxford University Press, 2015), 431–452.

25 Ilya Somin, "The Supreme Court of the United States," in *Courts in Federal Countries*, ed. N. Aroney and J. Kincaid (University of Toronto Press, 2017), 440–481, 448–453.

26 Robert Remini, *The Life of Andrew Jackson* (New York: Perennial, 2001), 245–246.

27 Eric Foner, *Reconstruction: America's Unfinished Revolution, 1863–1877*, 3rd edn. (New York: Harper Perennial, 2002).

28 Humphrey Desmond, "The Sectional Feature in American Politics," *Transactions of the Wisconsin Academy of Sciences, Arts and Letters* 8 (1888): 1–10, 10.

29 James Bryce, *The American Commonwealth*, 3 vols. (London: Macmillan, 1888), v.2.20.

30 On the relationship between democratization and elite bargaining, see: D.H. Donald, *An Excess of Democracy: The American Civil War and the Social Process* (Oxford: Clarendon Press, 1960).

31 Hamilton, Madison, and Jay, *The Federalist*, 375–376.

32 Alexander Keyssar, *The Right to Vote* (New York: Basic Books, 2009), ch. 2.

33 Walter Bagehot, *The English Constitution* (London: H.S. King, 1872), lvi–lviii, 222–227.

34 Bryce, *The American Commonwealth*, 1.83–85, 81.98–100, 101.150.

35 *Washington Times*, January 16, 1915, 3.

36 Robert Alleman and Jason Mazzone, "The Case for Returning Politicians to the Supreme Court," *Hastings Law Journal* 61.6 (2010): 1353–1406, Table A.

37 Arthur Schlesinger Jr., *The Age of Jackson* (Boston: Little, Brown, 1953), 54.

38 See David Hendrickson's discussion of the "*Staatsräison* of the American states-union": *Peace Pact: The Lost World of the American Founding* (Lawrence, KS: University Press of Kansas, 2003), xii and 271.

39 Peter Knupfer, *The Union as It Is: Constitutional Unionism and*

Sectional Compromise, 1787–1861 (Chapel Hill, NC: University of North Carolina Press, 1991).

40 Worthington Ford, *Writings of John Quincy Adams*, 7 vols. (New York: Macmillan Co., 1913), v.6: 129.

41 Turner, *Significance of Sections*, 50.

42 Julian Boyd, "Thomas Jefferson's 'Empire of Liberty,'" *The Virginia Quarterly Review* 24.4 (1948): 538–554, 547–548.

43 Paul Kramer, "Empires, Exceptions, and Anglo-Saxons: Race and Rule between the British and United States Empires, 1880–1910," *The Journal of American History* 88.4 (2002): 1315–1353.

44 Bryce, *American Commonwealth*, v.2.621.

45 Sudhindra Bose, *Fifteen Years in America* (Calcutta: Kar and Majumber, 1923), ch. 19.

46 Irwin S. Tucker, *A History of Imperialism* (New York: Rand School of Social Science, 1920), 5.

47 Frederick Jackson Turner, "The Significance of the Section in American History," *Wisconsin Magazine of History* 8.3 (1925): 255–280, 268.

48 Frank Baumgartner and Bryan Jones, *The Politics of Information* (University of Chicago Press, 2015), 117.

49 Historical Statistics of the United States, Series Aa142, Ea740, Ea748, Ea899, and Ed26.

50 Alasdair Roberts, *Four Crises of American Democracy: Representation, Mastery, Discipline, Anticipation* (Oxford University Press, 2017), 85–90.

51 Walter Trattner, *From Poor Law to Welfare State* (New York: Free Press, 1999), chs. 13 and 14.

52 Office of Management and Budget, *Historical Tables*, Table 3.1.

53 Remini, *Short History of the United States*, ch. 9.

54 R.E. McClendon, "Violations of Secrecy *in Re* Senate Executive Sessions, 1789–1929," *The American Historical Review* 51.1 (1945): 35–54, 37.

55 Kevin McGuire, "The Institutionalization of the US Supreme Court," *Political Analysis* 12.2 (2004): 128–142; Keith Whittington, *Repugnant Laws: Judicial Review of Acts of Congress from the Founding to the Present* (Lawrence, KS: University Press of Kansas, 2019), 27–29 and 176–177.

56 Michael Glennon, *National Security and Double Government* (Oxford University Press, 2015).

57 Data on White House personnel: www.presidency.ucsb.edu/statistics/.

58 *Historical Statistics of the United States*, Series Ea894 and Ea899.

59 Hugh Heclo, *A Government of Strangers: Executive Politics in Washington* (Washington: Brookings Institution, 1977), ch. 3.

60 Eric Kaufmann, *The Rise and Fall of Anglo-America* (Cambridge, MA: Harvard University Press, 2004), 177–203.

61 In his 1963 gubernatorial inaugural address, Wallace promised to defend "the Great Anglo-Saxon Southland."

62 George Sokolsky, "These Days," *Canton Repository*, August 25, 1948, 15.

63 Mary Dudziak, *Cold War Civil Rights: Race and the Image of American Democracy* (Princeton University Press, 2011).

64 Engerman and Gallman, *The Cambridge Economic History of the United States*.

65 Abraham Maslow articulated a theory about the "hierarchy of needs" in the early 1950s that was often used to explain the change in American politics: *Motivation and Personality* (New York: Harper, 1954).

66 Samuel Walker, *The Rights Revolution: Rights and Community in Modern America* (Oxford University Press, 1998).

67 V.O. Key, *Politics, Parties, and Pressure Groups*, 5th edn. (New York: Crowell, 1964), 341 and 386–387.

68 Arthur N. Holcombe, *The New Party Politics* (New York: W.W. Norton, 1933), 11.

69 V.O. Key, *American State Politics: An Introduction* (New York: Knopf, 1956), 26–28 and 50–51.

70 Schattschneider, *The Semisovereign People*, 86–96.

71 Daniel Bell, *The End of Ideology: On the Exhaustion of Political Ideas in the Fifties* (Glencoe, IL: Free Press, 1960), 64, 99–100, 251.

72 Commencement Address at Yale University, June 11, 1962.

73 William Safire, *Lend Me Your Ears: Great Speeches in History* (New York: W.W. Norton, 2004).

74 Richard Nixon, "Remarks on the NBC and CBS Radio Networks: The Nature of the Presidency, September 19, 1968," The American Presidency Project.

75 Generally, see: Ira Katznelson, *Fear Itself: The New Deal and the Origins of Our Time* (New York: Liveright, 2013).

76 Howard Odum, *The Way of the South: Toward the Regional Balance of America* (New York: Macmillan, 1947), 49, 232 and 241.

77 Juan Williams, *Eyes on the Prize: America's Civil Rights Years, 1954–1965* (New York, NY: Viking, 1987), chs. 4 and 7.

78 Julian Zelizer, *The Fierce Urgency of Now: Lyndon Johnson, Congress, and the Battle for the Great Society* (New York: Penguin Press, 2015), 8–9 and 169.

79 Trattner, *From Poor Law to Welfare State*, 325–327.

80 William Safire, "New Federalist Paper No. 1," *Publius* 2.1 (1972): 98–115, 100–101.

81 Topeka Messenger, "Nixon's Plan Called Phony," *Topeka Messenger*, September 5, 1969, 2.

82 For example, see: Patricia McGee Crotty, "The New Federalism Game: Primacy Implementation of Environmental Policy," *Publius* 17.2 (1987): 53–67.

83 Ellen Melton, "'Old South' Will Die, Negro Leader Says," *Daytona Beach Morning Journal*, October 3, 1955, 2.

84 Safire, "New Federalist Paper No. 1," 104.

85 Schattschneider, *The Semisovereign People*, 89.

86 Hedrick Smith, *The Power Game: How Washington Works* (New York: Random House, 1988), 27–28.

87 John Kenneth Galbraith, *A Tenured Professor* (Boston: Houghton Mifflin, 1990), 53.

88 Ronald Reagan, First Inaugural Address, January 20, 1981.

89 For employment data, see: *Historical Statistics of the United States*, Series Ea968. Expenditure as share of GDP: Office of Management and Budget Historical Tables, Table 3.1.

90 John Baker, "State Police Powers and the Federalization of Local Crime," *Temple Law Review* 72 (1999): 673–714, 674.

91 Thomas Birkland and Sarah DeYoung, "Emergency Response, Doctrinal Confusion, and Federalism in the Deepwater Horizon Oil Spill," *Publius* 41.3 (2011): 471–493, 477–479.

92 Andrew Rudalevige, "No Child Left Behind: Forging a Congressional Compromise," in *No Child Left Behind?*, ed. P. Peterson and M. West (Brookings Institution Press, 2003), 23–54, 24.

93 Alasdair Roberts, *The Collapse of Fortress Bush: The Crisis of Authority in American Government* (New York University Press, 2008), chs. 2 and 4.

94 Julian Zelizer, *The Presidency of Barack Obama* (Princeton University Press, 2018), ch. 3.

95 Carol Weissert and Matthew Uttermark, "Glass Half Full: Decentralization in Health Policy," *State and Local Government Review* 49.3 (2017): 199–214, 199.

96 Greg Goelzhauser and David Konisky, "The State of American

Federalism 2019–2020," *Publius: The Journal of Federalism* 50.3 (2020): 311–343.

97 Jocelyn Kiley, "In Polarized Era, Fewer Americans Hold a Mix of Conservative and Liberal Views," Pew Research Center, October 23, 2017.

98 Daniel Moskowitz, Jon Rogowski, and James Snyder Jr., *Parsing Party Polarization in Congress* (Cambridge, MA: National Bureau of Economic Research, 2019).

99 David Wasserman and Ally Flinn, *2017 Cook Political Report Partisan Voter Index* (Washington, DC: Cook Political Report, 2017).

100 Alan Abramowitz, *The Great Alignment: Race, Party Transformation, and the Rise of Donald Trump* (New Haven, CT: Yale University Press, 2018), 144–146; David Hopkins, *Red Fighting Blue: How Geography and Electoral Rules Polarize American Politics* (Cambridge University Press, 2017), 48–57.

101 Dante Scala and Kenneth Johnson, "Political Polarization Along the Rural-Urban Continuum? The Geography of the Presidential Vote, 2000–2016," *Annals of the American Academy of Political and Social Science* 672.1 (2017): 162–184.

102 Turner, *The Significance of Sections in American History*, 47–48.

103 Nolan McCarty et al., *Polarized America: The Dance of Ideology and Unequal Riches* (Cambridge, MA: MIT Press, 2006).

104 Cass Sunstein, *#Republic: Divided Democracy in the Age of Social Media* (Princeton University Press, 2017).

105 Bill Bishop and Robert Cushing, *The Big Sort: Why the Clustering of Like-Minded America Is Tearing Us Apart* (Boston: Mariner Books, 2009); Nolan McCarty et al., "Does Gerrymandering Cause Polarization?," *American Journal of Political Science* 53.3 (2009): 666–680.

106 "In a Politically Polarized Era, Sharp Divides in Both Partisan Coalitions," Pew Research Center, December 17, 2019; Hopkins, *Red Fighting Blue*, ch. 4.

107 Jill Lepore, *These Truths: A History of the United States* (New York: W.W. Norton, 2018), 656.

108 Alan Abramowitz and Steven Webster, "The Rise of Negative Partisanship and the Nationalization of US Elections in the 21st Century," *Electoral Studies* 41 (2016): 12–22, 15–16.

109 CBS News-YouGov Poll, February 5–8, 2021.

110 "Amid Campaign Turmoil, Biden Holds Wide Leads on Coronavirus, Unifying the Country," Pew Research Center, October 9, 2020.

111 Echelon Insights, Verified Voter Omnibus Survey, January 20–26, 2021.

112 Larry Diamond et al., "Americans Increasingly Believe Violence Is Justified If the Other Side Wins," *Politico Magazine*, October 2020.

113 American Perspectives Survey Topline Questionnaire, AmericanSurveyCenter.org, February 2021.

114 Hamilton, Madison, and Jay, *The Federalist*, 375–376.

115 Brendan Doherty, *The Rise of the President's Permanent Campaign* (Lawrence, KS: University Press of Kansas, 2012).

116 Pew Research Center, "Amid Campaign Turmoil, Biden Holds Wide Leads."

117 Alasdair Roberts, "The Hundred Day Mistake," *Wilson Quarterly*, Winter 2021.

118 Arthur Schlesinger, *A Thousand Days* (Boston: Houghton Mifflin, 1965), 17–18, 59–60 and 210–215.

119 Congressional Management Foundation, *Life in Congress: The Member Perspective* (Washington, DC: Congressional Management Foundation, 2021), 12–13.

120 Carl Hulse, "Why Trust Is in Short Supply on Capitol Hill," *New York Times*, August 1, 2021.

121 George Packer, "We Are Living in a Failed State," *The Atlantic*, June 2020.

122 Polling since the 1950s is summarized by the Pew Research Center: www.pewresearch.org/politics/2021/05/17/public-trust -in-government-1958–2021/.

123 Thomas Mann and Norman Ornstein, *It's Even Worse Than It Looks* (New York: Basic Books, 2013), 189.

124 David French, *Divided We Fall: America's Secession Threat and How to Restore Our Nation* (New York: St. Martin's Press, 2020).

125 Timothy Conlan and Paul Posner, "American Federalism in an Era of Partisan Polarization," *Publius* 46.3 (2016): 281–307.

126 Amy Gutmann and Dennis Thompson, *The Spirit of Compromise* (Princeton University Press, 2012), 179–180; Mark Levin, *The Liberty Amendments: Restoring the American Republic* (New York: Threshold, 2013), ch. 3; Lee Drutman, *Breaking the Two-Party Doom Loop* (Oxford University Press, 2020), 195–198; Akhilesh Pillalamarri, "Does America Need a Parliament?," *The National Interest*, December 14, 2020.

5 India: The Centralizing Reflex

1 Winston Churchill, *India: Speeches and an Introduction* (London: Butterworth, 1931), 123.

2 George Chesney, *Indian Polity: A View of the System of Administration in India*, 3rd edn. (London: Longmans, 1894), 398–399.

3 John Strachey, *India: Its Administration & Progress*, 3rd edn. (London: Macmillan, 1903), 2–3, 6–8, and 497.

4 Chesney, *Indian Polity*, 389; Lord Curzon, speech at the Delhi Durbar, January 1, 1903.

5 James Fitzjames Stephen, "Foundations of the Government of India," *The Nineteenth Century* 14 (1883): 541–550.

6 Strachey, *India: Its Administration & Progress*, 434.

7 Charles Buckland, *Sketches of Social Life in India* (London: W.H. Allen, 1884), 103–107.

8 Ilbert, *The Government of India* (Oxford: Clarendon Press, 1907), ch. 4.

9 Granville Austin, *Working a Democratic Constitution: The Indian Experience* (Oxford University Press, 1999), 68–74.

10 Proceedings of the Constituent Assembly of India, November 6, 1948.

11 Selig Harrison, *India: The Most Dangerous Decades* (Princeton University Press, 1960), 293.

12 Selig Harrison, "The Challenge to Indian Nationalism," *Foreign Affairs* 34.4 (1956): 620–636, 620.

13 Harrison, *India: The Most Dangerous Decades*, 338.

14 Generally, see: Rajni Kothari, "The Congress 'System' in India," *Asian Survey* 4.12 (1964): 1161–1173.

15 Walter Bagehot, *The English Constitution* (London: H.S. King, 1872).

16 Meghnad Desai, *The Rediscovery of India* (New Delhi: Allen Lane, 2009), 304.

17 The Listener, "India: Independence and After," *The Listener* (1960): 437–439.

18 Austin, *Working a Democratic Constitution*, ch. 29.

19 Deepak Gupta, *The Steel Frame: A History of the IAS* (New Delhi: Roli Books, 2019), 80–86.

20 G.M. Nandurkar, *Sardar Patel: In Tune with the Millions*, 2 vols. (Ahmedabad: Sardar Vallabhbhai Patel Smarak Bhavan, 1975), v.2: 143–146.

21 Tripurdaman Singh, *Sixteen Stormy Days: The Story of the First*

Amendment of the Constitution of India (Haryana: Penguin Random House India, 2020).

22 Akhil Ranjan Dutta, "'Indian State' and Colonial Apparatuses: Can Peace Be Achieved in Northeast India by Violating Peoples' Rights?," *The Indian Journal of Political Science* 73.2 (2012): 283–298, 287.

23 K.N. Rao, "The Constitution (Sixteenth Amendment) Bill, 1963," *Journal of the Indian Law Institute* 5.1 (1963): 153–158, 152.

24 Jawaharlal Nehru, *The Discovery of India* (Calcutta: Signet Press, 1946), 420.

25 Alternately, as quasi-federal: K.C. Wheare, *Federal Government*, 4th edn. (Oxford University Press, 1968), 27–28.

26 Constituent Assembly Debates, November 4, 1948.

27 Wheare, *Federal Government*, 27–28; Louise Tillin, *Indian Federalism* (Delhi: Oxford India, 2019), 24–34.

28 Austin, *Working a Democratic Constitution*, 157.

29 "Congress Manifesto," *Economic and Political Weekly* 1.5 (1966): 179–180, 179.

30 Nehru, *The Discovery of India*, 442.

31 Khilnani, *The Idea of India*, 74 and 79.

32 C.H.H. Rao, "Agriculture: Policy and Performance," in *The Indian Economy: Problems and Prospects*, ed. Bimal Jalan (Delhi: Penguin Books, 1992), 127–155, 128–130.

33 P.M. Bakshi, "Reservations for Backward Classes," *Journal of the Indian Law Institute* 27.2 (1985): 318–335, 318–320.

34 Jawaharlal Nehru, *Selected Works of Jawaharlal Nehru*, vol. 69 (New Delhi: Jawaharlal Nehru Memorial Fund, 1984), 21.

35 Marc Galanter, "Who Are the Other Backward Classes?," *Economic and Political Weekly* 13.43/44 (1978): 1812–1828, 1817–1819; *Report of the Commissioner for Scheduled Castes and Scheduled Tribes* (Delhi, 1960), 367.

36 Ram Bhagat, "Census and Caste Enumeration: British Legacy and Contemporary Practice in India," *Genus* 62.2 (2006): 119–134, 121–128.

37 Purushotham, *From Raj to Republic: Sovereignty, Violence, and Democracy in India* (Stanford University Press, 2021), ch. 5.

38 Austin, *Working a Democratic Constitution*, 157.

39 Jawaharlal Nehru, *Selected Works of Jawaharlal Nehru* (New Delhi: Jawaharlal Nehru Memorial Fund, 1984), v43:6.

40 John Harriss et al., *India: Continuity and Change in the 21st Century* (Cambridge, UK: Polity, 2020), 18–19 and 115.

41 Joseph Stauffer, "Sino-Indian Border Dispute–1962," *Naval War College Review* 19.9 (1967): 81–117.

42 Michael Ward and A.K. Mahajan, "Defense Expenditures, Security Threats, and Governmental Deficits: A Case Study of India, 1952–1979," *The Journal of Conflict Resolution* 28.3 (1984): 382–419, Table 3.

43 C.P. Cook, "India: The Crisis in Assam," *The World Today* 24.10 (1968): 444–448.

44 Desai, *Rediscovery of India*, 308 and 318.

45 Harrison, *India: The Most Dangerous Decades*, 306–307.

46 Satish Arora, "The Reorganization of the Indian States," *Far Eastern Survey* 25.2 (1956): 27–30, 27.

47 Sanjay Kumar, "Creation of New States: Rationale and Implications," *Economic and Political Weekly* 37.36 (2002): 3705–3709.

48 A.K.J. Wyatt, "New Alignments in South Indian Politics: The 2001 Assembly Elections in Tamil Nadu," *Asian Survey* 42.5 (2002): 733–753, 734–735.

49 Ram Joshi, "The Shiv Sena: A Movement in Search of Legitimacy," *Asian Survey* 10.11 (1970): 967–978, 969; K.C. Suri, "Telugu Desam Party: Rise and Prospects for Future," *Economic and Political Weekly* 39.14/15 (2004): 1481–1490, 1487.

50 Harrison, "The Challenge to Indian Nationalism," 620.

51 S.K. Agrawala, "Jawaharlal Nehru and the Language Problem," *Journal of the Indian Law Institute* 19.1 (1977): 44–67.

52 Yogendra Yadav, "Electoral Politics in the Time of Change," *Economic and Political Weekly* 34.34/35 (1999): 2393–2399, 2394.

53 Lloyd Rudolph and Susanne Rudolph, *In Pursuit of Lakshmi: The Political Economy of the Indian State* (University of Chicago Press, 1987), 227 and 238.

54 Jagdish Bhagwati, *India in Transition: Freeing the Economy* (Oxford University Press, 1993), 46–56 and 63–65.

55 "Humiliation of Hunger," *Economic and Political Weekly* 2.7 (1967): 398–400.

56 Paul Streeten and Michael Lipton, *The Crisis of Indian Planning: Economic Planning in the 1960s* (Oxford University Press, 1968), 4–5.

57 Paul McGarr, "After Nehru, What? Britain, the United States, and the Other Transfer of Power in India, 1960–64," *The International History Review* 33.1 (2011): 115–142, 118.

58 Norman Palmer, "India in 1975: Democracy in Eclipse," *Asian Survey* 16.2 (1976): 95–110, 282–284.

59 W.H. Morris-Jones, "Creeping but Uneasy Authoritarianism: India 1975–6," *Government and Opposition* 12.1 (1977): 20–41, 26.

60 Richard Kozicki, "The Demise of Indian Democracy," *Asian Affairs* 2.6 (1975): 349–362, 349.

61 Rahul Mukherji, *India's Economic Transition: The Politics of Reforms* (Oxford University Press, 2007), 9–10.

62 Samuel Paul and Subramanian Ashok, "Development Programmes for the Poor," *Economic and Political Weekly* 18.10 (1983): 349–358.

63 John Keay, *India: A History* (London: HarperPress, 2010), 552.

64 Rudolph and Rudolph, *In Pursuit of Lakshmi*, 139–141.

65 Amnesty International, "Detention Conditions in West Bengal," *Economic and Political Weekly* 9.38 (1974): 1611–1618, 1611.

66 Bhagwan Dua, "Presidential Rule in India," *Asian Survey* 19.6 (1979): 611–626, 614 and 620.

67 Stanley Wolpert, *A New History of India*, 6th edn. (Oxford University Press, 2000), 397–399.

68 Rosanna Ledbetter, "Thirty Years of Family Planning in India," *Asian Survey* 24.7 (1984): 736–758, 748–749.

69 Palmer, "India in 1975: Democracy in Eclipse," 103.

70 Morris-Jones, "Creeping but Uneasy Authoritarianism," 30.

71 Anthony Lukas, "India Is as Indira Does,"*New York Times*, April 4, 1976.

72 Christophe Jaffrelot and Patrinav Anil, *India's First Dictatorship: The Emergency, 1975–77* (London: Hurst & Company, 2021), ch. 9.

73 Sumit Ganguly and Rahul Mukherji, *India Since 1980* (Cambridge University Press, 2011), 70–77 and 84–95.

74 Sushil Khanna, "The Transformation of India's Public Sector," *Economic and Political Weekly* 50.5 (2015): 47–60, 51.

75 Indira Rajaraman, "Continuity and Change in Indian Fiscal Federalism," *India Review* 16.1 (2017): 66–84.

76 Hoshiar Singh, "Constitutional Base for Panchayati Raj in India: The 73rd Amendment Act," *Asian Survey* 34.9 (1994): 818–827.

77 Yadav, "Electoral Politics in the Time of Change," 2399.

78 Tillin, *Indian Federalism*, 122.

79 Yadav, "Electoral Politics in the Time of Change," 2397.

80 Navin Chawla, *Every Vote Counts: The Story of India's Elections* (Noida: HarperCollins, 2019), ch. 4; Milan Vaishnav, *When Crime Pays: Money and Muscle in Indian Politics* (New Haven, CT: Yale University Press, 2017).

81 Christophe Jaffrelot, "What's Left of the 'Mandal Moment', Politically and Socially, Now?," *Indian Express*, August 22, 2020.

82 Sanjay Ruparelia, "India's New Rights Agenda: Genesis, Promises, Risks," *Pacific Affairs* 86.3 (2013): 569–590, 572–582.

83 Such as the Right to Information Act, the National Rural Employment Guarantee Act, the Right to Education Act, and the Food Security Act.

84 Achin Vanaik, *The Rise of Hindu Authoritarianism: Secular Claims, Communal Realities* (London: Verso, 2017), ch. 1.

85 Desai, *Rediscovery of India*, 370–371, 384–385, and 393–401.

86 K.K. Kailash, "Middle Game in Coalition Politics," *Economic and Political Weekly* 42.4 (2007): 307–317.

87 Ashutosh Varshney, "Mass Politics or Elite Politics? India's Economic Reforms in Comparative Perspective," *The Journal of Policy Reform* 2.4 (1998): 301–335, 314–315.

88 K.P. Krishnan and T.V. Somanathan, "The Civil Service," in *Rethinking Public Institutions in India*, ed. D. Kapur et al. (Oxford University Press, 2017), 339–417.

89 World Bank data, inflation adjusted: data.worldbank.org/indicator/.

90 Christophe Jaffrelot and Sanskruthi Kalyankar, *To What Extent Is India a Union of States?* (Paris: Institut Montaigne, 2019), 10.

91 Sabyasachi Kar and S. Sakthivel, "Reforms and Regional Inequality in India," *Economic and Political Weekly* 42.47 (2007): 69–77, 77.

92 On the following, see: Michael Walton, "Inequities and India's Long-Term Growth: Tackling Structural Inequities," in *India 2039: An Affluent Society in One Generation*, ed. H. Kohli and A. Sood (Delhi: Sage, 2010), 67–100.

93 Nirvikar Singh et al., "Regional Inequality in India," *Economic and Political Weekly* 38.11 (2003): 1069–1073, Table 2.

94 Harinder Kohli and Anil Sood, *India 2039*, 43.

95 K. Nagaraj et al., "Farmers' Suicides in India: Magnitudes, Trends, and Spatial Patterns, 1997–2012," *Review of Agrarian Studies* 4.2 (2014): 53–83, 55 and 80–82.

96 Harriss et al., *India: Continuity and Change*, 181, 276–277.

97 Lant Pritchett, *Is India a Flailing State?* (Cambridge, MA: Harvard Kennedy School, 2009), 4.

98 Rumki Basu, *Democracy and Public Policy in the Post-Covid-19 World* (New York: Routledge, 2021), 205.

99 World Bank data in current US dollars: data.worldbank.org/indicator/.

100 Harriss et al., *India: Continuity and Change*, 285–291.
101 Generally: Harriss et al., *India: Continuity and Change*, ch. 9.
102 Puja Mehra, *The Lost Decade* (Gurgaon, Delhi: Penguin, 2019), 94.
103 Vaishnav, "The Decay of Indian Democracy."
104 In a 2009 survey, 43 percent of respondents agreed India "should be governed by a strong leader who does not have to bother about winning elections": Centre for the Study of Developing Societies, *2009 National Election Study Postpoll Findings* (Delhi, 2009), 80. Similar results were found in a 2019 survey.
105 Yadav, *Making Sense of Indian Democracy*, xiii–xxxi.
106 "Hindu Fevicol": Vinay Sitapati, *Jugalbandi: The BJP before Modi* (Gurgaon, Delhi: Penguin, 2020).
107 Generally, see: Vanaik, *The Rise of Hindu Authoritarianism*, ch. 1.
108 Desai, *Rediscovery of India*, 449.
109 Badri Narayan, *Republic of Hindutva* (Gurgaon, Delhi: Penguin, 2021).
110 Tariq Thachil, *Elite Parties, Poor Voters: How Social Services Win Votes in India* (Cambridge University Press, 2014).
111 Nussbaum, *The Clash Within*, ch. 1.
112 Alfred Stepan et al., *Crafting State-Nations: India and Other Multinational Democracies* (Baltimore, MD: Johns Hopkins University Press, 2010), ch. 2.
113 Christophe Jaffrelot and Cynthia Schoch, *Modi's India: Hindu Nationalism and the Rise of Ethnic Democracy* (Princeton University Press, 2021), ch. 2.
114 Indira Hirway, "Partial View of Outcome of Reforms and Gujarat 'Model,'" *Economic and Political Weekly* 48.43 (2013): 26–29, 27.
115 Neelanjan Sircar, "The Welfarist Prime Minister: Explaining the National-State Election Gap," *Economic and Political Weekly*, March 6, 2021.
116 Jaffrelot and Kalyankar, *To What Extent Is India a Union of States?*; Louise Tillin, "Why So Many Centre-State Tensions Are Breaking out in the Open Now," *Times of India*, November 3, 2020.
117 The Hindu, "'Infiltrators' Will Be Extradited by 2024," *The Hindu*, December 2, 2019.
118 Harriss et al., *India: Continuity and Change*, 120–133.
119 Human Rights Watch, *World Report 2021* (New York, 2021), 317–329.
120 "Rise in Sedition Cases in the Modi Era," Article 14, February 2, 2021.
121 Reporters Without Borders, *World Press Freedom Index: India Country Report* (Paris, 2021).

122 "Bachelet Dismayed at Restrictions on Human Rights NGOs," Office of United Nations High Commissioner for Human Rights, October 20, 2020.

123 "Power List 2015," *Indian Express*, February 28, 2015.

124 Raymond Zhong et al., "Micromanager-in-Chief: Modi Upends How India Is Run," *Wall Street Journal Asia*, March 10, 2017.

125 Milan Vaishnav, "The Decay of Indian Democracy," *Foreign Affairs*, March 18, 2021.

126 Alasdair Roberts, "Abolishing India's Planning Commission: The Results after Five Years," *Public Administration Review* 81.4 (2021): 799–805.

127 "In RTI Replies, Evidence of How Modi Dragged His Feet on Lokpal Appointment," *The Wire*, December 21, 2018; "Why India's Modi Wants to Increase Control over the Central Bank," *Reuters*, November 2, 2018; "What Has Changed in RTI Act?," *Indian Express*, July 22, 2019.

128 Rana Ayyub, "The Destruction of India's Judicial Independence Is Almost Complete," *Washington Post*, March 24, 2020.

129 Rishi Kishore, "BJP under Modi-Shah Has Adopted High Command Culture," *Scroll*, August 26, 2020.

130 Freedom House, *Freedom in the World 2021* (Washington, 2021), 2 and 7.

131 V-Dem Institute, *Democracy Report 2021* (University of Gothenberg, 2021), 20–21.

132 Mehra, *The Lost Decade*, 296.

133 Arvind Subramanian, *Of Counsel: The Challenges of the Modi-Jaitley Economy* (Gurgaon, Delhi: Penguin, 2018), 94 and 98–99.

134 Dinesh Unnikrishnan, "What Did RBI Advise Government on Demonetisation?," firstpost.com, April 13, 2018.

135 Shawin Vitsupakorn et al., *Early Experiences of Pradhan Mantri Jan Arogya Yojana in India* (Durham, NC: Center for Policy Impact in Global Health, 2021).

136 Soutik Biswas, "Narendra Modi: Pandemic and Sluggish Growth Dent Popularity," *BBC News*, August 23, 2021.

137 Rohan Venkatáramakrishnan, "How Big Is the Political Gap between North and South India?," *Scroll*, December 17, 2020.

138 Liz Mathew, "BJP Meet Reviews Party Activities in Five States," *Indian Express*, June 6, 2021.

139 James Manor, "Modi's Power and Cult Endanger the BJP," *The Wire*, September 3, 2021.

140 Sunil Khilnani, *The Idea of India* (New York: Penguin Books, 2003), 179.

6 China: Authoritarian Dilemmas

1 Ross Terrill, *The New Chinese Empire* (New York: Basic Books, 2003), 2–3.
2 Frederick Teiwes, "Mao and His Followers," in *A Critical Introduction to Mao*, ed. Timothy Cheek (Cambridge University Press, 2010), 129–168, 138; David Shambaugh, *China's Leaders: From Mao to Now* (Cambridge, UK: Polity, 2021), ch. 6.
3 François Bougon, *Inside the Mind of Xi Jinping* (London: Hurst, 2018), 28–29.
4 Yuri Pines, *The Book of Lord Shang* (New York: Columbia University Press, 2019), 11.
5 James Legge, *The Works of Mencius* (London: Trübner, 1861), 12; David Hinton, *Mencius* (Washington: Counterpoint, 1998), 26.
6 William Joseph, *Politics in China: An Introduction* (Oxford University Press, 2019), 23 and 45.
7 Agnieszka Joniak-Lüthi, "The Han 'Minzu,' Fragmented Identities, and Ethnicity," *The Journal of Asian Studies* 72.4 (2013): 849–871.
8 David Moser, *A Billion Voices* (Melbourne: Penguin, 2016), 6–7.
9 Jakub Grygiel, *Great Powers and Geopolitical Change* (Baltimore, MD: Johns Hopkins University Press, 2006), 144.
10 William Overholt, *China's Crisis of Success* (Cambridge University Press, 2018), ch. 3.
11 John Keay, *China: A History* (New York: Basic Books, 2009), chs. 15 and 16.
12 Letter to Simon North, April 19, 1916; Letter to Paul Reinsch, May 12, 1916. Willoughby Papers, William & Mary Libraries.
13 Yiching Wu, *The Cultural Revolution at the Margins* (Cambridge, MA: Harvard University Press, 2014), 18.
14 Allan Cole, "Political Contrasts: China, India, and Japan," *Journal of International Affairs* 17.2 (1963): 155–167, 156.
15 John Lewis, "China's Secret Military Papers," *China Quarterly*, 18 (1964): 68–78, 69.
16 Tang Tsou, "The Cultural Revolution and the Chinese Political System," *China Quarterly*, 38 (1969): 63–91.
17 Donald Whitaker and Rinn-Sup Shinn, *Area Handbook for the People's Republic of China* (Washington, DC: Government Printing Office, 1972), vii.

18 Jeremy Paltiel, "Jiang Talks Politics: Who Listens? Institutionalization and Its Limits in Market Leninism," *The China Journal*, 45 (2001): 113–121.

19 Xi Jinping, "Remarks to Political Bureau of the CPC Central Committee," xinhuanet.com, February 26, 2021.

20 Arthur Steiner, "Constitutionalism in Communist China," *American Political Science Review* 49.1 (1955): 1–21, 14.

21 Jiang Shigong, "Written and Unwritten Constitutions: A New Approach to the Study of Constitutional Government in China," *Modern China* 36.1 (2010): 12–46, 13.

22 William Joseph, "Ideology and China's Political Development," in *Politics in China*, ed. W. Joseph (Oxford University Press, 2019), 157–200.

23 Sebastian Heilmann, *China's Political System* (Lanham: Rowman & Littlefield, 2017), 141–142.

24 *People's Daily Online*, February 14, 2022.

25 Roel Sterckx, *Chinese Thought: From Confucius to Cook Ding* (London: Pelican, 2020), 107–114.

26 A. James Gregor and Maria Chang, "Anti-Confucianism: Mao's Last Campaign," *Asian Survey* 19.11 (1979): 1073–1092.

27 Bruce Dickson, *The Dictator's Dilemma: The Chinese Communist Party's Strategy for Survival* (Oxford University Press, 2016), 237–243.

28 Daniel Bell and Pei Wang, *Just Hierarchy: Why Social Hierarchies Matter in China and the Rest of the World* (Princeton University Press, 2020), 72–74.

29 Klaus Mühlhahn, *Making China Modern: From the Great Qing to Xi Jinping* (Cambridge, MA: Belknap Press, 2019), 154–169.

30 Orville Schell and John Delury, *Wealth and Power: China's Long March to the Twenty-First Century* (New York: Random House, 2013), 11.

31 Xi Jinping, *The Governance of China, Volume 1* (Beijing: Foreign Languages Press, 2014), 40–41 and 261.

32 Franz Schurmann, *Ideology and Organization in Communist China*, 2nd edn. (Berkeley, CA: University of California Press, 1968), 53–57.

33 Francis Fukuyama, *The Origins of Political Order* (New York: Farrar, Straus and Giroux, 2011), ch. 21.

34 Jonathan Fenby, *Modern China: The Fall and Rise of a Great Power* (New York: Ecco, 2008), chs. 20 and 21.

35 Immanuel Hsü, *The Rise of Modern China* (Oxford University Press, 1970), 778–779.

36 Associated Press, "TASS Says China Strife Described as Civil War," *Dallas Morning News*, September 24, 1967, 3.

37 Mühlhahn, *Making China Modern*, 473.

38 Resolution on Certain Questions in the History of Our Party since the Founding of the People's Republic of China, June 27, 1981.

39 Keay, *China: A History*, 526–532.

40 Kenneth Lieberthal, *Governing China: From Revolution through Reform*, 2nd edn. (New York: W.W. Norton, 2004), 152.

41 Cheng Li, "China's Communist Party-State," in *Politics in China*, ed. William Joseph (Oxford University Press, 2019), 201–237, 205, 217 and 228; Lieberthal, *Governing China*, 220–222; Heilmann, *China's Political System*, 115–118.

42 Cheng Li, *Chinese Politics in the Xi Jinping Era* (Washington: Brookings Institution, 2016), 13.

43 David Bachman, "The Limits on Leadership in China," *Asian Survey* 32.11 (1992): 1046–1062, 1046.

44 Lieberthal, *Governing China*, 152–155.

45 Andrew Nathan, "China's Changing of the Guard: Authoritarian Resilience," *Journal of Democracy* 14.1 (2003): 6–17, 7 and 16.

46 Shambaugh, *China's Leaders*, 236–237.

47 Dickson, *The Dictator's Dilemma*, 254–257.

48 Christopher Johnson and Scott Kennedy, "Xi's Signature Governance Innovation: The Rise of Leading Small Groups," Center for Strategic and International Studies, October 17, 2017.

49 Geremie R. Barmé, "The Ayes Have It," *China File*, October 21, 2017.

50 Andrew Wedeman, "Xi Jinping's Tiger Hunt: Anti-Corruption Campaign or Factional Purge?," *Modern China Studies* 24.2 (2017): 35–94.

51 Josh Chin, "Xi Jinping's Leadership Style," *Wall Street Journal*, December 15, 2021.

52 Richard McGregor, *Xi Jinping: The Backlash* (Melbourne: Penguin Books, 2019).

53 Theodore Chen and Wen-Hui Chen, "The 'Three-Anti' and 'Five-Anti' Movements in Communist China," *Pacific Affairs* 26.1 (1953): 3–23.

54 Lieberthal, *Governing China*, 135.

55 Alexander Woodside, *Lost Modernities: China, Vietnam, Korea, and the Hazards of World History* (Cambridge, MA: Harvard University Press, 2006), 80.

56 Caroline Tong et al., "Civil Service Reform in the People's Republic of China," *Public Administration and Development* 19.2 (1999): 193–206.

57 Susan Whiting, "The Cadre Evaluation System at the Grass Roots," in *Holding China Together*, ed. Barry Naughton and Dali Yang (Cambridge University Press, 2004), 101–119.

58 Fenby, *Modern China*, ch. 27.

59 World Bank data: data.worldbank.org/indicator/.

60 Fenby, *Modern China*, 567.

61 Rong Jian and Gloria Davies, "A China Bereft of Thought," in *Voices from the Chinese Century*, ed. T. Cheek et al. (New York: Columbia University Press, 2020), 72–103, 80–83.

62 Nis Grünberg and Katja Drinhausen, *The Party Leads on Everything* (Berlin: MERICS, 2019).

63 Scott Livingston, *The New Challenge of Communist Corporate Governance* (Washington, DC: Center for Strategic and International Studies, 2021).

64 The Economist, "China Takes Aim at Its Entrepreneurs," *The Economist*, November 12, 2020.

65 Sebastian Heilmann, "Policy Experimentation in China's Economic Rise," *Studies in Comparative International Development* 43.1 (2008): 1–26.

66 Ciqi Mei and Xiaonan Wang, "Wire-Walking: Risk Management and Policy Experiments in China," *Journal of Comparative Policy Analysis: Research and Practice* (2019): 1–23, 2 and 16.

67 Lieberthal, *Governing China*, 191.

68 World Bank data: data.worldbank.org/indicator/.

69 Edward Cunningham et al., *Understanding CCP Resilience: Surveying Chinese Public Opinion through Time* (Cambridge, MA: Ash Center for Democratic Governance and Innovation, 2020).

70 David Zweig, "China's Political Economy," in *Politics in China*, ed. William Joseph (Oxford University Press, 2019), 274–314, 303–304.

71 Björn Alpermann and Shaohua Zhan, "Population Planning after the One-Child Policy: Shifting Modes of Political Steering in China," *Journal of Contemporary China* 28.117 (2019): 348–366.

72 Dickson, *The Dictator's Dilemma*, 209.

73 Jidong Yang et al., "Income Inequality and Civil Disorder: Evidence from China," *Journal of Contemporary China* 29.125 (2020): 680–697, 681.

74 Feng Chongyi, "The Threat of Charter 08," in *Liu Xiaobo, Charter*

08 and the Challenges of Political Reform in China, ed. J.P. Béja et al. (Hong Kong University Press, 2012), 119–140.

75 Preamble to the constitution.

76 Dickson, *The Dictator's Dilemma*, 277.

77 Cunningham et al., *Understanding CCP Resilience*, 14.

78 George Magnus, *Red Flags: Why Xi's China Is in Jeopardy* (Yale University Press, 2018), ch. 7.

79 For an illustration, see: Winnie Yip et al., "10 Years of Health-Care Reform in China: Progress and Gaps in Universal Health Coverage," *The Lancet* 394.10204 (2019): 1192–1204.

80 Kerry Brown, *China's Dream: The Culture of Chinese Communism and the Secret Sources of Its Power* (Cambridge, UK: Polity, 2018), 167.

81 Dickson, *The Dictator's Dilemma*, 232–237.

82 Anne-Marie Brady, "Guiding Hand: The Role of the CCP Central Propaganda Department in the Current Era." *Westminster Papers in Communication and Culture* 3, no. 1 (2006): 58–77; David Shambaugh, "China's Propaganda System: Institutions, Processes and Efficacy," *China Journal* 57 (2007): 25–58; Margaret Roberts, *Censored* (Princeton University Press, 2018), 94–112.

83 David Bandurski, "Guidance of Public Opinion," ChinaMediaProject.org, November 5, 2013.

84 Press freedom rankings by Reporters Without Borders: rsf.org/en/ranking.

85 Shambaugh, "China's Propaganda System," 27.

86 Brady, "Guiding Hand," 62 and 66; Shambaugh, "China's Propaganda System," 53 and 55–58; Roberts, *Censored*, 99.

87 data.worldbank.org/indicator/.

88 Paul Mozur, "China's Internet Censors Play a Tougher Game of Cat and Mouse," *New York Times*, August 3, 2017.

89 Bill Taylor and Qi Li, "Is the ACFTU a Union and Does It Matter?," *Journal of Industrial Relations* 49.5 (2007): 701–715; Nanlai Cao, "Chinese Religions on the Edge: Shifting Religion-State Dynamics," *China Review* 18.4 (2018): 1–10.

90 Heike Holbig and Bertram Lang, "China's Overseas NGO Law and the Future of International Civil Society," *Journal of Contemporary Asia* (2021): 1–28.

91 "China Schools: 'Xi Jinping Thought' Introduced into Curriculum," *BBC News*, August 25, 2021.

92 Eva Pils, "China's Human Rights Lawyers: Rifts and Schisms in an Era of Global Human Rights Backlash," *Made in China Journal* 6.1 (2021): 108–113.

93 Adrian Zenz, "China's Domestic Security Spending," 18.4 (2018): 5–11, Table 1.

94 Suzanne Scoggins, *Policing China: Street-Level Cops in the Shadow of Protest* (Ithaca, NY: Cornell University Press, 2021), ch. 1.

95 Jean Mittelstaedt, "The Grid Management System in Contemporary China," *China Information* (May 2021).

96 Dahlia Peterson, *Designing Alternatives to China's Repressive Surveillance State* (Washington, DC: Center for Security and Emerging Technology, 2020).

97 Katja Drinhausen and Vincent Brussee, *China's Social Credit System* (Berlin: Mercator Institute for China Studies, 2021).

98 Xinhua News Agency, "Xi Stresses Unity for Tibet, Vows Fight against Separatism," *China Daily*, August 26, 2015.

99 Xing Lu, *The Rhetoric of Mao Zedong* (University of South Carolina Press, 2017), ch. 7.

100 Eric Schluessel, *Land of Strangers: The Civilizing Project in Qing Central Asia* (New York: Columbia University Press, 2020), 216.

101 Gardner Bovingdon, "Xinjiang," in *Politics in China*, ed. William Joseph (Oxford University Press, 2019), 487–516, 493–502.

102 Sheena Greitens et al., "Counterterrorism and Preventive Repression: China's Changing Strategy in Xinjiang," *International Security* 44.3 (2020): 9–47, 10–11.

103 Michael Clarke, "In Xinjiang, China's 'Neo-Totalitarian' Reality," *The Diplomat*, March 10, 2018.

104 Ondrej Klimes and Joanne Finley, "China's Neo-Totalitarian Turn and Genocide in Xinjiang," Society and Space, December 7, 2020.

105 Xiaoyuan Liu, *To the End of Revolution: The Chinese Communist Party and Tibet, 1949–1959* (New York: Columbia University Press, 2020).

106 Xinhua News Agency, "Xi Stresses Unity for Tibet."

107 Claude Levenson, "Tibet: A Neo-Colonial Genocide," in *Forgotten Genocides*, ed. René Lemarchand (University of Pennsylvania Press, 2011), 91–105.

108 Louisa Brooke-Holland, *Hong Kong: The Joint Declaration* (London: House of Commons Library, July 5, 2019).

109 Preamble and Article 45 of the Basic Law of The Hong Kong Special Administrative Region, 1990.

110 "China Says Sino-British Joint Declaration on Hong Kong No Longer Has Meaning," *Reuters News*, June 30, 2017.

111 Human Rights Watch, *Dismantling a Free Society: Hong Kong One Year after the National Security Law* (New York, 2021).

112 Elaine Pearson, "What Jimmy Lai's Arrest Means," Human Rights Watch, August 12, 2020.

113 David Sacks, "What Xi Jinping's Major Speech Means for Taiwan," Council on Foreign Relations, July 6, 2021.

114 Hubei Province Health Commission, *Report on the Fifth Plenary Session of the Nineteenth Central Committee*, January 7, 2021.

115 John Bryan Starr, *Understanding China*, 3rd edn. (New York: Hill and Wang, 2010), 138.

116 Ye Zhou, Speech to the Shanghai New Fourth Army History Research Association, January 7, 2021.

117 Yafei He, "Ushering in a New Chapter," ChinaUSFocus.com, February 26, 2021.

118 For example: Susan Shirk, *China: Fragile Superpower* (Oxford University Press, 2007); Elizabeth Economy, "China's Inconvenient Truth," *Foreign Affairs*, May 28, 2021.

119 John Chin, "The Longest March: Why China's Democratization Is Not Imminent," *Journal of Chinese Political Science* 23.1 (2018): 63–82; Branko Milanović, *The Haves and the Have-Nots: A Brief and Idiosyncratic History of Global Inequality* (New York: Basic Books, 2011), ch. 1.

120 Roger Garside, *China Coup: The Great Leap to Freedom* (Oakland: University of California Press, 2021).

7 The European Union: Cohesion without Coercion

1 Margaret Thatcher, Speech to College of Europe, September 20, 1988.

2 Phrases are drawn from the British Newspaper Archive.

3 "Barroso: European Union Is 'Non-Imperial Empire,'" Euractiv, July 10, 2007.

4 Declaration on European Identity, December 14, 1973.

5 The EU itself distinguishes between the union as a "form of legal organization" and as a "political project": eur-lex.europa.eu/summary/glossary/.

6 Judgment of the European Court of Justice, *Flaminio Costa v. ENEL*, July 15, 1964.

7 Erika Tóth, "National Cultures and European Identity: The Process of 'Engrenage' among European Commission Civil Servants," *Society and Economy* 29.3 (2007): 413–431.

8 Jonathan Olsen, *The European Union: Politics and Policies*, 7th edn. (New York, NY: Routledge, 2021), 105.

9 Margaret Thatcher, *Statecraft: Strategies for a Changing World* (London: HarperCollins, 2002), ch. 10.

10 Luis Martín-Estudillo, *The Rise of Euroskepticism* (Nashville, TN: Vanderbilt University Press, 2018), 202.

11 Rachel Donadio, "Richard Clarke's Unsecret Agent," *New York Observer*, April 5, 2004, 1.

12 Viktor Orbán, Speech on the Future of the European Union, June 19, 2021.

13 Mateusz Morawiecki, Statement to European Parliament on the Rule of Law Crisis in Poland, October 19, 2021.

14 Roman Joch, "Are We Barbarians?," *Aspen Review Central Europe*, March 15, 2017.

15 Conclusions of the Presidency, European Council in Copenhagen, June 1993.

16 Tobias Lock, "Why the European Union Is Not a State," *European Constitutional Law Review* 5.3 (2009): 407–420, 414.

17 Olsen, *The European Union*, 251–255.

18 Robert Schütze, *European Union Law* (Oxford University Press, 2021), 345–6.

19 Wojciech Kosc, "Poland Faces Blowback over Its Migrant Policy," *Politico Europe*, September 30, 2021.

20 European Court of Auditors, *Implementation of the 2014 Staff Reform Package at the Commission* (Luxembourg: European Court of Auditors, 2019), 5.

21 Schütze, *European Union Law*, 385–388.

22 Tanja Börzel, *Why Noncompliance: The Politics of Law in the European Union* (Ithaca, NY: Cornell University Press, 2021), 13.

23 *Tools for Ensuring Implementation and Application of EU Law* (Luxembourg: European Parliament, 2013).

24 José Manuel Barroso, State of the Union 2012 Address, September 12, 2012.

25 Declaration on the Granting of Independence to Colonial Countries and Peoples, December 14, 1960.

26 Robert Young, *The Secession of Quebec and the Future of Canada* (Montreal: McGill-Queen's University Press, 1998), 93 and 154.

27 Jason Sorens, *Secessionism: Identity, Interest, and Strategy* (Montreal: McGill-Queen's University Press, 2012), 189.

28 *Army and Navy Chronicle*, December 12, 1839, 392.

29 Data from the Fragile States Index: fragilestatesindex.org.

30 World Bank data on government effectiveness: info.worldbank.org/governance/wgi.

31 Börzel, *Why Noncompliance*, 3–4, 31–32 and 97–98.

32 Theda Skocpol, *States and Social Revolutions* (Cambridge University Press, 1979), 29.

33 John McCormick, "What Has the European Union Ever Done for Us?," in *The State of the Union(s)*, ed. Joaquín Roy (Miami: University of Miami, 2011), 38.

34 Remarks by President Obama and Prime Minister David Cameron in Joint Press Conference, June 5, 2014.

35 Antony Jay, *Oxford Dictionary of Political Quotations*, 4th edn. (Oxford University Press, 2010), 174.

36 Charles Forelle, "Three's a Crowd," *Wall Street Journal*, March 29, 2010.

37 Samuel Gregg, *Becoming Europe* (New York: Encounter Books, 2013), ch. 1.

38 Peter van Ham and Richard Kugler, *Western Unity and the Transatlantic Security Challenge* (Garmisch-Partenkirchen: George C. Marshall Center, 2002), 2.

39 Michael Hirsh, "How the US Got 9/11 Wrong," *Foreign Policy*, September 7, 2021.

40 Bagehot, *The English Constitution*, 226.

41 Bryce, *The American Commonwealth*, v1.249 and v1.342.

42 Eric O'Connor, "A Salutary Shock: The European Suffrage Movement and Democracy in the European Community, 1948–1973," *Journal of Contemporary European Research* 10.1 (2014): 57–73, 67.

43 Émile Noel, "Some Reflections on the Preparation, Development and Repercussions of the Meetings between Heads of Government," *Government and Opposition* 11.1 (1976): 20–34, 22.

44 TEU Article 15.

45 Schütze, *European Union Law*, Figure 1.1.

46 Michael Brenner, "EC: Confidence Lost," *Foreign Policy* 91 (1993): 24–43, 27.

47 John Hulsman and William Schirano, "The European Union Is Dead," *The National Interest* 81 (2005): 61–66, 62 and 65.

48 Agniezka Smolenska, "EU Bank Regulation after the Great Financial Crisis," in A. Drach and Y. Cassis, *Financial Deregulation: A Historical Perspective* (Oxford University Press, 2021), 163–166.

49 Jeffry Frieden, *Global Capitalism* (New York: W.W. Norton, 2020), chs. 17, 20 and 21.

50 Ali Ai-Eyd and Sylvia Gottschalk, "The Stability and Growth Pact

and Slow Growth in Europe," *National Institute Economic Review*, 192 (2005): 23–32, 26–27.

51 David Ignatius, "A Tea Party for Europe," *Washington Post*, February 11, 2010.

52 Charles Kupchan, "As Nationalism Rises, Will the European Union Fall?," *Washington Post*, August 29, 2010.

53 Alasdair Roberts, "'An Ungovernable Anarchy': The United States' Response to Depression and Default, 1837–1848," *Intereconomics* 45.4 (2010): 196–202.

54 Frank Rövekamp, *The Evolution of the European Stability Mechanism* (Tokyo: Asian Development Bank Institute, 2020), 1–3.

55 Markus Brunnermeier et al., *The Euro and the Battle of Ideas* (Princeton University Press, 2016), ch. 15.

56 Adriaan Schout and Cathelijn Padberg, *Monitoring and Enforcement in the European Union* (The Hague: Clingendael Institute, 2019).

57 Vestert Borger, *The Currency of Solidarity: Constitutional Transformation During the Euro Crisis* (Cambridge University Press, 2020), 21.

58 Phillip Connor, "Illegal Migration to EU Rises for Routes Both Well-Worn and Less-Traveled," Pew Research Center, March 18, 2016.

59 "IOM Counts 3,771 Migrant Fatalities in Mediterranean in 2015," iom.net, January 5, 2016.

60 Eurostat data: ec.europa.eu/eurostat/web/main/data/database.

61 Andrea Dernbach, "Germany Suspends Dublin Agreement for Syrian Refugees," *Der Tagesspiegel*, August 26, 2015.

62 Jules Johnston, "The 10 Most Apocalyptic Warnings of the EU's Demise," *Politico*, October 28, 2015.

63 Vit Novotny, *Reducing Irregular Migration Flows through EU External Action* (Brussels: Wilfried Martens Centre for European Studies, 2019), 4 and 15.

64 European Commission, *Progress Report on the Implementation of the European Agenda on Migration* (Brussels: October 16, 2019), 2–3.

65 Department of Homeland Security, *Estimates of the Unauthorized Immigrant Population Residing in the United States* (Washington, 2021).

66 Sanjeev Tripathi, *Illegal Immigration from Bangladesh to India: Toward a Comprehensive Solution* (Delhi: Carnegie India, 2016).

67 Kam Wing Chan and Will Buckingham, "Is China Abolishing the Hukou System?," *The China Quarterly* 195 (2008): 582–606.

68 Georgi Gotev, "MEPs Fear Brexit Will Trigger 'Perfect Storm' and EU Breakup," euractiv.com, February 17, 2016.

69 Matthew Goodwin, "What a Le Pen Win Would Look Like," *New York Times*, March 23, 2017.

70 Speech at the Annual General Meeting of the Hellenic Federation of Enterprises, June 21, 2016.

71 Country summaries for Eurobarometer 95, Spring 2021.

72 Viktor Orbán, Speech at the Bálványos Free Summer University and Youth Camp, July 26, 2014.

73 See the Freedom House report on Hungary: freedomhouse.org.

74 Freedom House report on Poland: freedomhouse.org.

75 Renáta Uitz, *Funding Illiberal Democracy: The Case for Credible Budgetary Conditionality in the EU* (Vienna: Central European University, 2020), 8.

76 Ulrich Sedelmeier, "Political Safeguards against Democratic Backsliding in the EU," *Journal of European Public Policy* 24.3 (2017): 337–351.

77 Henry Foy and James Shotter, "Top EU Court Tells Poland to Pay €1m a Day for Ignoring Court Order," *Financial Times*, October 27, 2021.

78 European Parliament, *Understanding the EU Rule of Law Mechanisms* (Brussels: Members' Research Service, 2016), 6.

79 European Commission, *2020 Rule of Law Report*, September 30, 2020, 20–21.

80 Kim Scheppele et al., "EU Values Are Law, after All," *Yearbook of European Law* 39 (2021): 3–121, 38–39.

81 Neil Kirst, "Rule of Law Conditionality: The Long-Awaited Step Towards a Solution of the Rule of Law Crisis in the European Union?," *European Papers* 6.1 (2021): 101–110.

82 Scheppele et al., "EU Values Are Law, after All," 10 and 120.

83 Jan-Werner Müller, "Should the EU Protect Democracy and the Rule of Law inside Member States?," *European Law Journal* 21.2 (2015): 141–160.

84 Joseph Weiler, "Some Iconoclastic Views on Populism, Democracy, the Rule of Law and the Polish Circumstance," in *Defending Checks and Balances in EU Member States*, ed. Armin von Bogdandy et al. (Berlin: Springer, 2021), 3–13, 10–11. Orbán's Fidesz retained power in an April 2022 election. Observers from the Organization for Security and Co-operation in Europe judged that the election was largely free and well administered, although "marred by the absence of a level playing field."

85 Martti Ahtisaari et al., *Report on the Austrian Government's Commitment to the Common European Values* (Strasbourg: European Court on Human Rights, 2000), 33.

86 Lili Bayer, "As EU Seeks Talks, Poland Risks Unraveling the Bloc's Legal Order," *Politico Europe*, October 26, 2021.

87 Leonard Seabrooke and Eleni Tsingou, "Europe's Fast- and Slow-Burning Crises," *Journal of European Public Policy* 26.3 (2019): 468–481, 468.

88 Ramona Coman et al., *Governance and Politics in the Post-Crisis European Union* (Cambridge University Press, 2020), xiii–xiv, 2 and 45.

89 Erik Jones et al., "Failing Forward? The Euro Crisis and the Incomplete Nature of European Integration," *Comparative Political Studies* 49.7 (2015): 1010–1034, 1027.

90 Leon N. Lindberg, "Decision Making and Integration in the European Community," *International Organization* 19.1 (1965): 56–80, 79–80.

91 Stephen Graubard, "Preface," *Daedalus* 108.1 (1979): v–xi, ix.

92 John Gillingham, *European Integration, 1950–2003: Superstate or New Market Economy?* (Cambridge University Press, 2003), 497.

93 Lindberg, "Decision Making and Integration in the European Community," 56.

94 Erik Jones, "European Crisis, European Solidarity," *Journal of Common Market Studies* 50.s2 (2012): 53–67, 66.

95 Ramona Coman et al., "The European Union as a Political Regime, a Set of Policies and a Community after the Great Recession," in *Governance and Politics in the Post-Crisis European Union*, ed. R. Coman et al. (Cambridge University Press, 2020), 1–30, 1.

96 Berthold Rittberger, *Building Europe's Parliament: Democratic Representation Beyond the Nation State* (Oxford University Press, 2005), ch. 6.

97 Michael Burgess, "Introduction: Federalism and Building the European Union," *Publius* 26.4 (1996): 1–15, 3.

8 The COVID Test

1 Peter Baldwin, *Fighting the First Wave: Why the Coronavirus Was Tackled So Differently across the Globe* (Cambridge University Press, 2021), 286.

2 Murad Banaji and Aashish Gupta, "Estimates of Pandemic Excess Mortality in India Based on Civil Registration Data," *medRxiv*, October 1, 2021.

3 This timeline is drawn from: *Covid-19: The Authoritative Chronology, December 2019–March 2020* (Geneva: Independent Panel for Pandemic Preparedness and Response, 2021).

4 Huaiyu Tian et al., "An Investigation of Transmission Control Measures During the First 50 Days of the Covid-19 Epidemic in China," *Science* 368.6491 (2020): 638–642, 368.

5 Ilan Alon et al., "Regime Type and Covid-19 Response," *FIIB Business Review* 9.3 (2020): 152–160, 158.

6 Generally, see: Chris Buckley and Steven Lee Myers, "As New Coronavirus Spread, China's Old Habits Delayed Fight," *New York Times*, February 1, 2020; Tom Mitchell et al., "What Went Wrong in Wuhan?" *Financial Times*, October 17, 2020.

7 Patricia Thornton, "Crisis and Governance: SARS and the Resilience of the Chinese Body Politic," *China Journal*, 61 (2009): 23–48.

8 Mi Liu et al., "Influenza Activity During the Outbreak of Coronavirus Disease 2019 in Chinese Mainland," *Biosafety and Health* 2.4 (2020): 206–209, Figure 2.

9 Tian et al., "An Investigation of Transmission Control Measures During the First 50 Days of the Covid-19 Epidemic in China," 368.

10 World Health Organization, *Report of the WHO-China Joint Mission on Coronavirus Disease 2019 (Covid-19)* (Geneva, February 28, 2020), 16.

11 Human Rights Watch, *World Report 2021* (New York, 2021); "China 2020," Amnesty International, April 7, 2021; Baldwin, *Fighting the First Wave*, 104.

12 Xingjie Hao et al., "Reconstruction of the Full Transmission Dynamics of Covid-19 in Wuhan," *Nature* 584.7821 (2020): 420–424; Shengjie Lai et al., "Effect of Non-Pharmaceutical Interventions to Contain Covid-19 in China," *Nature* 585.7825 (2020): 410–413.

13 Appraisals of China's performance might be more tempered if events of 2022 were taken into account. Chinese leaders persisted with a strict lockdown policy during an Omicron-variant wave, despite rising public frustration and economic costs. Some critics wondered whether other countries had developed more sophisticated long-term strategies for dealing with the virus. It was not possible, at time of writing, to consider this question closely. It remained true that the total Chinese death count was orders of magnitude lower than in other superstates.

14 World Health Organization, *Report of the WHO-China Joint Mission*, 20.

15 Nicholas Christakis, *Apollo's Arrow: The Profound and Enduring Impact of Coronavirus on the Way We Live* (New York: Little, Brown, 2020), 156; Bob Woodward, *Rage* (London: Simon & Schuster, 2020), xix.

16 Gottlieb, *Uncontrolled Spread*, 88–90.

17 Lawrence Wright, *The Plague Year: America in the Time of Covid* (New York: Knopf, 2021), 244; Christakis, *Apollo's Arrow*, 153–154.

18 Gottlieb, *Uncontrolled Spread*, 251–253, 290–293; Christakis, *Apollo's Arrow*, 164–166.

19 Max Fisher, "Stephen K. Bannon's CPAC Comments, Annotated and Explained," *New York Times*, February 24, 2017.

20 In a June 2020 survey, more than ninety percent of likely Trump voters expressed approval of his handling of the pandemic: "Trump vs. Biden Voters on the Most Important Issues in Their Vote Choice," Politico, June 30, 2020, 5.

21 Bryan Walsh, "The US Divide on Coronavirus Masks," *Axios*, June 24, 2020.

22 "States That Issued Lockdown and Stay-at-Home Orders in Response to the Coronavirus (Covid-19) Pandemic," ballotpedia.org.

23 William Galston, "For Covid-19 Vaccinations, Party Affiliation Matters More Than Race and Ethnicity," Brookings Institution, October 1, 2021.

24 Leo Lopez et al., "Racial and Ethnic Health Disparities Related to Covid-19," *JAMA* 325.8 (2021): 719–720; Brea Perry et al., "Pandemic Precarity: Covid-19 Is Exposing and Exacerbating Inequalities in the American Heartland," *Proceedings of the National Academy of Sciences* 118.8 (2021).

25 Michael Lewis, *The Premonition: A Pandemic Story* (New York: W.W. Norton, 2021), 113, 163 and 182.

26 Matt McKillop and Vinu Ilakkuvan, *The Impact of Chronic Underfunding on America's Public Health System* (Washington, DC: Trust for America's Health, 2019), 4.

27 Rhea Farberman et al., *Ready or Not: Protecting the Public's Health from Diseases, Disasters and Bioterrorism* (Washington, DC: Trust for America's Health, 2019), 26.

28 Government Accountability Office, *COVID-19: Continued Attention Needed to Enhance Federal Preparedness, Response, Service Delivery, and Program Integrity*, GAO-21–551 (Washington, 2021), 128–136.

29 Nathaniel Weixel and Peter Sullivan, "Top Health Officials Brief Senators on Coronavirus as Infections Spread," *The Hill*, January 24, 2020.

30 "Coronavirus Cases in US and Europe Confirmed," *CNBC*, February 21, 2020.

31 "Transcript for the CDC Telebriefing Update on COVID-19," Centers for Disease Control, February 26, 2020.

32 "Transcript of Coronavirus Task Force Briefing," *C-SPAN*, February 29, 2020.

33 Generally, see: Gottlieb, *Uncontrolled Spread*, ch. 5.

34 Wright, *The Plague Year*, 111.

35 T. Alex Perkins et al., "Estimating Unobserved Sars-Cov-2 Infections in the United States," *Proceedings of the National Academy of Sciences* 117.36 (2020): 22597–22602.

36 On the following, see generally: Wright, *The Plague Year*, 58–66; Gottlieb, *Uncontrolled Spread*, chs. 6 and 7.

37 Gottlieb, *Uncontrolled Spread*, 332, 336–337, 388.

38 See ourworldindata.org/explorers/coronavirus-data-explorer.

39 Wright, *The Plague Year*, 150. Gottlieb, *Uncontrolled Spread*, 249–251.

40 Graison Dangor, "CDC's Six-Foot Social Distancing Rule Was 'Arbitrary,' Says Former FDA Commissioner," *Forbes Magazine*, September 19, 2021; Emily Anthes, "Three Feet or Six? Distancing Guideline for Schools Stirs Debate," *New York Times*, March 16, 2021.

41 Jeneen Interlandi, "Can the CDC Be Fixed?," *New York Times*, June 16, 2021.

42 "Most Americans Say Federal Government Has Primary Responsibility for Covid-19 Testing," Washington, DC, Pew Research Center, May 12, 2020; "Americans Want the Federal Government to Help People in Need," Center for American Progress, March 10, 2021.

43 Jeannie Gersen, "Who's in Charge of the Response to the Coronavirus?" *The New Yorker*, April 19, 2020.

44 Tad DeHaven, "Disaster Response and Federalism," Cato Institute, October 31, 2012.

45 Sarah Gordon et al., "What Federalism Means for the US Response to Coronavirus Disease 2019," *JAMA Health Forum*, May 8, 2020.

46 Lena Sun et al., "A Plan to Defeat Coronavirus Finally Emerges, but It's Not from the White House," *Washington Post*, April 10, 2020.

47 Karen DeSalvo et al., "Public Health COVID-19 Impact Assessment: Lessons Learned and Compelling Needs," *NAM Perspectives* (April 2021); McKillop and Ilakkuvan, *The Impact of Chronic Underfunding on America's Public Health System.*

48 Michelle Mello et al., "Attacks on Public Health Officials During Covid-19," *JAMA* 324.8 (2020): 741–742.

49 See generally: NITI Aayog, *Strategy for New India @75* (Delhi: NITI Aayog, 2018), chs. 27 to 30.

50 M.P.R. Mohan and Jacob Alex, "COVID-19 and the Ambit of the Disaster Management Act," *The Week*, April 26, 2020.

51 As assessed by Oxford University researchers: www.bsg.ox.ac .uk/research/research-projects/covid-19–government-response -tracker.

52 Committee on Health and Family Welfare, *Report on the Outbreak of Pandemic Covid-19 and Its Management* (Delhi: Rajya Sabha, November 21, 2020), 5–11.

53 Richard Horton, *The Covid-19 Catastrophe* (Cambridge, UK: Polity, 2020), 72.

54 "Is India Testing Enough for Coronavirus Cases?" *Scroll*, March 14, 2020.

55 Jayati Ghosh, "A Critique of the Indian Government's Response to the COVID-19 Pandemic," *Journal of Industrial and Business Economics* 47 (2020): 519–530.

56 "4,000 Rules in 4 Months: Are Civil Servants Creating Chaos in India's Covid-19 Management?" *The Print*, May 4, 2020.

57 Harsh Mander, *Locking Down the Poor* (Delhi: Speaking Tiger, 2021), 92 and 208; Munieshwer Sagar, "Containment Zones Remain on Paper in Chandigarh," *Hindustan Times*, January 5, 2022; Sravasti Dasgupta and Angana Chakrabarti, "4,501 Containment Zones but Little Is Contained," *The Print*, November 20, 2020.

58 Mander, *Locking Down the Poor*, 2.

59 M. Vidyasagar et al., *Progression of the COVID-19 Pandemic in India: Prognosis and Lockdown Impacts* (Hyderabad: IIT Hyderabad, October 17, 2020); Manindra Agrawal, Madhuri Kanitkar, and M. Vidyasagar, "Modelling the Spread of Sars-Cov-2 Pandemic – Impact of Lockdowns & Interventions," *Indian Journal of Medical Research* 153.1–2 (2021), 175–181.

60 Soutik Biswas, "Coronavirus: Are Indians More Immune to COVID-19?" *BBC News*, November 2, 2020.

61 "Prime Minister Modi's Address at the Davos Dialogue," Government of India Press Information Bureau, January 28, 2021.

62 The Hindu, "BJP Hails PM for 'Defeating' COVID-19," *The Hindu*, February 21, 2021.

63 Vidya Krishnan, "India's COVID-19 Taskforce Did Not Meet in February, March Despite Surge," *The Caravan*, April 22, 2021.

64 "We Are in the Endgame of COVID-19 Pandemic: Health Minister Harsh Vardhan," *India Today*, March 7, 2021.

65 Data on confirmed cases: who.int/region/searo/country/in.

66 "India Records World's Biggest Single-Day Rise in Coronavirus Cases," reuters.com, April 22, 2021.

67 Thomas Abraham, "What Has Gone Wrong with India's Vaccination Programme?" *The India Forum*, April 21, 2021.

68 G.S. Mudur, "How India Landed in Covid Vaccine Mess," *The Telegraph*, April 19, 2021.

69 Shahid Jameel, "How India Can Survive the Virus," *New York Times*, May 13, 2021.

70 "COVID-19 Situation under Control in India: Health Minister Harsh Vardhan," livemint.com, *Mint*, March 30, 2021.

71 Neetu Chandra Sharma, "No Need of Total Lockdown, India Equipped to Handle 2nd COVID Wave: PM Modi," *Mint*, April 9, 2021.

72 Press Trust of India, "Covid Strikes Back, Ind Vs Eng T20 Ties in Ahmedabad Minus Fans Now," *Outlook*, March 15, 2021.

73 "BJP Makes a Delayed U-Turn, Modi Says Kumbh Attendance Should Now Be 'Symbolic,'" *The Wire*, April 17, 2021.

74 Sayed Quadri and Prasad Padala, "An Aspect of Kumbh Mela Massive Gathering and COVID-19," *Current Tropical Medicine Reports* 8.3 (2021): 225–230, 227.

75 Ian Rocha et al., "Kumbh Mela Religious Gathering as a Massive Superspreading Event," *American Journal of Tropical Medicine and Hygiene* 105.4 (2021): 868–871.

76 Manish Anand, "With 23 Rallies in Whirlwind Election Tours, There's No Stopping of PM Modi Even in Pandemic," *New Indian Express*, April 5, 2021.

77 "EC Curtails Period of Campaign for West Bengal Polls in 'Larger Public Interest,'" *Outlook*, April 16, 2021.

78 Monideepa Banerjie, "'Have Witnessed Such a Rally for the First Time': PM Modi in Bengal," ndtv.com, April 18, 2021.

79 The Wire, "IMA VP Says PM Modi a 'Super Spreader,'" *The Wire*, April 28, 2021.

80 Committee on Health and Family Welfare, *Report on the Outbreak*

of Pandemic COVID-19 and Its Management, 26; "State after State Shut Down Special COVID Centres Just before Second Wave," *Indian Express*, April 26, 2021.

81 Committee on Health and Family Welfare, *Report on the Outbreak of Pandemic Covid-19 and Its Management*, 27; Harikishan Sharma, "April, November Last Year: Officials, House Panel Flagged Oxygen Need, Shortage," *Indian Express*, April 23, 2021.

82 Arvind Gunasekar and Deepshikha Ghosh, "India Oxygen Export Rose over 700% in January 2021 Vs 2020 Amid Pandemic," ndtv. com, April 21, 2021.

83 Lazaro Gamio and James Glanz, "Just How Big Could India's True COVID Toll Be?" *New York Times*, May 25, 2021.

84 Abhishek Anand and Arvind Subramanian, *Three New Estimates of Deaths in India During the Pandemic* (Washington, DC: Centre for Global Development, July 21, 2021), 18.

85 K.S. Komireddi, "Modi Fiddles While India Burns," *Foreign Policy*, April 30, 2021.

86 Jennifer Rankin, "Coronavirus Could Be Final Straw for EU, European Experts Warn," *Guardian*, April 1, 2020.

87 "WHO Director-General's Opening Remarks at the Media Briefing on COVID-19, 13 March 2020," World Health Organization, March 13, 2020.

88 Articles 6(a) and 168, Treaty on the Functioning of the European Union.

89 Jillian Deutsch, "Coronavirus Exposes Flaws with EU's Infectious Disease Agency," *Politico*, October 18, 2020.

90 Mara Sanfelici, "The Italian Response to the COVID-19 Crisis," *The International Journal of Community and Social Development* 2.2 (2020): 191–210, 197.

91 "Coronavirus: The World in Lockdown in Maps and Charts," *BBC News*, April 7, 2020.

92 Daniel Gordon et al., "Cross-Country Effects and Policy Responses to Covid-19 in 2020: The Nordic Countries," *Economic Analysis and Policy* 71 (2021): 198–210, 201.

93 Corona Commission, *Summary of Second Interim Report* (Stockholm, October 29, 2021) 2 and 7. Also see: Baldwin, *Fighting the First Wave*, 79–81.

94 Kai Kupferschmidt, "Can Europe Tame the Pandemic's Next Wave?" *Science*, September 1, 2020.

95 Frederik E. Juul et al., "Mortality in Norway and Sweden During the COVID-19 Pandemic," *Scandinavian Journal of Public Health*

NOTES TO PAGES 157–158

(October 5, 2021); Ida Seing et al., "Social Distancing Policies in the Coronavirus Battle: A Comparison of Denmark and Sweden," *International Journal of Environmental Research and Public Health* 18.20 (October 2021): 10990.

96 Peter Wise, "How Portugal Turned Back Coronavirus Tide That Swamped Its Neighbour," *Financial Times*, May 3, 2020.

97 Sabine Kuhlmann et al., "Tracing Divergence in Crisis Governance: Responses to the COVID-19 Pandemic in France, Germany and Sweden Compared," *International Review of Administrative Sciences* 87.3 (2021): 556–575.

98 Amie Tsang, "E.U. Seeks Solidarity as Nations Restrict Medical Exports," *New York Times*, March 7, 2020.

99 Annalisa Cangemi, "Covid-19, Nei Sondaggi Sale Fiducia Nel Governo Conte (29,2%): +4 Punti in Un Mese," fanpage.it, March 13, 2020.

100 Jillian Deutsch and Sarah Wheaton, "How Europe Fell Behind on Vaccines," *Politico Europe*, January 27, 2021.

101 Adam Tooze, *Shutdown: How Covid Shook the World's Economy* (London: Allen Lane, 2021), 133–134.

102 Shaun Walker and Jennifer Rankin, "Hungary Passes Law That Will Let Orbán Rule by Decree," *Guardian*, March 30, 2020.

103 Rankin, "Coronavirus Could Be Final Straw"; Luuk van Middelaar, *Pandemonium: Saving Europe* (Newcastle upon Tyne: Agenda Publishing, 2021), 2–3.

104 Euronews, "EU Will Lose Its 'Raison d'etre' If It Fails to Help During Covid-19 Crisis, Italy's PM Warns," euronews.com, March 28, 2020.

105 David Herszenhorn, "Virtual Summit, Real Acrimony: EU Leaders Clash over 'Corona Bonds,'" *Politico Europe*, March 26, 2020; Pedro Sánchez, "Europe's Future Is at Stake in This War against Coronavirus," *Guardian*, April 5, 2020.

106 "George Soros Says Coronavirus May Spell the End of the EU," *Daily Mail*, May 22, 2020.

107 Generally, see: Middelaar, *Pandemonium*, 55–80; Sarah Wolff and Stella Ladi, "European Union Responses to the COVID-19 Pandemic," *Journal of European Integration* 42.8 (2020): 1025–1040, 1027–1029.

108 Jack Ewing, "Europe's Central Bank Vastly Expands Stimulus Measures," *New York Times*, March 18, 2020.

109 Bjarke Smith-Meyer, "EU Triggers Deficit Rules 'Escape Clause' to Boost Public Spending," *Politico Europe*, March 20, 2020.

110 Matina Stevis-Gridneff, "E.U. Backs Half-Trillion Euro Stimulus, but Balks at Pooling Debt," *New York Times*, April 9, 2020.

111 Jacob Funk Kirkegaard, "Europe's Big Fiscal Deal Leaves Some Tough Decisions Ahead," Peterson Institute for International Economics, July 29, 2020.

112 Ben Hall et al., "Is the Franco-German Plan Europe's 'Hamiltonian' Moment?" *Financial Times*, May 21, 2020.

113 Jeremy Cliffe, "What Europe Can Learn from Alexander Hamilton," *New Statesman*, December 5, 2018.

114 Gideon Rachman, "Why the European Commission Failed the Vaccine Challenge," *Financial Times*, February 1, 2021.

115 Paul Krugman, "Vaccines: A Very European Disaster," *New York Times*, March 18, 2021.

116 Steven Erlanger, "Vaccine 'Fiasco' Damages Europe's Credibility," *New York Times*, April 2, 2021.

117 Greg Heffer, "COVID-19: EU Chief Ursula Von Der Leyen Admits UK 'Speedboat' Can Act Faster Than Bloc over Vaccines," *Sky News*, February 5, 2021.

118 Elena Sánchez Nicolás, "EU Targets Vaccinating 70% of Adults by Summer," *EU Observer*, January 20, 2021.

119 Luuk van Middelaar, "Faced with Covid, Europe's Citizens Demanded an EU Response – and Got It," *Guardian*, December 29, 2021.

120 Gerardo Fortuna, "The EU's New Body to Prevent the Next Pandemic," EURACTIV Media Network, September 14, 2021.

121 Alberto Alemanno, "Towards a European Health Union: Time to Level Up," *European Journal of Risk Regulation* 11.4 (2020): 721–725.

122 Jillian Deutsch, "Europe's 'Health Union' Prepares for Its First Feeble Steps," *Politico Europe*, September 1, 2021.

123 Amartya Sen, *Development as Freedom* (Oxford University Press, 1999), 16.

124 Gabriel Cepaluni, Michael Dorsch, and Réka Branyiczki, "Political Regimes and Deaths in the Early Stages of the Covid-19 Pandemic," *APSA Preprints* (December 2020).

125 Justin Esarey, "The Myth That Democracies Bungled the Pandemic," *The Atlantic*, October 4, 2021.

9 How to Rule a Superstate

1 Raymond Pearl, *The Biology of Population Growth* (New York: Knopf, 1925), 173.

2 O.E. Baker, "Land Utilization in the United States: Geographical Aspects of the Problem," *Geographical Review* 13.1 (1923): 1–26, 5.

3 J.B. Bury, *History of the Later Roman Empire*, 2 vols. (London: Macmillan, 1923), v.1:311.

4 I have borrowed the phrase "creedal passion" from Samuel Huntington, although I do not use it the same way. See: Michel Crozier, Samuel Huntington, and Joji Watanuki, *The Crisis of Democracy* (New York University Press, 1975), 59–118.

5 Christopher Ansell, *The Protective State* (Cambridge University Press, 2019).

6 This is a common expression in scholarly work since the 1980s, referring alternately to nations, states, and provinces.

7 For example, see: Susan Herbst, *A Troubled Birth: The 1930s and American Public Opinion, Chicago Studies in American Politics* (University of Chicago Press, 2021).

8 Alexander George, "The 'Operational Code': A Neglected Approach to the Study of Political Leaders and Decision-Making," *International Studies Quarterly* 13.2 (1969): 190–222, 191. Other scholars wrote about the "political mind" of the Soviet ruling group: their "patterns of thought, ways of perceiving the world, psychological attitudes, ideological premises, and working theories": Robert Tucker, *The Soviet Political Mind* (New York: W.W. Norton, 1971), ix.

9 Ronald Robinson and John Gallagher, *Africa and the Victorians* (New York: St. Martins Press, 1961), 20–21.

10 Mitchell Dean, *Governmentality: Power and Rule in Modern Society*, 2nd edn. (Thousand Oaks, CA: Sage, 2010), 24–25.

11 Jawaharlal Nehru, *Selected Works of Jawaharlal Nehru, Second Series, Volume 16 Part 1* (New Delhi: Jawaharlal Nehru Memorial Fund, 1984), 165.

12 Xi Jinping, *The Governance of China* (Beijing: Foreign Languages Press, 2014), v1:304.

13 Lothar Brock, *Fragile States: Violence and the Failure of Intervention* (Cambridge, UK: Polity, 2012), 14.

14 Jon Meacham, *Destiny and Power: The American Odyssey of George Herbert Walker Bush* (New York: Random House, 2016), xxii.

Index